WORLD WAR I

A Compact History

WORLD WAR I

A Compact History

by Grace P. Hayes

Introduction by Colonel R. Ernest Dupuy

Hawthorn Books, Inc.
Publishers
New York

WORLD WAR I: A COMPACT HISTORY

1   2   3   4   5   6   7   8   9   10

The author and publisher wish to thank the following copyright holders for permission to include the maps listed below:

The maps on pages 8, 27, 42, 52, 119, 192, 215, 233, 264, 284, 287, 290, and 305 are reproduced by permission of McGraw-Hill Book Company, Inc., from *Military Heritage of America,* by R. Ernest Dupuy and Trevor N. Dupuy. Copyright © 1956 by the McGraw-Hill Book Company, Inc.

The maps on pages 16, 99, and 103 are reproduced by permission of Prentice-Hall, Inc., from *Sea Power: A Naval History,* by E. B. Potter and Chester W. Nimitz. Copyright © 1960.

The maps on pages 62, 65, 76, 138, 141, and 147 are reproduced by permission of Charles Scribner's Sons from *The World Crisis,* Vol. VI, by Winston Churchill. Copyright © 1931 by Charles Scribner's Sons; renewal copyright © 1959 by Winston S. Churchill.

The maps on pages 176 and 177 are reproduced by permission of Harvard University Press from *The Naval History of World War I,* Vol. I, by Thomas G. Frothingham. Copyright © 1926.

The maps on page 309 are reproduced by permission from "The Campaign in German East Africa," by C. E. Hamshere, in *History Today,* April, 1965.

For

Martha and Benjamin

Foreword

There is no easy answer to the question of why World War I happened. No list of reasons and causes is entirely adequate to explain the pressures of fact and belief and prejudice and conflicting values and economics and diplomacy that contributed to shattering the peace the main belligerents had known since 1871. But in 1914 the bits and pieces had created a situation that made war imminent, and it took only a small spark to set it off.

The spark, and much of the tension that existed all over Europe, resulted mainly from the existence of numerous minority groups who by earlier wars and treaties had been divided and dominated by stronger peoples. Among the minorities were nine ethnic groups in Austria-Hungary; an assortment divided among the nations in the Balkans; the Poles, who were split three ways by Prussia, Austria, and Russia; the Baltic Estonians, Latvians, and Lithuanians; and, most resentful of all of foreign domination, the French in Alsace and Lorraine. From the time those two provinces of France were taken by Prussia after the Franco-Prussian War in 1871, no French government forgot that they must be regained. The basic antagonism of France and Germany was one of the prime reasons for the existence in 1914 of the Triple Alliance—Germany, Austria-Hungary, and Italy—and the Triple Entente—France, Great Britain, and Russia. Designed for mutual support in war, these and other agreements brought the nations to war like soldiers assembling for mail call.

Perhaps the most striking thing about World War I is the futility of it all, the enormous waste of men and matériel in a war that settled nothing. Thousands upon thousands of young men were sent to their deaths to little purpose. The war had its heroes and its moments of glory, but they are obscured in the larger picture of destruction and gore. This book has room for little of the glamour that occasionally appeared or the personal courage and

vii

individual bravery that proved the virtue of man in the midst of evil of man's making. This is a narrative of the progression of main events from the beginning to the end. Perhaps a rereading of the story of that "war to end all wars" will advance the purpose the war was supposed to have accomplished.

In preparing this book I have been greatly assisted by my colleagues in the Historical Evaluation and Research Organization, Mrs. Gay M. Hammerman and Mr. Frank Pichini, and particularly by its President and Executive Director, Colonel Trevor N. Dupuy, whose confidence, knowledge, and advice have been vital throughout.

G. P. H.

Contents

Introduction

In 1914 the political structure of the society of nations, teetering on the pinnacle of power balance, came shivering down like a house of cards. Before World War I ended, three great empires had dissolved in the bloodbath, obliterating with them the last decadent vestiges of the Holy Roman Empire, while a new force in world power structure was slowly rising on the leverage provided by the doctrines of Karl Marx. Finally, and this must never be forgotten, it was only after a million Americans had crossed the Atlantic that the issue was decided.

Five years after the guns of August, 1914, first spoke, the victors gathered about the council table in Versailles, reshuffled the deck, and then erected another world political structure, even more shaky than its predecessor—so shaky, indeed, that in 1939 it, too, collapsed in a catacylsm of even greater proportions. So immense was this second global struggle that it and its effects have to some extent obscured the earlier conflict.

From the historian's standpoint this is unfortunate. World War I was a significant milestone on the highway of world events. It marked the end of one epoch and the beginning of another. The aftermath of World War I was a curtain-raiser for World War II, and as drafted in the Treaty of Versailles, it also became the fertile forcing-bed for the dragon's teeth sown during 1914–1918.

This is the word picture that Grace Hayes has painted in simple, stark brushstrokes. It should serve for the edification of generations to whom the names of battles and of leaders and heads of state who strutted the boards during what our British friends called "The Great War," and wishful-thinking Americans dubbed "the war to end all wars," have unfortunately been almost blotted out.

Mrs. Hayes is to be congratulated. In a highly readable fashion she has compressed the multitudinous details of a catastrophic struggle.

Colonel R. Ernest Dupuy

WORLD WAR I

A Compact History

1

Beginning

THE EVENTS AT SARAJEVO

Emperor Franz Joseph in his old age had no son to succeed him on the throne of the Austro-Hungarian Empire. His only son, Rudolph, had died many years earlier in a murder-suicide pact with a young baroness. So it was that in 1914 the emperor's nephew, the Archduke Franz Ferdinand, was in line for his uncle's throne.

Franz Ferdinand, strong-minded and quick-tempered, had developed a keen interest in the problems of the Slavic minorities in Austria-Hungary, and he intended to do something about them. To his uncle his views were incomprehensible and deplorable. Franz Ferdinand's marriage to Sophie Chotek was also unpopular with Franz Joseph, for although she came from a noble family she was not of royal birth. This meant, according to the rules of the Hapsburg court, that she and their children were deprived of the usual titles and privileges, including succession to the throne.

In June, 1914, Franz Ferdinand went to Bosnia-Herzegovina, newest province of his uncle's empire, to inspect major army maneuvers, as part of his job as head of Austria-Hungary's army and navy. The inspection over, the archduke and his wife proceeded to the capital city, Sarajevo, for an official welcome.

Elaborate preparations had been made for the occasion, and people lined the streets to see the distinguished visitors. Scattered among the crowd were seven pro-Slav fanatics, most of them very young, who were committed to assassinate the archduke. Franz Ferdinand's well-known interest in creating a third, Slavic, state equal to the Austrian and Hungarian states of Austria-Hungary, although inspired by a genuine interest in improving the lot of the Slavic people, was inadmissable to the fanatics. They saw in it a direct threat to the movement for Slavic independence and union with Serbia, and they did not intend that the archduke become emperor.

As the procession of automobiles carrying the party wound through the streets of Sarajevo, the seven conspirators waited at strategic spots along the route. The first young man made no move as the archduke's automobile passed through his range. The second took aim and threw the bomb he had been concealing, only to have it deflected by the arm of the alert archduke and explode in the street, wounding three members of the party and several spectators. Accelerating, Franz Ferdinand's driver rushed his passengers to the city hall, passing three more conspirators on the way.

After a brief stop Franz Ferdinand insisted on being taken to the hospital to see how the injured were faring. The couple reentered their car and were driven on a route that took them past the sixth conspirator, who, like the first, did nothing. Shortly thereafter the driver made a wrong turn. As he stopped to correct his route, the car presented a perfect target to the seventh, and most determined, of the would-be assassins. Taking careful aim, Gavrilo Princip fired two bullets from his gun. They found their targets, killed the archduke and his wife, and ignited the fuse of World War I.

REACTION IN VIENNA

There was little sorrow, official or unofficial, in Vienna over the archduke's death. Only the dead couple's children and a few friends and close associates mourned. The old emperor expressed the view that a wise Providence had removed his dangerous nephew from the scene. Foreign rulers were discouraged from attending the funeral. In Britain King George V decreed seven days' mourning; Czar Nicholas II of Russia called for twelve; and President Woodrow Wilson sent an official cable of sympathy. But no one anticipated the dreadful drama about to be played.

Behind the scenes the first act was already taking shape. Princip and the other conspirators captured at Sarajevo were Bosnians, and there was no clear evidence that Serbia had played any role in the crime. But there seemed a good possibility that the plot had been brewed in Serbia, and Austrians who had long advocated a punitive war with Serbia promptly pushed for revenge.

General Franz Conrad von Hötzendorf, Chief of the Austro-Hungarian Staff, an able soldier and a war hawk, called for immediate mobilization against Serbia. Count Leopold von Berchtold, Austrian Foreign Minister, favored sending an army straight to Belgrade. But Conrad opposed such action, knowing that the army was not ready to go to war without mobilization. Von Berchtold himself realized that he must first be sure he had support, at least from the German allies. Opposed to any threatening moves was Count István Tisza, Hungarian Prime Minister, who feared a countermove by Russia should Serbia be attacked, but his views failed to carry the day.

Von Berchtold dispatched an envoy to Germany, and the Austrian ambassador called on the Kaiser to ask the fatal question: Could Austria-Hungary count on German support if she mobilized against Serbia? Wilhelm's answer was clear. "Even if matters went to the length of war between Austria-Hungary and Russia," the Austrian ambassador reported, "Germany, in her customary loyalty as our ally, would stand at our side." Having thus pledged his nation to support Austria-Hungary in whatever course she selected, the Kaiser left for a long-planned cruise on the North Sea.

THREATS AND MOBILIZATION

An unannounced military attack on Serbia was not in accordance with good international behavior. So the Austrian Ministerial Council, now united in the view that Serbia was responsible and must be punished, drew up an ultimatum. It was delivered to the Serbian government at 6 P.M. on July 23, 1918.

The terms were severe and deliberately intended to be unacceptable. The Serbian government must suppress all propaganda and subversive activities against Austria-Hungary, must investigate and take legal action in the Sarajevo murders, and must accept the "participation" and "collaboration" of Austro-Hungarian officials in the investigations. This was a clear threat to

Serbian sovereignty. Serbia had forty-eight hours to return an answer.

The Austro-Hungarian demands were widely publicized. All over Europe the reaction was one of outrage. British diplomats at once tried hard to mediate the dispute. But by that time only Serbia could try to change the course of events. Drained of men and weapons by the recent Balkan Wars, Serbia might have accepted all the demands, had not Russia assured her she would support her if she did not give in. A fear that high-ranking Serbian officials might be involved in the conspiracy also influenced the government to hold back. The reply that went to Austria-Hungary nevertheless was conciliatory. It rejected outright the demands for participation in the investigation, but otherwise Austria's demands were accepted with few qualifications.

As soon as the Austrian ambassador to Belgrade saw the reply, he knew his government would not accept it. Accordingly he burned his code books and left for Vienna. In Serbia orders went out to start mobilizing.

Von Berchtold, upon receiving a report of Serbia's response, convinced the emperor that Austria must mobilize too. Russia was bound to come to Serbia's aid, and Austria-Hungary must be prepared to defend herself.

Events were moving rapidly. Sir Edward Grey, British Foreign Secretary, increased his efforts to mediate. Even from his friends, however, he received little support. Kaiser Wilhelm was still at sea. Whether he was given little information intentionally or unintentionally is not clear, but in any case he was not kept fully informed. When he came hurrying back from his vacation he found things at a serious pass, even though to him it seemed that the Serbian reply was satisfactory. Too late, he and his ministers tried to dissuade Von Berchtold from going to war.

For three days Austria-Hungary delayed. Frantic messages passed from capital to capital. Rumor flew even faster as fears increased. Finally, on July 28, Von Berchtold's government declared war on Serbia. Later that day German Chancellor Theobald von Bethmann-Hollweg warned Von Berchtold that if Austria-Hungary did not compromise she must reckon with "a gradual revulsion of public opinion . . . in all of Europe." The following day Von Bethmann-Hollweg cabled: "We must refuse to let ourselves be drawn . . . by Vienna into any general conflagration because she has ignored our advice." But Austrian guns had already bombarded the Serbian capital, Belgrade.

To understand what happened next it is necessary to know something of the significance of mobilization in Europe in 1914. Active warfare did not start with a single order. Before armies could fire they had to be moved into position by a lengthy and involved process that included thousands of telegraphed orders to civilian reservists; loading and unloading of railroad freightcars full of weapons, ammunition, food, uniforms, and equipment for millions of men; and complex shuttlings of other railroad cars across many miles of track, much of which had been built for the purpose. Mobilization was a chain reaction that, once started, could not readily be halted before shots had been fired. No nation could permit another to mobilize across its borders without calling up its own forces to defend itself against the threat. Germany had no plan for mobilizing as a diplomatic weapon or precautionary measure; for her, mobilization automatically meant war.

As the crisis grew, the Russian Foreign Minister, Sergei Sazonov, mindful that his country was obligated by treaty to support Serbia, prepared to come to her aid. Thinking it possible to mobilize only part of the Russian Army, on the night of July 29 he convinced the Russian generals to agree to a partial mobilization, against Austria only. In reality, however, there was no administrative machinery in existence in Russia (or any other nation, for that matter) for any less than total mobilization. If Russia mobilized against Austria she would mobilize against Germany as well. Her military leaders were struggling with the problem of calling up only part of the Russian Army when Von Bethmann-Hollweg warned from Berlin that Russian mobilization would be countered by German mobilization. But word of the shelling of Belgrade had already reached St. Petersburg, and Russian leaders were convinced there was no turning back. Reluctantly, the Czar was persuaded to order general mobilization on Thursday, July 30. As red posters announcing the order began to go up all over Russia the following day, Austria-Hungary too ordered full mobilization.

The German government reacted to news of Russian mobilization on July 31 by declaring a "Threatening Danger of War" and dispatching an ultimatum to Sazonov. He must call off mobilization within twelve hours, or else. To Paris, too, went an ultimatum. France must say within eighteen hours whether she would stay neutral if Germany attacked Russia. The French Cabinet had already decided to mobilize, when the German ambassador, Baron Wilhelm Eduard von Schoen, delivered the ultimatum to French Premier René Viviani. When Von Schoen returned for an answer, it was simply, "France will act in accordance with her interests." The French order for general mobilization went out at 4 P.M. on August 1. Shortly thereafter Germany too ordered general mobilization. An hour later the German ambassador in St. Petersburg, Count Friedrich von Pourtales, handed Sazonov a declaration of war and then burst into tears.

2

The Lines Are Drawn

While the tears were flowing in St. Petersburg, the first German troops were marching into neutral Luxembourg, setting in motion Germany's long-prepared contingency war plan. The first town they occupied was Trois Vierges (Three Virgins), and the innocence of the name emphasized for newspaper readers everywhere the Germans' ruthless violation of neutral nations to achieve their ends.

THE GERMAN PLAN

More than a decade earlier, General Count Alfred von Schlieffen, Chief of the German General Staff, had drafted a strategic war plan. Recognizing that the alliance of France and Russia meant that if Germany went to war with one she would find herself fighting both, the plan was designed to defeat France quickly while massive, sluggish Russia was still mobilizing. It called for a wide sweep of five German armies through Belgium and the Netherlands, deep into France. Penetrating beyond Paris, the Germans would cut back behind the French left flank and attack the main body of the French decisively from the rear. Since the French could be expected to attack into Alsace-Lorraine, a smaller German force would hold them in that area, withdrawing slowly in order to keep the French force occupied away from the main German attack. While this operation was in progress, a delaying force would hold the Russians in East Prussia. The force would be increased to deal with Russia after France had been defeated.

Von Schlieffen's successor as Chief of the German General Staff in 1905, General Helmuth von Moltke, nephew of Germany's

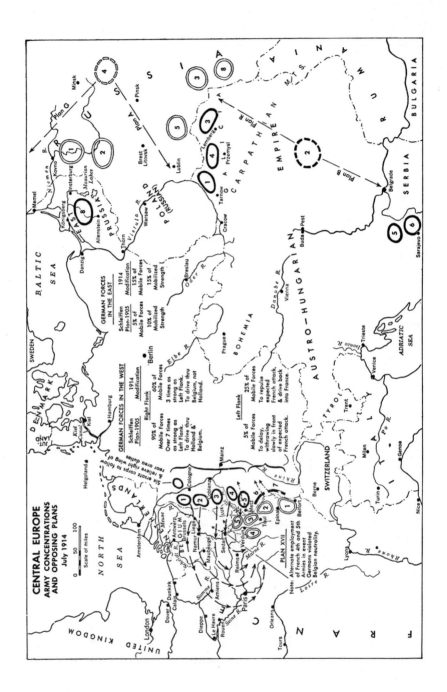

CENTRAL EUROPE
ARMY CONCENTRATIONS
AND OPPOSING PLANS
July 1914

Scale of miles
0   50   100

GERMAN FORCES IN THE WEST

Schlieffen Plan—1905	1914 Modification
Right Flank 90% of Mobile Forces Over 7 times as strong as Left Flank. To drive thru Holland & Belgium.	60% of Mobile Forces 3 times as strong as Left Flank. To drive thru Belgium, not Holland.
Left Flank 5% of Mobile Forces To delay, withdrawing slowly in front of expected French attack.	25% of Mobile Forces To repulse expected French attack & drive back into France.

Six ersatz corps to follow & relieve right wing of rear area duties.

GERMAN FORCES IN THE EAST

Schlieffen Plan—1905	1914 Modification
5% of Mobile Forces 10% of Mobilized Strength	15% of Mobile Forces 15% of Mobilized Strength

PLAN XVII.

Note: Alternate employment of French 4th and 5th Armies in event Germans violated Belgian neutrality.

great general in the Franco-Prussian War, had modified the plan. Knowing that the Russians were working on a speeded-up mobilization plan, he strengthened the German holding force assigned to East Prussia. He also increased the strength of his left wing on the Western Front, both to decrease the danger of a French breakthrough into Alsace and to gain for himself the possibility of a double envelopment if it proved possible to swing around the French right flank as well as the left. Finally, Von Moltke decided not to violate Dutch territory and so made it necessary for the entire right wing of the German attack to push through the narrow frontier of little Belgium on its way to Paris.

To carry out the plan, Germany in 1914 had the best-trained and best-equipped army in all of Europe, that is to say, in all the world. It was not the biggest. When fully mobilized, Russia had 114 infantry divisions as against 87 German. But the German Army was better organized and much more capably led. It was trained primarily in offensive tactics; but the German General Staff had efficiently planned for all contingencies, and defensively, too, the German Army was the most efficient in the world.

Execution of the German war plan necessitated violation of a treaty that had been in existence since 1839, a treaty signed by France, Germany, Great Britain, Russia, and Austria, guaranteeing the neutrality of Belgium. Recognizing that the obvious pathway from Germany to France was across Belgium and that Belgian ports would be useful for an invasion of England, the treaty was designed to prevent larger nations from so taking advantage of Belgian territory. No one knew in the summer of 1914 whether Britain would uphold the treaty and react to a German invasion of Belgium. But German leaders considered the risk worth taking, and many thought that Britain, whose traditional strength was on the sea, could have little effect on the outcome of a short war on land.

THE FRENCH PLAN

The French also had drawn a plan, and, as Von Schlieffen had assumed, it was designed primarily to retake Alsace and Lorraine. It had evolved through a series of plans since the humiliating military defeat of 1870–1871, until the version that was current in 1914 was numbered XVII.

Plan XVII had been completed under the leadership of General Joseph Jacques Césaire Joffre, commander in chief of the French Army. Big, imperturbable, silent if he had nothing to say, always ready to listen, terrible in his anger when aroused, Joffre was a man of clear vision and great courage. But his plan paid little heed to the possibility that the Germans might attack through neutral Belgium. Joffre's predecessor as commander in chief, General Victor Michel, had tried to sell this idea and been replaced for doing so.

Plan XVII called for the five French armies to be deployed along the border from Belfort near the Swiss frontier to Hirson, on the Belgian border. Two thirds of the French-Belgian border were left unprotected. The armies were to attack in two major thrusts through Alsace and Lorraine, south and north of the fortified German area of Metz-Thionville. If the Germans should invade Belgium, two of the northern French armies would strike instead through Luxembourg and the Ardennes Forest.

There was no part for the British written into Plan XVII, but in prewar conversations it had been agreed that the British Expeditionary Force would be sent to France immediately in case of war and placed on the left of the French line. This would extend it a short distance beyond Hirson.

THE ULTIMATUM TO BELGIUM

The German minister to Belgium received a sealed envelope from his government on July 29, 1914, with instructions not to open it until he was given orders to do so. Inside was the German ultimatum to Belgium: Let German armies march through your country or take the consequences! Like the other steps in the war plan, presentation of the ultimatum had been carefully timed. Movements of French armies near the Belgian border were cited to justify the demand for passage, but the letter had actually been composed by the German government two days before Austria declared war on Serbia.

On Sunday, August 2, the day after Germany had ordered mobilization and declared war on Russia, the German minister in Brussels received his orders, opened the envelope, and presented the ultimatum. King Albert and his government never hesitated.

With only six Belgian divisions to face scores of German ones, Belgium's choice was between handing over the country to the Germans and risking destruction of her army and devastation of her land. Bravely, the king rejected the ultimatum.

Scrupulously devoted to maintaining Belgium's obligations as a neutral, King Albert refused to ask aid from France and Britain before German troops actually crossed his frontier. Nor had his General Staff made contingency plans with either nation. Belgian armies were so deployed that they were equally ready, and equally unready, for attack by either France or Germany. But now the chips were down, and when Albert took over as commander in chief of his army as prescribed in the Belgian Constitution, he knew which were his friends.

On August 4, German cavalry troops, carrying lances, sabers, pistols, and rifles, rode in formation across the Belgian border. Behind them came infantrymen, on foot and by automobile, singing as they came. Their first objective was to seize the bridges across the Meuse before they could be destroyed, and then push on to capture Liège. Thousands of German soldiers were on Belgian soil that evening when Baron von Schoen handed French Premier Viviani a declaration of war. French military aviators had committed hostile acts on German territory, it said. Von Schoen, who knew as well as Viviani that the accusations were false, could not conceal his unhappiness.

BRITAIN ACTS

With German troops actually in Belgian territory on August 4, King Albert appealed to France and Britain for help. For the past several days the British Cabinet had been discussing the situation in great earnestness, and the Foreign Secretary, Sir Edward Grey, had been using all the channels he had to try to avert what was rapidly becoming inevitable. At the direction of Winston Churchill, First Lord of the Admiralty, the British Grand Fleet had moved quietly to bases at Scapa Flow on July 29, and other units of the Royal Navy were alerted for war.

Grey had attempted on July 31 to obtain assurances from France and Germany that they would respect Belgian neutrality. From France the reply was affirmative; the German Foreign Secretary, Gottlieb von Jagow, had refused to answer. On August 2 the British Cabinet voted to defend the French coast with the Royal Navy, although two members resigned over this commitment to semibelligerence. When word of the German ultimatum to Belgium arrived, the Cabinet decided to intervene if Belgian neutrality were violated. Prime Minister Herbert Asquith authorized the War Office to call up the Reserves and the Territorials (a sort of National Guard), who were to defend the British Isles if the Regular Army went to France.

On August 3, Grey addressed the House of Commons for over an hour, reporting the measures already taken and prospects for the future. His oratory carried the Members with him. The country rallied behind him, and the two Cabinet members who had resigned rejoined the government. The following day the British ambassador in Berlin, Sir Edward Goschen, informed the German government that unless Germany agreed by midnight to respect the neutrality of Belgium the British government would "take all steps in their power to uphold the neutrality of Belgium and the observance of a treaty to which Germany is as much a party as ourselves." But Von Jagow informed him it was already too late. German troops had indeed entered Belgium. Later in the evening when Goschen called on Chancellor von Bethmann-Hollweg, he found him furious at the British action. In words that echoed and reechoed against him during the four bloody years of war he deplored the fact that Britain was about to go to war for "a scrap of paper." Did the British ambassador realize the dreadful consequences of this stubbornness? Goschen did indeed. But, he said, fear of the consequences was no excuse for breaking Britain's solemn word.

Midnight came and went, and Britain was at war. The next morning the Kaiser sent word to King George that he was giving up his honorary British titles of Field Marshal and Admiral. Shortly thereafter Goschen was handed his passport.

Having declared war, the British government lost no time in sending British soldiers to fight. On August 5 the War Council agreed to send four infantry divisions and a cavalry division at once to France, leaving two to follow later. Commander of this British Expeditionary Force would be Field Marshal Sir John French. Four days later the first of a long stream of transport ships crossed the English Channel. Guarded by ships of the Royal Navy, they delivered their valuable cargo unchallenged and indeed undetected. The soldiers moved promptly into position beside the French near Maubeuge and Le Cateau.

THE WORLD AT WAR

In the next few days the nations lined up. On one side were the Central Powers: Austria-Hungary and Germany. On the other were the Allies: Belgium, England, France, Montenegro, Russia, and Serbia. Italy had announced that since Austria had attacked Serbia she was not bound to stand by her treaty obligations, and she had declared herself neutral. This was a convenient excuse, for in 1902 Italy and France had signed a secret treaty in which they agreed not to participate in any war against one another.

World War I had begun. Before it ended, more than four years later, 93 percent of the world's population would have been involved in it. Almost five million Allied soldiers would have died, and about three million of the Central Powers. They would have fought on many fronts, on land and sea and, for the first time, in the air; on the Western Front in France and the Eastern Front in Poland, Russia, and the mountains of Austria and the Balkans; in Italy, Turkey, Palestine, Mesopotamia, and Africa; in the far China Sea, the Mediterranean, and the North Sea; in the Atlantic, Pacific, and Indian Oceans. Had anyone been told what it was that was starting in August, 1914, he would not have believed it, but, of course, no one could tell.

3

War Begins at Sea

TURKEY'S POSITION

The first dramatic action of World War I was already being played at sea as the hours ticked by in the countdown that sent Britain to war. The players included Britain, Germany, and a third nation which had been in the thoughts of both from the beginning of the crisis, Turkey.

Straddling the Straits of the Dardanelles and the Bosporus, in the far northeastern corner of the Aegean Sea, Turkey controlled the only warm-water route of communications between the western Allies and Russia. By no other route could the Allies send Russia adequate supplies, and it was to their distinct advantage to keep it open. Germany was as well aware of this as the Allies were, and naturally hoped to gain control of it herself. Moreover, her own communications to the Middle East (it was called the Near East at the time) went by land across Turkey. For some years before the war Germany had been cultivating Turkey as a potential ally, one strategically situated to menace British interests in the Middle East and pro-Allies nations in the Balkans.

Germany had gained a military advantage in Constantinople, for only a year before the war began a German military mission had started to reorganize the Turkish Army. A British naval mission was working in similar fashion with the Turkish Navy, but despite the fact that Germans and Turks distrusted each other, the influence of the German soldiers far outweighed that of the British sailors. Still, until the assassination of Franz Ferdinand loosened the bonds that had been holding the military might of Europe in check, neither Germany nor Britain had shown much interest in joining a military alliance with Turkey.

As July's crisis deepened, the advantage to Germany of controlling the Dardanelles in the event of war with Russia, and the desirability of having an ally who could move into the Balkans from the southeast should war come there, became clear. Kaiser Wilhelm accordingly directed his ambassador in Constantinople to do his utmost to reach a treaty agreement with the Young Turks who were in control in Turkey. The Turkish government well knew that the Russians had always wanted direct control over their warm-water entrance and that Turks alone might be unable to prevent a direct Russian move to take the Bosporus and the Dardanelles. Consequently, when Austria declared war on Serbia, an act that was almost certain to be followed by the involvement of Russia, the Turks asked Germany for a secret agreement for mutual support should either nation go to war with Russia. German agreement was given on the same day it was asked, July 28, but the secret covenant was not signed until August 2 in Constantinople.

Many months before this, the Turkish government had ordered two modern battleships to be built in British shipyards and had conducted a nationwide fund drive to pay for them. More than five hundred Turkish sailors had arrived in England in the summer of 1914 and were awaiting permission to take possession of the first of the ships, the *Reshadieh,* already completed and moored in the River Tyne. As the First Lord of the Admiralty, Winston Churchill, surveyed the property of the Royal Navy and its state of readiness for war during the days of mounting tensions, he viewed with mistrust the release of these brand-new vessels to a nation which might put them to use against his own. Consequently, on July 28 he directed his planners to count them in with the complement of British dreadnoughts. Three days later he called for strong military guards to prevent the Turks from boarding. On August 3, Grey, expressing his government's sincere regret, officially informed the Turkish government that its ships had been commandeered. This addition to Britain's naval strength was welcome indeed. The Turks understandably viewed the action in a different light. German-financed propaganda in Constantinople seized on the story and heightened the Turks' resentment. Sooner than those ships could have arrived from Britain, however, the Turkish Navy had been presented with two replacements.

THE SHIPS AT SEA

The approach of war found the French Army physically divided. Over eighty thousand French soldiers were in Algeria. Most of them would be needed at home if war came with Germany, and French war plans called for their immediate transfer across the Mediterranean to take their places in the battle line. Since the transports would be tempting targets for enemy warships, most of the ships of the French Navy were assigned to protect them. They could rely for support on the Malta-based ships of the British Mediterranean Fleet—the speedy battle cruisers *Inflexible, Indomitable,* and *Indefatigable,* four armored cruisers, four light cruisers, and fourteen destroyers.

Since Austria's fleet was small and kept safely within the Adriatic Sea, the chief threat to the safe passage of the French troops in August, 1914, was posed by two German warships which were then in Mediterranean waters, the battle cruiser *Goeben* and the light cruiser *Breslau.* Both ships could have caused disaster to the French transports, and for this reason the British Admiralty was watching them closely as the inevitability of war increased.

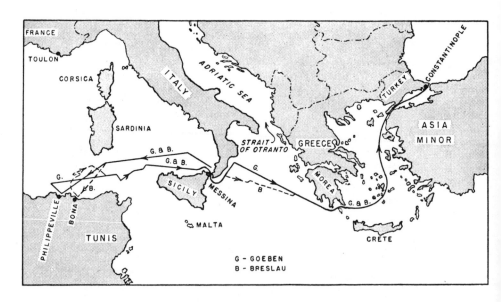

Escape of the "Goeben" and the "Breslau," 1914

Ever since the tragedy at Sarajevo the commander of the *Goeben,* Admiral Wilhelm Souchon, had been preparing his ships and their crews for war. The *Goeben,* launched in 1912, had been troubled by leaky boilers. Had events turned out differently she would have gone to Kiel in October for repairs. As soon as news of the assassination reached Souchon at Haifa, he requested that parts, and men to install them, be provided for him at Pola, the chief port of Austria on the Adriatic. As soon as he could get his ship to Pola he put all available men to work at top speed.

Souchon was no less aware than the British of the hazards of remaining in the Adriatic. The British Mediterranean vessels would have little difficulty in keeping the German ships bottled up where they could serve no useful purpose and present no hazard to Allied shipping. Where else could he go? Escape through the narrow Strait of Gibraltar or through the Suez Canal was probably out of the question, although perhaps he could make it before the actual declaration of war. Unless Italy stood beside Germany —and this seemed increasingly unlikely—Souchon could count on only two ports in the whole area that were large enough to shelter his ships and not subject to Allied domination or influence. Pola was one; the other was Constantinople, and Constantinople's welcome was by no means sure.

Souchon decided against risking confinement to the Adriatic. As soon as the major part of the repairs were finished he got up steam and sailed for Brindisi, on Italy's heel, seeking to fill up with coal. But the Italians refused to supply him, and he continued on, joined now by the *Breslau,* and headed for Messina, on the northeast tip of Sicily.

In command of the British ships in the Mediterranean was Admiral Sir Berkeley Milne, mediocre and cautious to a fault. On July 30 he received orders from the Admiralty to help the French and if possible bring "to action individual fast German ships, particularly *Goeben,* which may interfere." He was warned, however, "except in combination with the French as part of a general battle, do not at this stage be brought to action against superior forces." To the Admiralty this meant to avoid taking on the Austrian fleet single-handed. Unfortunately Milne and his subordinates interpreted it otherwise.

As the days passed Churchill and the First Sea Lord, Prince Louis of Battenberg, watched anxiously and tried to keep Milne in position to attack the German ships as soon as war was declared. Souchon, having taken on coal from some German merchant vessels at Messina, had headed for the Algerian ports of Bône and Philippeville.

Milne had sent Rear Admiral Sir Ernest Troubridge, his second in command, with the bulk of the British fleet, to guard the entrance to the Adriatic. Then, realizing that Souchon was heading west, Milne detached the two large battle cruisers, *Indomitable* and *Indefatigable,* and sent them at full speed to look for him. While they were rushing west, French warships were steaming south, to take their positions as guardians of the invaluable transports.

As the ships of three nations steamed through the night, Souchon's radiomen received an important message for him from home. A treaty had been signed in Constantinople. He should proceed there at once. But Constantinople was far away, and Souchon's target was almost within reach. He continued on his way, determined to fire his guns at least once before he headed for what might prove to be confinement for the rest of the war. As dawn lighted the coast of North Africa, shells from the *Goeben* descended on Philippeville, and from the *Breslau* on Bône. Forced to be satisfied with this minimal action, Souchon turned and headed back to Messina. He could not hope to make it to Constantinople without more coal.

At 9:30 A.M. on August 4, lookouts on the *Indomitable* and the *Indefatigable* sighted the *Goeben* and *Breslau* on an opposite course about eight thousand yards away, well within range of the British guns. But orders from the Admiralty were clear. No attack should be made until the ultimatum to Germany expired at midnight. Admiral Milne ordered guns trained and ready, and the ships passed silently, without the customary exchange of salutes. As the German ships hurried off, Milne ordered his ships about and hastened after them. All day the British ships, joined in the afternoon by the light cruiser *Dublin,* chased after the not-yet-enemy Germans, holding their fire. In London the periodic reports from Admiral Milne kept Churchill and his staff on tenterhooks, and only after soul-searching discussions did they refrain from unleashing the naval guns.

By almost superhuman effort, Souchon drove his ship at maximum speed, about twenty-four knots with his still-leaking boilers. This was good enough to outdistance the British in the late afternoon. Helped by an evening fog, the *Goeben* and *Breslau* disappeared. Milne, who was aboard the *Inflexible*, sent the *Indomitable* to Bizerte to coal. Since the Admiralty had directed Milne to respect the six-mile limit of neutral Italy, he kept his ships at sea and did not attempt to follow Souchon to Messina, where Milne correctly surmised the *Goeben* and *Breslau* had gone. Incorrectly, however, he expected that, before the expiration of the twenty-four-hour limit international law allowed for refueling in a neutral port, the Germans would attempt a dash to the west, perhaps even to escape past Gibraltar. Consequently he kept the three battle cruisers near the northwestern exit of the Strait of Messina and sent a single light cruiser, the *Gloucester*, Captain Howard Kelly commanding, to maintain a watch at the southern and eastern exit.

While the British vessels waited impatiently, Souchon was bending every effort to refuel his ships, driving his men in the hot August sun to transfer the coal from German—and reportedly one British—merchant ships to the two naval vessels. At noon on August 6 he called a halt, gave the weary men a few hours of rest, and then at 5 P.M. was on his way. While in Messina, Souchon had received two messages from Grand Admiral Alfred von Tirpitz, Secretary of State for the Navy. The first message informed him that for political reasons it was inadvisable to try to go to Constantinople. The second reported that the Austrians could give him no help in the Mediterranean, and left it to him to decide where to go. He scarcely hesitated. He would go to the Dardanelles despite orders, and "force the Turks, even against their will, to spread the war to the Black Sea against their ancient enemy, Russia."

As the *Goeben* emerged from the Straits and headed, it appeared, toward the Adriatic Sea, the waiting *Gloucester*'s lookouts spotted her and reported at once both to Milne, still expecting the Germans to head in the opposite direction, and to Troubridge, who, with four armored cruisers and eight destroyers, was patrolling south of Corfu, off the island of Cephalonia. Kelly's light cruiser was no match for the *Goeben*, although she could probably have fought fairly evenly with the *Breslau*. He re-

mained out of range, but followed the Germans as they headed
north, then turned east and southeast toward a prearranged rendezvous with a collier off the southern tip of Greece.

Admiral Troubridge undoubtedly could have intercepted the
ships had he acted immediately upon receipt of the report from
Kelly that Souchon was altering course. Troubridge waited, however, until he was convinced it was not a sham. Just after midnight he turned south, thinking to meet the Germans in the early
light of dawn, when he could perhaps approach undetected and
offset the advantage of longer range held by the *Goeben*. This disadvantage in range weighed heavily on his mind, for he had been
ordered by the Admiralty not to engage superior forces, and
Troubridge viewed the *Goeben* as a "superior force." As the sky
began to lighten and he was still not within view of the Germans,
the likelihood of his getting within range before the *Goeben*'s
guns had sunk his smaller armored cruisers seemed more and
more remote. Just after 4 A.M. he signaled to Milne that he was
abandoning the search.

As the *Goeben,* joined by the *Breslau,* which had taken a more
direct route, approached the Greek coast in the morning hours of
August 7, only the *Gloucester* still clung to the trail, despite recent orders from Milne "gradually to drop astern to avoid capture." Souchon could not stop for fuel in view of the enemy. So as
he approached the Greek coast he sent the *Breslau* back to maneuver closer to the *Gloucester* and divert her. Kelly took the opportunity to open fire, determined to force the *Goeben* to turn and
protect the *Breslau*. Both the German ships returned his fire, but
neither side scored. Kelly dropped back, and the Germans sped
on. At 4:30 P.M. on August 7, Kelly abandoned the chase, and the
Goeben sailed on into the Aegean to the island of Denusa, where
she met her collier late in the afternoon of August 9.

Milne, meanwhile, finally decided to head east in search of the
Goeben. He was halfway to Cape Matapan when an erroneous report that war had begun with Austria diverted him from his
course and sent him toward the Adriatic. By the time this error
was rectified and he resumed the eastward search, he was much
too late. He entered the Aegean early in the morning of August
10, at almost the same time that Souchon was leaving Denusa. At
8:30 that evening the German ships entered the Dardanelles.

Milne was forty miles north of Denusa at noon the following day before he received the news from the Admiralty.

The passage of the *Goeben* and the *Breslau* through the Dardanelles was a triumph for the Germans, and particularly for the German ambassador in Constantinople, Baron von Wangenheim. While the British felt secure in the knowledge that the Treaty of Paris of 1856 and the Treaty of London of 1871 both forbade passage of warships through the Straits of the Dardanelles except in peacetime with the express permission of the Turkish Sultan, Von Wangenheim had been scheming to circumvent the treaties. He saw in the presence of the two ships an opportunity to push the reluctant Turks toward war. Capitalizing on the British seizure of the two new Turkish warships in England, Von Wangenheim proposed that as replacements the Turkish government buy the *Goeben* and the *Breslau*. No money need be involved, and it would hardly be an inconvenience to Germany since the ships had little chance of escaping from the Mediterranean and could most usefully be sent to Constantinople. Von Wangenheim managed to persuade the Turkish leaders to accept this scheme. So it was that when Admiral Souchon arrived off the entrance to the Straits and asked permission to pass through, hopeful but completely uncertain what the answer would be, permission was granted. Although few were fooled by the fictitious purchase, the *Goeben* was renamed *Yavuz Sulten Selim* and the *Breslau, Midilli,* and the German crews, including Admiral Souchon himself, took to wearing fezzes when they went ashore.

The arrival of the ships did not cause the Turks to declare war, as Von Wangenheim had hoped, but it did insure that Turkey could not long stay neutral and would ultimately go to war on the German side. It also effectively ended all possibility of the Allies' sending supplies in quantity to Russia. The results of this victory without a battle were probably more far-reaching than any other single event of World War I.

4

First Battles in the West

LIÈGE

The first serious obstacle in the path of the German invasion of France was the fortified Belgian area of Liège. Since the German General Staff had altered Von Schlieffen's original plan to avoid violating neutral Netherlands territory, the advance had to pass between the Belgian-Dutch border and the broken, forested terrain of the Ardennes area and to cross the Meuse River. In the middle of the passageway, astride the Meuse, lies the industrial city of Liège. Five bridges crossed the Meuse in and around the city, which was also at a junction of four railroad lines which the Germans must control in order to supply their armies in Belgium and France.

For defense Liège was ringed by twelve mutually supporting concrete forts, designed by the great fortifications engineer Henri Brialmont, and built in the 1880's. It was generally considered the strongest position in Europe. The forts at Liège were almost entirely underground, with retractable guns—four hundred of them —observation towers, and huge underground barracks, magazines, corridors, and ramps. In the center of the ring of forts were the city and the citadel, the latter a more traditional fortress used largely as the area army headquarters. In charge of the Belgian defense was General Gérard Mathieu Leman. He had forty thousand men in the garrison and orders from King Albert to "hold to the end."

On August 5 the Germans, having crossed the Belgian border the day before, presented Leman with a surrender ultimatum. He refused it and prepared to defend his forts.

The Germans detailed six brigades of the Second Army as a

special Army of the Meuse under General Otto von Emmich to take Liège. Once the city's five bridges were in German hands the First and Second Armies could pass through on their way to France. The plan was to send a cavalry force across the river north of Liège. It would swing around the west side of the city and attack the forts from that direction while infantry penetrated between the forts and captured the city. Artillery, including—if they were ready in time—specially built 42-centimeter (16.6-inch) howitzers and 30.5-centimeter (12-inch) mortars, would support the attack and blast the forts to rubble.

The initial German attacks made little progress, for Belgian troops had entrenched between the forts, and they held the Germans from marching through the ring. The forts proved impregnable to light artillery. Piles of German corpses built up before them, victims of one of the new and basic weapons of World War I, the machine gun. The German attack stalled temporarily, long enough for the Allied press to proclaim a great Belgian victory.

Among the staff officers attached to the Army of the Meuse was Major General Erich Ludendorff, a brilliant soldier who as a member of the German General Staff had carefully planned the seizure of Liège. He was accompanying the 14th Brigade, in the center of the German line, on the night of August 5. Morale was low among the troops as rumor magnified the facts of the strong Belgian resistance. When word reached Ludendorff that the brigade commander, General von Wussow, had been killed, Ludendorff seized command, rallied the men, and ordered them to attack. Skillfully he led them as they pushed their way through the defenses between two of the forts, and in the afternoon of August 6 gained the heights across the river from the citadel of Liège. Although the rest of the German attackers were still halted, General Leman decided not to sacrifice the Belgian 3rd Division, which was defending the area, and ordered it to withdraw to Louvain. He refused to surrender the forts, however, and the German attack continued.

Although only the 14th Brigade had penetrated the circle of forts, and none of the forts had yet fallen, Ludendorff and General von Emmich, who had joined him, entered the city of Liège on August 7, accepted the surrender of the citadel, and arrested the burgomaster. Still the forts held out, and the Germans waited for their big guns to be brought up. On August 12 the ninety-eight-ton forty-two-centimeter howitzers started firing their eighteen-hundred-pound high explosive shells at the forts. One by one the forts were blasted to bits. In the ruins of the last to fall, General Leman was found unconscious. He was carried off to spend the rest of the war as a German prisoner. The way was now open for the German advance to proceed across Belgium.

The Germans had expected the Belgians to yield their country without a fight. They were outraged at the losses they suffered at Liège and at Haelen, where on August 12 Belgian riflemen soundly defeated some of the finest squadrons of German cavalry. Even more outrageous, it seemed to the Germans, was the armed resistance they encountered from Belgian civilians. The jumpy, green German troops shot many of these *franc tireurs,* as well as innocent bystanders, providing a basis for Allied propaganda stories of atrocities against the Belgians.

In view of King Albert's insistence on Belgian neutrality, Ludendorff considered the resistance unfair. In the memoirs he published after the war he wrote plaintively of the blasted bridges and the tunnels dynamited by the Belgians as the Germans approached. "Why didn't they destroy the bridges near the French border if they were really neutral?" he wondered. Even the delay at Liège held up the German advance for only two days beyond schedule, however. General Alexander von Kluck's First Army and General Karl von Bülow's Second pushed ahead into southern Belgium against little resistance. Brussels was occupied on August 20, and the Belgians withdrew to the fortress of Antwerp.

ÉLAN IN ALSACE

The five French armies had taken their positions in the first days of August in numerical order from the Swiss border on the south (right) to Hirson on the north (left). As they prepared to carry out Plan XVII and strike at once at Alsace, no amount of reports of Germans massing on the Belgian border could have changed Joffre's mind. Even when German troops marched into Belgium he did not consider changing his plans in order to meet them.

The first offensive into Alsace was carried out at the far right of the French line by two elements of General Auguste Dubail's First Army, the VII Corps and 8th Cavalry Division. Its objective was the capture of Mulhouse and Colmar, and then an advance to the Rhine just below the Swiss border. In the early morning of August 7 the VII Corps advanced with bayonets fixed on the town of Altkirch, which they captured after a six-hour battle. Mulhouse was taken without a shot, for the Germans had withdrawn farther north to guard the frontier. They hurried back, however. Welcoming celebrations were scarcely over when the Germans attacked, on the morning of August 9. The French fought stubbornly until the next morning, when, despite a reserve division which was rushed to the area, they avoided envelopment by retreating back across the frontier.

By this time persistent reports were reaching Joffre's headquarters at Vitry-le-François of a strong buildup of German forces on the French left, ready to flood into the plain of Flanders. Still the French commander remained intent on freeing Alsace and Lorraine and proceeded with plans for the offensive prescribed by Plan XVII. His next move was to add one regular and three reserve divisions to the VII Corps to form a new Army of Alsace, which he put under the command of General Paul Marie Pau, popular one-armed veteran of the Franco-Prussian War.

5

The Battles at the Western Frontiers

ALSACE AND LORRAINE

On August 14 General Joffre launched his main offensives. In the first action, Dubail's First Army, with the new Army of Alsace on its right, was to capture Sarrebourg and advance toward Strasbourg, while the Second Army, commanded by Joffre's deputy, General Noel Marie Joseph Edouard de Curières de Castelnau, attacked on the left toward Morhange. Facing them were the German Sixth Army under Colonel General Josias von Heeringen and the Seventh Army under Crown Prince Rupprecht of Bavaria.

As the French crossed into the provinces, visible for miles in their red *pantalons,* their spirits were high. They were going to regain for France the land she had lost in the Franco-Prussian War. But they soon ran into fire from machine guns and light artillery, for the Germans were falling back in accordance with their plan, and fighting a delaying action that proved costly to the French. For four days the Germans withdrew. The French, though suffering heavy casualties, advanced confidently if wearily. Then, on August 20, the Germans counterattacked. Fighting was very heavy. The First Army pulled back, and two corps of the Second Army were driven back in great disorder. Only the XX Corps, commanded by General Ferdinand Foch, stood firm until ordered by De Castelnau to withdraw. The Germans pursued slowly. After five days the French established their defense on the wooded heights known as the Grande Couronne, east and northeast of the rail center of Nancy.

The ease with which the French attack had been repulsed seemed to Von Moltke and his staff to offer great possibilities. The plan had been to halt, once the French offensive was repulsed in Lorraine, and, leaving enough forces in the area to defend the German position, to shift all that could be released to aid in the major advance on the right. Now there appeared a possibility of breaking through on the left and, in combination with the right-wing offensive, executing a great double envelopment. Von Moltke decided to take advantage of the opportunity. He told Rupprecht to continue the offensive, using the Sixth and Seventh Armies.

The French offensive in Lorraine had failed, but it had succeeded in tying down German forces which, under the original German plan, would have been available to strengthen the right wing. There they might have had a decisive influence on the outcome.

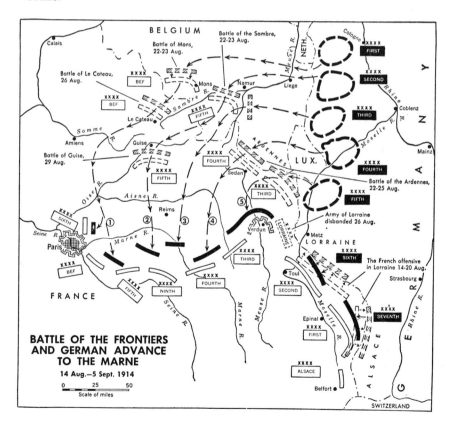

**BATTLE OF THE FRONTIERS
AND GERMAN ADVANCE
TO THE MARNE**

14 Aug.–5 Sept. 1914

THE ARDENNES

The original French plan included an offensive by the Fifth
and Third Armies, with the Fourth as reserve, north and south of
Metz, completely avoiding Belgian territory, unless the Germans
first violated it. When the Germans attacked at Dinant on August
15, however, Joffre was persuaded that the Metz plan, for which
he was preparing, would have to be changed. Despite consistent
intelligence reports of the overwhelming strength of the German
advance into Belgium, Joffre believed that the demonstrated
strength of the German left in Lorraine and right in Belgium indicated that the center must be weak. He would proceed with the
plan to attack, but move the offensive up to the Belgian frontier.

In accordance with his interpretation of the situation, Joffre
shifted the Fifth Army, commanded by General Charles L. M.
Lanrezac, north to the junction of the Sambre and the Meuse, and
ordered the Fourth Army, under General Fernand de Langle de
Cary, and the Third Army, under General Pierre Ruffey, to proceed with an attack across the southeast corner of Belgium, including part of the formidable Ardennes Forest. On the right of
the Third Army Joffre formed a new army of reserve divisions,
the Army of Lorraine, commanded by General Joseph Maunoury.

On the other side of the front in this area were the German
Fifth Army, commanded by Crown Prince Wilhelm, son of the
Kaiser, and Fourth Army, under Duke Albrecht of Württemberg.
These formed the pivot around which the whole right wing of the
German front turned. On August 19 they received orders to ad-
vance, the Fourth against Neufchateau, and the Fifth against
Virton, Longwy, and Montmedy. Two days later advance units of
both the French and the German forces met in the morning fog.
By the next morning the two forces had squared off for battle.

On both sides activity was hampered by the nature of the terrain in which they fought. Narrow forest roads through the thick
woodland of the lower Ardennes Forest made communications extremely difficult. Hills and valleys offered cover for snipers. Heat
added to the discomfort, and hand-to-hand fighting with revolvers
and bayonets increased the horror. The fighting centered in four
actions, near the villages of Virton, Tintigny, Rossignol, and

Neufchateau. The Germans had dug in as soon as the commanders realized a battle was developing. But the French, neither equipped with picks and shovels nor trained in their use, advanced with fixed bayonets as they had been taught, into the deadly rain of machine-gun fire. At Virton the French light artillery piece, the seventy-five-millimeter gun, proved its worth by enabling the French VI Corps to capture a German corps. Elsewhere, however, the French were repulsed at heavy loss. De Langle's troops were stopped at Tintigny, and a French Algerian division was virtually annihilated at Rossignol. It was clear to the two commanders that their offensive was dead. After attacking again on August 24, on Joffre's orders, the French streamed back in retreat west of the Meuse and established themselves with their right flank on the fortress of Verdun.

As the French Third Army fled through the Ardennes, back toward Verdun, Crown Prince Wilhelm's Fifth Army pursued past the important iron and steel center of Longwy. Wilhelm was acclaimed by the German press as the conqueror of Longwy, and an idealized bust of him bearing that legend was placed before the Eberlein Museum in Berlin.

THE SAMBRE

Lanrezac had moved toward the Sambre-Meuse angle, meanwhile, with orders to attack north across the Sambre or east across the Meuse, depending on where the German forces were. Actually they were coming from both directions, General Karl von Bülow's Second Army from the north and Colonel General Baron Max von Hausen's Third Army from the east. On Von Bülow's right was General Alexander von Kluck's First Army.

Lanrezac was worried, for this left flank was unprotected. The Belgians had withdrawn to Antwerp, and the British Expeditionary Force, which was supposed to have taken a position on Lanrezac's left, was not yet there. Sir John French insisted that his men could not be ready for action before August 24, and Lanrezac's efforts to persuade him to move up sooner had failed. Neither commander spoke the other's language. This handicap served to aggravate a natural feeling of antipathy between the two men.

Von Bülow had been placed over Von Kluck shortly before this.

The German High Command had reasoned that the British would land at the Channel ports, Ostend, Calais, and Dunkirk, where they could attack the flank of the German right wing. To avoid the possibility that in response to such an attack Von Kluck's First Army might swing to the right and open a gap between itself and Von Bülow's Second, it was desirable that one man control both armies. Von Bülow, seeing a chance to envelop Lanrezac's Fifth Army, ordered Von Kluck to attack from the west while he himself attacked from the north and General Max von Hausen from the east.

Late in the afternoon of August 21, while the huge German siege guns were beginning to reduce the forts at Namur to rubble, Lanrezac's men took up positions on the high ground south of the Sambre River. Trained for the offensive, the French soldiers did not dig in or fortify their line with barbed wire. When troops of the German Second Army seized bridges across the river and attacked, the French charged in the best French tradition, and were pushed back.

The following day Von Bülow attacked across the Sambre with three corps, joined late in the day by Von Hausen. All across the French Fifth Army front the Germans pushed hard against the French. On the far left General C. C. Sordet's Cavalry Corps fell back, leaving the flank exposed. When Lanrezac asked Sir John French to strike at Von Bülow's right flank, French refused, promising only to hold the line of the Mons Canal for twenty-four hours. On the Fifth Army right flank General Louis Franchet d'Esperey's I Corps counterattacked and held its line on the Meuse, while the other corps were being driven back.

Franchet d'Esperey was hoping to attack north and envelop Von Bülow's left flank, when word came that the German Third Army had crossed the Meuse farther south, where it would threaten the rear of the French Fifth. Without approval from Lanrezac, Franchet d'Esperey hurried south, sending a brigade under an aggressive young commander, Charles Mangin, to throw them back.

Mangin succeeded, but Lanrezac did not know it when he received word that the Ardennes offensive had failed and he could not count on De Langle's support on his right flank. He did not know what the British were doing on his left. Concluding that his situation was precarious, he sought and received permission to withdraw.

BRITISH RIFLES AT MONS

The British Army, though small, was a precision instrument, built on rigorous individual training in rifle marksmanship. It was ready to go where needed to protect the Empire, and ideally suited for trouble-shooting, for putting down a mutiny in India or dealing with warring African tribesmen. Britain had no conscription, and none of her reservists had been sent to France with the British Expeditionary Force. The foreboding of the Secretary of State for War, Field Marshal Lord Horatio H. Kitchener, at placing this band of 125,000 men in the midst of the clash of European armies of millions was well justified.

After the five divisions of the BEF landed in France they concentrated in the vicinity of Le Cateau, on the left of the French Army as planned. Field Marshal Sir John French had orders to cooperate with the French, but he was not under French command. His headquarters were only thirty-five miles from General Lanrezac's, and the two generals should have been fighting one coordinated battle, but they were not. Neither knew much of what the other was doing.

On August 22 the British took up a position on the Mons Canal, an extension of the line of the Sambre, on Lanrezac's left flank, covering a thirty-five-mile front, with the cavalry division in reserve to exploit a breakthrough. On the left was the II Corps, commanded by General Sir Horace Smith-Dorrien; on the right was Lieutenant General Sir Douglas Haig's I Corps.

Early on Sunday morning, August 23, the British at Mons were struck by the main body of the German First Army. Strongest of the German armies, the First was on the right wing and had the all-important mission of sweeping wide around the Allied armies and trapping them. Von Kluck was farther east than had been intended, partly because the Germans, too, had command problems. Von Bülow, anticipating battle with Lanrezac on the Sambre, lost his perspective, and thinking mainly of his own situation he or-

dered Von Kluck to change his direction of advance from south-
west to south, passing near Mons and Maubeuge. The aggressive
Von Kluck, imbued with the central idea of the Von Schlieffen
Plan, insisted on maintaining his wide westward sweep, but he
was overruled. Neither of the German generals knew that the
British were already stationed in his path. By changing plans
Von Kluck lost the opportunity to envelop the British left flank.

This was mining country and, though level, was broken by
houses, factories, ditches, pit heads, and slag heaps. The two armies scarcely saw each other before the Germans ran headlong
into the British II Corps. Smith-Dorrien's men greeted the enemy
with aimed rifle fire of such speed and accuracy that the Germans
thought they faced an army of machine-gunners. Actually the
British, like the Germans, had only two machine guns per battalion. German infantry tactics were not markedly superior to the
French, although they relied on artillery preparation rather than
the initial charge with the naked bayonet, but they too moved forward in masses. The cliché "mowed down," with its association
with fields of cut grain, was grimly appropriate when these masses were swept by fire such as that of the British infantry.

The devastating casualties suffered by the Germans in the
morning engagement caused Von Kluck to reorganize and to prepare a coordinated attack, with artillery giving close support to
the infantry. In renewed attacks the artillery took its toll, and by
nightfall the British had fallen back three miles, blowing up two
important bridges behind them. Proud of their showing against
the renowned German army, they were eager to resume the battle
the next day.

Von Kluck, meanwhile, realizing that he had unwittingly
launched a frontal attack on a strong enemy, came up with a new
plan. His two flanking corps had not been involved in the fight.
Now he would use them in a double envelopment while holding
steady with his center.

By this time the British realized that they were badly outnumbered. At eleven o'clock that night came the news that General
Lanrezac was moving the French Fifth Army back, on their right
flank. Sir John, not wanting to leave his flank exposed, had no
choice but to withdraw also. Orders reached Haig in good time,
but difficulty in finding Smith-Dorrien's headquarters to deliver

the message so delayed his withdrawal that his men, who had done most of the fighting on the twenty-third, had to withdraw under heavy fire.

So ended the Battle of Mons and began the more harrowing retreat. The "contemptible little army," as the Kaiser had called the British Expeditionary Force, had fought well, had delayed the Germans for one day, and was now swept up in the general Allied flood ebbing southwest, toward Paris.

6

The German Advance
to the Marne

PLANS

On August 25 Joffre directed the Third, Fourth, and Fifth French Armies and the British Expeditionary Force to continue their disengagement southwestward while the French First and Second Armies in Alsace and Lorraine held in place. The withdrawing forces were to be prepared to counterattack when the general line Abbeville-Amiens-Laon-Verdun had been reached. This counterattack would be essentially a Von Schlieffen-type movement in reverse, with Verdun as the axial point.

In order to accomplish this task Joffre needed more strength on the left flank, to reinforce the French Fifth Army and the BEF. Hurriedly he sent Sordet's Cavalry Corps and three Territorial divisions under General Albert d'Amade to fill the space between the BEF and the sea. By withdrawing units from the right flank and drawing on reserves from France's interior, he formed two new armies, the Sixth and the Ninth. The Sixth Army, commanded by General Maunoury, was to assemble in the Amiens vicinity, west of Von Kluck's First Army, preparatory to an attack on the German right flank. The Ninth, commanded by General Foch, was to secure a gap that had developed between the French Fourth and Fifth Armies during the retreat.

Meanwhile Von Moltke evaluated his commanders' reports at Coblenz (over one hundred miles from the nearest section of the front) and concluded that French resistance was on the verge of collapse. He was worried by reports of a Russian victory at Gumbinnen in East Prussia. Consequently, in accordance with his interpretation of Von Schlieffen's plan that reinforcements should be sent east as soon as it was apparent that the French were incapable of resistance, he ordered two corps, one each from the Second and Third Armies, to the Eastern Front. This transfer, combined with the forces already sent to reinforce the Sixth and Seventh Armies and to besiege Antwerp and the French fortress of Maubeuge, reduced the strength of the German right flank from sixteen to eleven corps at a time when Joffre was reinforcing his left flank.

On August 28 Von Moltke ordered his five right-flank armies to continue their advance to envelop the French forces. The First Army was to march to the Seine southwest of Paris; the Second was to strike directly for the capital city; the other three armies of the right wing were to advance to the Marne. The Sixth and Seventh Armies on the east flank were to complete the double envelopment by continuing their assault toward the Moselle.

LE CATEAU

The British southwesterly retirement from Mons was difficult. Von Kluck, believing that the Channel ports of Boulogne and Calais were British bases of operation, relentlessly drove his troops forward in an attempt to turn the BEF's west flank and sever its line of communications. The weary British II Corps, on the left of the line, was especially harassed and was forced to fight rearguard actions throughout August 24 and 25. By evening of the twenty-fifth the exhausted troops, closely pursued by German units, tenuously occupied the line Le Cateau–Inchy–Caudry, with the I Corps continuing the line eastward to the Landrecies-Maroilles area.

The retreat was supposed to continue the following day, but because the troops were exhausted and refugees and French troops moving to reinforce the Allied left flank had choked the lines of retreat, Smith-Dorrien decided that he would hold the Le Cateau line during the twenty-sixth and withdraw under cover of darkness the following night. Haig's I Corps, on the other hand, followed Field Marshal French's orders and resumed the retreat before daybreak on August 26, leaving the right flank of the II Corps exposed.

Von Kluck had not expected the British to remain in position during the twenty-sixth, but when informed that his leading units had encountered the British position, he ordered a general attack. The British II Corps, forced to fight both in front and on the right against the overwhelming strength of the German First Army, managed to hold the center of the line throughout most of the day. In the early afternoon the 5th Division, on the right flank, sustained heavy casualties and lost most of its artillery when it had to withdraw under heavy fire to avoid annihilation. On the left General Sordet's French cavalry came riding up and occupied the Germans while the 4th Division extricated itself from threatened envelopment.

After the battle Von Kluck's own losses, the darkness, and the almost complete exhaustion of his troops mitigated against an immediate pursuit. This delay allowed Smith-Dorrien's corps to break contact and continue the retreat. During the Le Cateau engagement the British lost almost eight thousand men (of forty thousand committed) and thirty-eight guns. The toll might have been higher had Von Kluck used more of his divisions against the British. His two right-flank corps, attempting to complete the envelopment of the BEF, had been engaging French Territorial elements protecting the Allied left flank, and two other corps had been busy elsewhere. Thus Von Kluck never had more than three divisions of infantry engaged against the British II Corps; however, he did concentrate the artillery power of five divisions.

BATTLE OF GUISE

While fighting raged at Le Cateau, Joffre conferred with French, Lanrezac, and D'Amade. After hearing the commanders' reports, he decided that the Allied forces probably could not be organized for an attack, and that the retreat would have to be continued for a few more days. Then the proposed offensive would be begun farther south. The situation looked even worse when Joffre received a pessimistic report on the Battle of Le Cateau that questioned the viability of the BEF as a fighting force. Since an intact BEF was a necessary component in the counterattack plan, Joffre ordered Lanrezac to pivot his Fifth Army west at once and attack the flank of the German First Army to relieve pressure on the British.

Still closely pursued from the north by Von Bülow's Second Army, Lanrezac reluctantly initiated a redeployment plan. He ordered the XVIII and III Corps to turn west and prepare to strike toward St. Quentin, while the X Corps fanned out, facing north, and defended the original Fifth Army front. The reserve, I Corps, commanded by General Louis Franchet d'Esperey, was to be ready to move to either front depending on the course of the battle. Lanrezac also asked French to mount a diversive action to hold Von Kluck's First Army in place. French refused. Since Lanrezac's action was designed to relieve pressure on the British, to take full advantage of the respite French felt that his troops shouldn't engage in battle. Moreover, he wanted to be in a position to escape to the sea in case of a total French collapse. This refusal added more fuel to the already blazing fire of distrust and antipathy that had developed between the two commanders.

The French strike west toward St. Quentin was a dismal failure. On August 29 Von Bülow ordered a general attack along his Second Army front. The right flank of the French III Corps (the northernmost of the western-facing corps) came under fire, and all westward movement of the unit ceased. The XVIII Corps commander, informed that the corps on his right had dropped back, leaving his flank unsupported, abandoned vigorous attack. At the end of the day's battle, during which Von Kluck's First Army forces were not even engaged, Lanrezac's two left-flank corps, instead of attacking, were defending the Oise River line.

The heaviest action of the day occurred near Guise along the original Fifth Army front. Von Bülow's initial assault pushed back the French X Corps as well as the right flank of the III Corps. The reserve I Corps, under Franchet d'Esperey, was sent in between the X and III Corps and ordered to counterattack. In a vicious strike in the center of the line, the French threw back the Germans, giving the French their first tactical success of the war. However, Lanrezac's army was deployed in an almost untenable position. Because of the withdrawal of the BEF on his left and the Fourth Army on his right, both of his flanks were exposed. Therefore, with Joffre's permission, Lanrezac continued the retreat the following day. Von Bülow's army, in no condition to pursue after this setback, remained near the Oise for thirty-six hours, allowing both the BEF and the French Fifth Army to continue their retreat unhindered. Thus the action accomplished

Joffre's purpose even though the battle didn't follow the attack plan.

After Le Cateau Von Kluck, no longer subordinate to Von Bülow, pushed his First Army on to the southwest on the heels of the British but not quite catching them. His right-wing forces encountered parts of the new French Sixth Army and drove them back. Von Kluck believed that he had destroyed the fighting capability of the BEF and that the French Fifth Army was the only remaining unit on the Allied left that was still capable of resistance. Consequently, when Von Bülow asked him for help in exploiting the Second Army's "victory" at Guise, Von Kluck agreed. This would mean abandonment of the encirclement of Paris in favor of encirclement of the Fifth Army, for he would wheel his army to the southwest toward Noyon and Compiègne and pass east, instead of west, of the city. But it promised the defeat of the French armies.

When Von Moltke was told of the change of plans he hastened to approve it, although actually Von Kluck had already started to move. Von Moltke had been worried about gaps which had developed between the four armies on the right, and Von Kluck's move would bring them closer together. It also promised the quick victory the Germans sought.

Meanwhile Joffre was beginning to see how his revised plans could be put into effect. On September 1 he issued orders to continue the retreat as far as the Seine River if necessary in order to remove the Fifth Army from all danger of envelopment. Maunoury's Sixth Army was to assemble in and around Paris and prepare to strike east against the right flank of the German First Army if it continued its southeastward advance. If Von Kluck moved west again, Maunoury was to attack his left flank, in an attempt to cut him off from the main body of the German armies.

At this juncture Joffre was not sure to what extent he could count on British participation in his counteroffensive scheme. He had intended French's BEF to be the principal blocking force in front of Von Kluck's army when Maunoury launched his counterattack. But French was withdrawing southwest as quickly as he could, and it appeared he wanted no part of any counterattack plans. Rumors of the tension between the two commanders reached the British Cabinet, and Lord Kitchener sent a message asking French if he was conforming to Joffre's plan. Upon receiving an unsatisfactory reply, Kitchener went to Paris and conferred with both Joffre and French. After these conversations French seemed more cooperative and wired Joffre, suggesting that it was time for the Allies to stop and fight.

From August 30 through September 2, Von Kluck drove his weary troops southeast. The speed of his advance, and Von Bülow's delay after Guise, meant that the German Second Army, now moving south, was more than a day's march behind the First. It appeared to Von Kluck that he and Von Bülow had an opportunity to envelop the French Fifth Army, his First striking the left flank, while the Second came in from the front. By September 2 Von Kluck's IX Corps was straddling the Marne River near Chateau-Thierry. His leading units were actually *behind* the French Fifth Army's left flank, and almost fifteen miles south of Von Bülow's right. The First Army's right flank and center had crossed the Oise and were advancing toward the Ourcq River, pressing the British, who were on the Marne, just east of Paris.

That night Von Kluck was ordered by Von Moltke to follow the Second Army in echelon and screen its right wing while advancing east of Paris. Von Moltke, aware of French reinforcements near Paris, thought Von Kluck's forces would contain the French near Paris while the rest of the invading armies continued the envelopment program. Separated from the battlefield, however, he did not know that Von Bülow was far behind Von Kluck, nor did he notify Von Kluck of the new French forces in Paris.

Von Kluck knew that if he halted and tried to follow Von Moltke's orders it would take two days for Von Bülow's division to catch up. He was not aware of the situation near Paris and believed that his army was the only one that was in a position to drive the French east away from the capital. Von Kluck therefore decided on September 3 to press across the Marne with three corps, to fulfill what he thought was the spirit of Von Moltke's attack plan, while leaving two corps north of the Marne to contain any movement from Paris.

Joffre, by September 3, knew that Maunoury's Sixth Army would be afforded an opportunity to strike eastward against Von Kluck's advancing right wing. Since his own right-wing armies were in good positions that enabled them to hold any assaults by the German Sixth and Seventh Armies, Joffre withdrew more units from them and reinforced Foch's Ninth and Maunoury's Sixth Armies near Paris. He then reshuffled his commanders, most notably replacing Lanrezac by Franchet d'Esperey. The new Fifth Army commander got along with Field Marshal French, and this presaged a period of better BEF–Fifth Army coordination. Between Paris and Verdun the Allies were now in numerical superiority over their tiring foes.

The French government fled to Bordeaux on September 2, leaving the impression that the French were resolved to continue the fight regardless of the fate of Paris. This attitude was also reflected by the actions of General Joseph-Simon Gallieni, the military governor of Paris, who announced that he was prepared to hold the city "to the bitter end."

At about this time Von Moltke decided that his right-wing armies were not strong enough to break the Allied forces near Paris. Since his central armies had seen little serious fighting lately, on September 4 he issued new orders. The Third, Fourth, and Fifth Armies were to assault the French center, the Fourth and Fifth striking southeast toward the Sixth and Seventh Armies, which were to renew their offensive in Lorraine and the Vosges. The First and Second Armies were not to attack but to halt and protect the German right flank against the Allied forces around Paris.

Von Kluck, when he received the orders, couldn't believe that his army was to face Paris from positions between the Marne and Oise Rivers, for four of his five corps were already south of the Marne, marching toward the Seine. Only his reserve corps, the IV, was north of the Marne, near Meaux. Von Kluck decided that Von Moltke did not understand the situation. He continued his advance. Only when a staff officer sent by Von Moltke explained the situation on September 5 did Von Kluck realize the danger. He then ordered two corps back across the Marne and waited before shifting his entire army backward.

7

The Battle of the Marne

PLANS

Despite the long retreat the Allied armies had just made, Joffre was determined that they should stand and fight, for he knew that the Germans were no less exhausted and that his forces on the left now outnumbered theirs. He had been receiving reports on the activities of the German armies, and particularly of Von Kluck as he headed southeast. Maunoury's Sixth French Army was stationed east of Paris, and Joffre intended to use it to attack Von Kluck's right flank if opportunity offered. Finally he decided to strike on September 6.

On September 4 the order went out. Maunoury was to advance east from Paris, northeast of Meaux, to cross the Ourcq River toward Chateau-Thierry. The British Expeditionary Force was to strike northeast from its position between the Seine and the Marne Rivers. The Fifth would strike north. Together they would try to envelop the German First Army. The French Ninth Army would cover the right flank of the Fifth, while the Fourth and Third, on its right, held their ground.

BATTLE OF THE OURCQ

Maunoury began moving his army east from Paris to his assigned line of departure (Lizy-Mayen-Multien) on September 5. At the same time, General Hans von Gronau, commanding the IV Reserve Corps on the right wing of the German First Army, was proceeding toward Barcy, north of Meaux, across the path of the French Sixth Army. Becoming concerned about reports of movements on his extreme right, Von Gronau decided to find out what was going on by attacking west in the early afternoon.

41

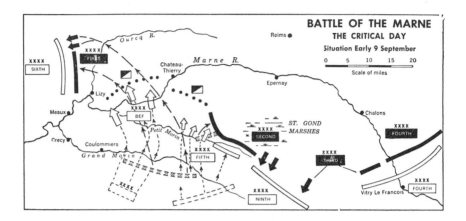

Von Gronau's attack met Maunoury head-on, and the German force pushed back the surprised Frenchmen, who had not expected action until the next day. Despite the initial success, Von Gronau, realizing that he faced a numerically superior force, prudently withdrew to a good defensive position and notified Von Kluck. Not knowing how much was behind the units Von Gronau had encountered, Von Kluck sent him one corps.

The next day Maunoury attacked in strength. With the help of another corps that Von Kluck sent to the front, the Germans held the French attack, but it was not until a copy of Joffre's attack order was found on the battlefield that Von Kluck realized that a major offensive was in progress. Thereupon he moved the rest of his army north to the Ourcq and prepared to attack Maunoury. This widened the gap between the First and Second Armies, but it didn't bother Von Kluck. The British, who were in a position to come between the two German armies, had been retreating since Le Cateau, and he didn't think they were any threat.

Maunoury continued to press his attack on September 7 and 8, reinforced by Sordet's Cavalry Corps and two divisions, including two regiments that General Gallieni rushed to the front from Paris in buses and taxicabs. By September 9 Maunoury had committed the last of his reserves and had to pass to the defensive. Von Kluck, with his army assembled west of the Ourcq, was poised for an attack on Maunoury when he was ordered by Von Moltke to withdraw to the Aisne River.

BATTLE OF THE PETIT MORIN

The French Fifth Army struck north in accordance with Joffre's orders on September 6. Initially it encountered units of Von Kluck's army that were on their way to assist Von Gronau. The action was minor, and both armies continued on their way, Franchet d'Esperey's men approaching the right wing of the German Second Army and the gap between the two. On September 7 Von Bülow realized that his right flank was being enveloped. He ordered his units on that wing back behind the Petit Morin River to avoid encirclement. This movement, while it saved the right flank of the German Second Army, widened the gap in the German line to almost twenty-five miles, a gap that was covered by only two small, thinly spread German cavalry corps. The French Fifth Army, slow to follow the retreat of Von Bülow's right, attacked the Petit Morin line on September 8 without success. That night, however, Franchet d'Esperey mounted a daring attack that forced the Second Army's right back almost six miles farther, to a position facing west. This further widened the gap between the First and Second German Armies, and again placed Franchet d'Esperey's army in an excellent position to envelop the German Second's flank.

The British Expeditionary Force, slow-starting, moved northeast into the gap between the German armies on Franchet d'Esperey's left. On September 7 the British crossed the Marne River, sweeping aside opposition from the German cavalry units. But under Sir John French's cautious leadership, the British took three days to advance twenty-five miles. By the time they were in position to threaten the German First Army, Von Kluck had realized his danger and was able to withdraw the bulk of his forces.

BATTLE OF THE ST. GOND MARSHES

General Foch's French Ninth Army struck north on September 6, from positions in the St. Gond Marshes, his left flank advancing toward the left of Von Bülow's Second Army. The rest of Foch's front faced Von Hausen's Third Army, which was advancing to the south on Von Bülow's left. There was a twelve-mile gap in the Third Army front because almost half the army had been sent to reinforce Duke Albrecht of Württemberg's Fourth Army. Fortunately for both sides, this gap matched one between Foch's right wing and the left wing of General de Langle de Cary's Fourth Army.

Attacked on the left by Von Bülow and on the right by Von Hausen, the French fell back to a stronger position and stood their ground on September 7, with strong support from their light artillery. In the early morning moonlight of September 8, Von Hausen attacked with four divisions and pushed Foch's right wing back in confusion. When notified of the precarious situation of his troops, Foch ordered them, still reeling back, to attack. Although poorly organized, this counterattack halted the German advance. According to undocumented popular reports it was on this occasion that Foch wired Joffre, "My right gives. My center yields. Situation excellent. I shall attack."

Still further attacks on the following day by Von Hausen, assisted by some of Von Bülow's units, again pushed most of Foch's units back. But with some help from Franchet d'Esperey and the inspiration of an aggressive, confident commander, the line held.

VITRY-LE-FRANÇOIS

General de Langle de Cary's Fourth Army was to the right of the Ninth Army, its front extending from Vitry-le-François to the vicinity of Revigny. When the Fourth attacked on September 6, it ran headlong into the German Fourth Army, which was also attacking. There was a gap to the right of the French Fourth Army as well as to the left, but Albrecht and Crown Prince Wilhelm, who commanded the German Fifth Army to the east, couldn't agree on how to exploit the two openings. Consequently, the French and Germans fought bitterly along the front for days, neither giving ground. The Germans finally decided to attack on the French right flank, but by then reinforcements from Lorraine had arrived to fill the gap on De Langle's left, and he had stretched his front eastward and closed that gap as well.

THE THIRD ARMY FRONT

The French Third Army, now commanded by General Maurice Sarrail, held the Allied line on De Langle's right, between Revigny and Verdun. An attack by Sarrail on the German Fifth

Army on September 6 was countered by a German attack. Crown Prince Wilhelm hoped to envelop Sarrail's left near Revigny but never succeeded, partly because of his arguments with Albrecht. Wilhelm's left was east of Verdun, and he sent a corps around the fortress with orders to cross the Meuse River twenty miles south and attack the French Third Army from the rear. This move was thwarted. Even though the Meuse River line was lightly held, a French cavalry division and the garrison at Fort Troyon on the Meuse restrained the Germans until reinforcements arrived.

NANCY AND THE VOSGES

On September 4 the German Sixth and Seventh Armies again tried to smash through the French defenses on the right of the Allied line. The main German effort was against De Castelnau's Second Army at Nancy. On several occasions during the battle De Castelnau requested permission to withdraw, but Joffre ordered him to hold on. By September 10 the negligible German gains sustained Von Schlieffen's theory that attacks in Lorraine would be difficult, and Von Moltke, although slow to accept this theory, finally ordered the attack to stop.

THE HENTSCH MISSION

The decisive action of the Battle of the Marne occurred just east of Paris. Von Moltke, separated from the front during the battle, and lacking good communications, had no real picture of the fighting as it was taking place. It was not until September 8, two days after Joffre's plan had been put into effect, that the German commander had enough information at his disposal to realize that there was a dangerous gap between the First and Second German Armies, and that the British were approaching it. At that point Von Moltke finally acted. He sent Lieutenant Colonel Richard Hentsch, a member of the General Staff, to the front. Hentsch's orders were oral and no one knows quite what they were.

Hentsch visited the headquarters of the Third, Fourth, and Fifth Armies on September 8 and sent back optimistic reports to his commander. That evening he arrived at the Second Army headquarters and found Von Bülow in the midst of a crisis. The Second Army commander was especially concerned about the French threat to his army's right flank. Despite his limited successes against Foch, Von Bülow thought it was time to withdraw both his army and Von Hausen's Third. That night when Von Bülow learned that Franchet d'Esperey's night attack had penetrated his line, he ordered his right flank to withdraw. Hentsch apparently approved this withdrawal in Von Moltke's name.

The next morning, when Hentsch arrived at the First Army headquarters on the Ourcq River, he had to deal with a staff officer, because Von Kluck was near the front, directing his troops in an attack on Maunoury's Sixth Army. That front seemed to be in good shape, but the left flank was now being threatened by the approaching British, and Von Kluck was pulling it back. In Von Moltke's name, Hentsch ordered an immediate withdrawal before the First Army should become entirely trapped.

Von Moltke received Hentsch's report on September 10 and at once ordered the First, Second, and Third Armies to pull back; the other armies were to stop where they were. He then went himself to inspect the battle area. So unfavorable did it appear to him that he ordered a general withdrawal. The front line was to entrench in as strong a line as possible between Noyon and Verdun. Action broke off as the Germans pulled back, for the Allied troops were exhausted after their three weeks of marching and fighting and did not have the energy to pursue vigorously.

EVALUATION

The Battle of the Marne was a great strategic victory for the Allies, for it halted the Germans and ended the threat of envelopment. The casualties suffered there by both sides brought the total for a little over a month of war to about a quarter of a million each. The Germans were defeated not only by the greater staying power of the Allies and the superiority of the Allied leaders but by their own strategic shortcomings, which permitted the gaps in their line and the lack of cooperation among their leaders. Joffre showed his skill in making his armies turn about and attack all along the front at the same time. Von Moltke, on the other hand, demonstrated his lack of control over his armies. They probably were saved from disaster only by his recognition of the correct moment to retreat. The defeat was costly for him, for on September 14 the Kaiser relieved him of his duty, replacing him with tall, good-looking, and capable General Erich von Falkenhayn.

8

First Battles on the Eastern Front

There is little doubt that the Battle of the Marne would have gone differently if Von Moltke had not decided he should send two corps to the Eastern Front. However, at the time he did it Von Moltke thought the Western Front was safely in German control. The Eastern Front was a different story.

The eastern boundaries of the Central Powers stretched like two arms around Russian Poland, which pushed Russia's frontier west 250 miles in a great semi-ellipse toward the heart of Germany. North of this bulge East Prussia extended Germany's Baltic coastline east beyond the Niemen River; south of it the frontier of Austria-Hungary's province of Galicia ran east and then south to the border of neutral Rumania. The whole area offered a variety of attractive military possibilities. If the Russians could drive north 80 miles from the border of Poland to the Baltic Sea at Danzig, they could sever East Prussia from Germany. A similar drive to the west would give them control of the raw materials and industry of Silesia. And the plains of Galicia, separated by the imposing Carpathian Mountains from the rest of Austria-Hungary, invited Russian attack from the north. On the other hand, a German drive south from East Prussia, converging with an Austrian drive north, could cut Poland's base with Russia. In fact, all four of these possibilities were being planned by the opposing sides.

EAST PRUSSIA

The original Von Schlieffen Plan had assumed that Russia, big and only partially industrialized as she was, would be so slow to mobilize that victory would be won in the west before she put a significant force in the field. Consequently, only about fifty thousand German troops were to be deployed on the Russian front, to fight a holding action while the bulk of the German Army overwhelmed the French on the Western Front. It might be necessary for the troops in the east to withdraw to the Vistula River, abandoning East Prussia; but, before the Russians could advance farther, German units, fresh from their victory in the West, could be shifted east to drive them back.

Von Moltke was more sensitive than his predecessor to the objections of Prussian nationalists to a plan that almost certainly would result in alien boots tramping across Prussian soil. He was also aware that Russian plans for mobilization had been speeded up. He therefore increased the size of the blocking force on the Eastern Front to about 200,000 men. Events were to prove the wisdom of this decision.

The German troops in the east were organized as the Eighth Army, commanded by General Max von Prittwitz. Von Prittwitz's mission was not one for a man of weak moral courage. He was to defend East and West Prussia from a Russian invasion, while at the same time not allowing his army to be overpowered or bottled up in the heavily fortified area around Königsberg, the capital of East Prussia. Only in the event of engaging a "greatly superior Russian force" was he authorized to retreat to the Vistula River. Von Prittwitz could count, however, on some Austro-Hungarian assistance, since the four Austrian armies mobilizing in Galicia would force the Russians to mass defensive forces in southern Poland. It was hoped that these Austrian armies could invade Poland before Russian armies could complete their mobilization. The other two armies of Austro-Hungarian Chief of Staff General Franz Conrad von Hötzendorf would be invading Serbia.

Behind the frontiers of Prussia and Austria-Hungary was an extensive network of railroads which were an essential element in all the German and Austrian war plans. No less than seventeen lines, capable of carrying five hundred troop trains a day, led from Germany to the Russian frontier. Seven lines crossed the Carpathians from Hungary into Galicia. Many connecting lines made it almost as easy to move troops from one section of the frontier to another. The Russians also had six lines to the front, but few north-south connections to facilitate movement behind the front lines.

Russia's alternatives were obvious, and her war plans were based on them. One, in case of an all-out German attack, called for withdrawal from Poland until enough strength had been assembled for an offensive. The other, recognizing the vulnerability of the Polish salient, provided for simultaneous attacks on East Prussia and Galicia to protect Russia's flanks before she launched an attack in strength west across the salient, into the rich German province of Silesia. It was the latter plan which was put into effect by the Grand Duke Nicholas, commander in chief of the Russian forces in August, 1914.

A large portion of the eastern frontier of East Prussia was shielded by the natural defense of the Masurian Lakes, which extend from Augerburg to the Russian border south of Johannisburg. Instead of trying to cross that area, the Russians divided their forces and attacked around the ends of the lakes with the two armies of the Northwest Army Group under General Yakov Zhilinsky. The First Army, commanded by General Pavel K. Rennenkampf, attacked north of the lakes through the thirty-four-mile-wide Insterburg Gap, while the Second Army, commanded by General Alexander Samsonov, crossed the border from Poland west of the Masurian Lakes. Since the Russians expected the German Eighth Army to concentrate in the north to stop Rennenkampf and to protect Königsberg, Samsonov was to move rapidly north and cut off the Germans from the rear. Together the Russian armies would seize control of the mouth of the Vistula River and isolate the rich agricultural region of East Prussia from the rest of Germany.

Russia had started mobilizing before the declaration of war, and the process was partially completed when the Germans marched into Belgium and the French found themselves under heavy pressure on the Western Front. When the French government begged the Russians for an early offensive that would draw some German forces away from them, Czar Nicholas agreed. On August 13 Grand Duke Nicholas ordered the Northwest Army Group to advance to the attack. Advance they did, inadequately equipped, short of food, and deficient in plans and equipment to coordinate the action of the two armies.

Von Prittwitz had rightly guessed that Rennenkampf's army would invade sooner than Samsonov's and had concentrated three of his corps in position to resist an invasion from the east. The fourth, the XX Corps under General Friedrich von Scholtz, was near Allenstein, preparing to meet Samsonov. Von Prittwitz had the advantage of reading most of the Russian orders, for the Russians, short of communications personnel and equipment, sent them by radio in uncoded messages. The German commander was unaware, however, that although he had ordered his three corps to form behind the Angerapp River, the I Corps was not following orders. Its Prussian commander, General Hermann von François, was unwilling to give up the Prussian territory east of the Angerapp, and he had moved farther forward, to Stallupönen, near the border.

On August 17 the Russian III Corps met the waiting units of Von François's I Corps near Stallupönen. In the fighting that followed, the Russian corps lost about 3,500 men and was thrown back to the frontier. The Russian First Army advance halted, and the victorious Von François withdrew to Gumbinnen to join the other German corps. The following day Rennenkampf again cautiously began to advance beyond Stallupönen toward Insterburg.

Von Prittwitz was not entirely happy with the action at Stallupönen. He had figured from Russian orders that he had five days in which to handle Rennenkampf before he would have to shift at least some of his northern corps to help the XX contend with Samsonov. Therefore Von Prittwitz had been anxious to fight a decisive battle as soon as possible. Now Rennenkampf had been delayed a day, and intercepted messages indicated that he had ordered his units not to attack on August 20 as Von Prittwitz anticipated. In response to a suggestion from Von François, whose I Corps was east of the river near Gumbinnen, Von Prittwitz decided to attack himself, despite the objections of his operations officer, Lieutenant Colonel Max Hoffmann. Hoffmann argued that the other two corps were not yet ready, but Von Prittwitz decided to go ahead.

On August 20 the Germans attacked: I Corps on the left, XVII Corps under General August von Mackensen in the center, and I Reserve Corps under General Otto von Below on the right. The Russian XX Corps on the right of the Russian line wilted away under the fury of Von François's attack, and the German left advanced more than five miles. The I Reserve Corps on the right held its own against the Russian IV Corps but made no progress. In the center, however, Von Mackensen's XVII Corps was repulsed by the Russian III.

The situation looked grim to the Germans by evening, when word reached Eighth Army headquarters that Samsonov had already crossed the Prussian border. This was too much for Von Prittwitz. Seeing no possibility of retrieving Gumbinnen or sending reinforcements to Von Scholtz before Samsonov attacked, he called Von Moltke at Coblenz and told him that he was retreating to the Vistula River. With his present complement of troops he doubted whether he could hold even that line.

After his conversation with Von Moltke, Von Prittwitz conferred with Hoffmann and changed his plans, but no one informed Von Moltke. The German Chief of Staff had already decided that Von Prittwitz was too weak a general and must be replaced by someone who could fight. So he called on General Ludendorff, hero of the German assault at Liège, to take over as Chief of Staff in the East, and because he needed someone of higher rank as commander, he called General Paul von Hindenburg from retirement. The wisdom of his choice would soon be proved.

In his next decision, however, Von Moltke's wisdom failed, not entirely because of his own shortcomings but because no one bothered to tell him what was actually happening on the Eastern Front. Believing that Von Prittwitz was in retreat to the Vistula with Samsonov and Rennenkampf in pursuit, Von Moltke took two corps and a cavalry division from the Western Front and sent them east. Thus the Russians had achieved their chief purpose in invading East Prussia early. They had caused the Germans to weaken their effort in the west in time to help the faltering French and British.

TANNENBERG

When Von Prittwitz consulted his staff, he soon changed his mind about retreating to the Vistula. As Hoffmann pointed out to him, Samsonov was already closer to the Vistula than the Eighth

Army was and could easily intercept the Germans as they tried to retreat. Von Prittwitz was persuaded by Hoffmann's arguments and accepted a new plan. A single cavalry division was to be left facing Rennenkampf, while the I Corps and the 3rd Reserve Division would go by rail to join the XX Corps near Allenstein. The XVII and I Reserve Corps would march west slowly, able to delay Rennenkampf if he decided to advance, or to be shifted south if they were needed against Samsonov.

Ludendorff met Von Moltke at Coblenz on August 22 and was informed of the situation in the east as Von Moltke understood it. Immediately Ludendorff sent a message to Eighth Army headquarters to halt the retreat to the Vistula and concentrate against the Russian Second Army at Allenstein, leaving only a covering force in front of Rennenkampf, exactly what the Eighth Army was already doing. When Von Hindenburg and Ludendorff arrived at the field headquarters the following day, they realized at last what the situation was.

Samsonov's two center corps, the XV and the XXIII, tired after their long march to the frontier, and existing on greatly reduced rations, met the German XX Corps entrenched midway be-

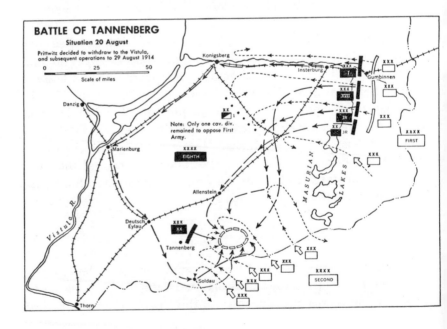

BATTLE OF TANNENBERG

Situation 20 August

Prittwitz decided to withdraw to the Vistula, and subsequent operations to 29 August 1914

0   25   50
Scale of miles

Note: Only one cav. div. remained to oppose First Army.

tween Soldau and Allenstein, on August 24. The battle, known as Orlau-Frankenau, was indecisive. Although the Russian forces greatly outnumbered the German, lack of adequate reconnaissance and control prevented Samsonov from massing them at critical positions where he might have gained the advantage. When Von Scholtz moved one of his divisions back to a stronger position, the Russians, as the Germans learned from intercepted messages, interpreted this as a general withdrawal to the west and set off in pursuit. Since Rennenkampf was moving very slowly, Von Hindenburg ordered the XVII and I Reserve Corps to march south and intercept the VI Russian Corps, on the right flank of Samsonov's army. The Germans were thus spread in a large crescent, the XVII, I Reserve, XX, and I Corps from left to right, and Samsonov was marching right into its center. When his scouts reported the buildup of the German I Corps on his left, Samsonov requested permission from Zhilinsky to shift his line of advance to avoid it, but Zhilinsky, 160 miles to the rear with only a general notion of what was going on, refused.

The first German attack, by Von François, came on August 25 near Soldau. The following day, after his heavy artillery had arrived on the battlefield, Von François struck again and drove the Russian I Corps from the field. On the right wing on the same day the Russian VI Corps was attacked northeast of Allenstein, near Bischofsburg, by the German XVII and I Reserve Corps. The Russians broke and fled back across the border. The three corps in the Russian center, the XIII, XV, and XXIII, were in peril, with both flanks exposed.

Samsonov seems not to have realized his situation immediately, for he ordered an attack in the center on August 28, but the German XX Corps counterattacked and drove the Russian center back. Samsonov's messages to Rennenkampf and Zhilinsky begging for Rennenkampf to come to his aid began to stream into German radio receivers. But no help was coming. Most of Samsonov's army was by this time in retreat.

On the German right Ludendorff ordered a simple envelopment, with the I Corps swinging close behind the Russian left flank to trap the XXIII Corps. But Von François ignored the order and drove straight east in an attempt to spread the net as wide as possible. By the end of August 29, a thin line of German troops had completely cut off the southern escape route of the entire Russian Second Army. On the left wing of the German line, however, the corps of Von Mackensen and Von Below held back, not wishing to move too far from Rennenkampf's threatening position, and most of two of the Russian corps managed to escape. Samsonov, accompanying his troops as they tried to flee on August 29, disappeared, probably committing suicide in despair over the collapse of his army.

The Germans closed in from west, east, and north, capturing 125,000 men and five hundred guns, almost half of the Second Army. German losses were a little more than 10,000. Tactically, Tannenberg was one of the most decisive battles of World War I. Although Russia helped save France by her early invasion of East Prussia, it was at enormous sacrifice. Thereafter no Russian army would face the Germans with confidence.

AUSTRIAN PLANS

While the Russian First and Third Armies were being kept busy in East Prussia, others were achieving better results in Galicia, where Austria-Hungary's Chief of Staff, Field Marshal Franz Conrad von Hötzendorf, had his hands full. When Serbia rejected Austria's ultimatum in July, Conrad ordered Austrian Plan B into effect. This called for sending three armies against Serbia, while the other three Austrian armies protected the Galician borders against any Russian invasion. It was expected that the defeat of Serbia would take only about three weeks. Then a concentrated effort could be made against slowly mobilizing Russia. But after the mechanism of Plan B was started, Conrad changed his mind and decided to shift one army, the Second, sending it also against Russia and only two armies against Serbia. The Second Army was already concentrating north of Belgrade, and part of it was committed in Serbia; so Conrad ordered those units to leave Serbia and join the rest. The whole army would then move north to the Galician front.

SERBIA

Although Serbia was a small country, its people were confident that the invading Austrians could not win an easy victory. Their army, though small, was tough, and it had a most capable commander. General Radomir Putnik was in Austria in July, 1914, being treated by Austrian doctors for a chronic illness. Aware of his whereabouts when the ultimatum was delivered to Serbia, the Austrian government placed him temporarily under arrest, and then sent him back to Serbia. This action was shortsighted, for Putnik, ill though he was, knew the topography of his country so well and was such a skilled strategist that he very ably directed the Serbian Army, seldom having to leave his quarters.

Serbia, remote from her allies, had only one tiny neighbor on whom she could count for support, Montenegro, on her western border. North of Montenegro, and bordering Serbia on the west and north, was Austria-Hungary, on the far bank of three rivers, the Drina on the west and the Sava and Danube on the north. On the east was Bulgaria, whose government had immediately declared neutrality; on the south was Greece, and then Albania, both still silently neutral.

So Serbia was alone. But Putnik had long since worked up a plan for her defense. Leaving only light covering forces on the Austrian borders, and a small force on the Bulgarian frontier in case Bulgaria should relinquish her neutrality in favor of the Central Powers, he concentrated his armies in northwest Serbia to await Austrian moves. Nor had he long to wait. On August 12, 1914, the first Austrian invaders crossed the frontier.

The IV Corps of the Austro-Hungarian Second Army crossed the Sava River and soon captured Sabac, while the Fifth pushed across the Drina. The following day Putnik gathered his forces and counterattacked in earnest. Inferior though the equipment of the Serbs was, most of the troops were veterans of the Balkan Wars, and their spirits were high. Slowly they pushed the Austrians back across the rivers, and the Austrian commander, General Oskar Potiorek, ordered all his troops to withdraw.

Potiorek's troops crossed the Drina and the Sava a second time on September 8. The Serbs counterattacked on the sixteenth and drove the Austrians back toward Bosnia, but Austrian bridgeheads were left behind on both rivers. At this point Putnik decided to withdraw a bit, to avoid being trapped in northwestern Serbia. He moved his forces back to a front running north and south through Valjevo. Almost two months passed before the Austrians tried again in Serbia, for their main attention was fully occupied in Galicia.

GALICIAN BATTLES

Conrad had decided not to wait until the Second Army could reach the Polish border. With the other three armies, he had crossed into Russian Poland on August 22, eager to help the Germans in East Prussia by occupying Russian troops, and confident that Russian mobilization would be incomplete for another month. Conrad's plan was to advance with the First and Fourth Armies through Lublin and Kholm toward Brest Litovsk, where he thought the Russians would concentrate, while the Third Army took up a defensive position east of Lvov. When the Second Army arrived it would come into the line to the right of the Third. Both armies would then advance northeastward into Russian territory on the right of the first two.

Unknown to Conrad, however, the Russian Southwest Army Group, commanded by General Nikolai Ivanov, was already preparing to attack Galicia. Ivanov expected the Austrians to concentrate their strength around Lvov, and he sent his strongest armies, the Third and Eighth, to that sector to strike the Austrian front while the Fourth and Fifth advanced from the Lublin-Kholm area in order to envelop the Austrians' left and attack their rear. Just over the Russian border the advancing Austrian First Army, under General Viktor Freiherr von Dankl, stumbled onto the Russian Fourth, under General Anton Salza, in the vicinity of Kraśnik.

For most of three days the two armies maneuvered in the area between the Wieprz and Vistula Rivers. By August 25, however, the ten divisions of the Austrian Army began to overpower the Russian six. Salza's center was driven back almost seven miles, and his right flank was enveloped by the Austrian left. Only Conrad's order to Von Dankl to slow the advance until his right wing could be protected by the Austrian Fourth Army saved the Russians from disaster. Ivanov promptly replaced Salza with General Aleksei Ewerth and ordered the Fifth Army under General Wenzel von Plehve, which was east of the Fourth, to swing right and assault the Austrian First Army on the right flank and the rear.

On August 26, while moving to execute this order, the Russian Fifth Army collided with the Austrian Fourth, commanded by

General Moritz von Auffenberg, near Komarow. Both commanders underestimated the forces opposing them. Von Auffenberg,
facing the left wing of the Russian Army, decided he could envelop
both flanks, not realizing that he was facing a numerically superior force. Plehve thought he was confronting only the flank
guard of the Austrian First Army and continued to advance. Confused fighting went on until August 30, when Von Auffenberg
succeeded in driving back both of the Russian flanks. For a time
he threatened to encircle Plehve's army, but the Russian realized
his danger and ordered a withdrawal. His escape was facilitated
by rumors that reached the commanders of Von Auffenberg's
flank corps that Russian forces were closing in on them. Both left
and right corps ceased attacking and withdrew. By the following
day, when the rumors were laid to rest, Plehve had gone.

Meanwhile, to the southeast, the Austrian Third Army, under
General von Brudermann, reinforced by a corps-sized force commanded by General Hermann Kövess von Kövessháza, had advanced about twenty miles east of the Gnila Lipa River. There
they were attacked on August 26 by lead elements of the Russian
Third and Eighth Armies, commanded by Generals Nikolai Russki and Aleksei Brusilov, both much more capable than the Russian commanders in East Prussia. The Russians, with a three-
to-one numerical superiority and prepared for battle, quickly
overwhelmed the surprised Austrians, forcing Conrad to order a
retreat to the Gnila Lipa River line.

Ivanov did not realize the full import of this success. Thinking
that the Third and Eighth Armies had met up with the main
Austrian force, he ordered them to halt in order to close ranks
and prepare for a major battle. The advance was resumed on August 30. Attacking with full strength, the Russians this time
smashed the Austrians, who fled from Lvov in great confusion,
with the Russians following close behind.

By this time the Austrian Second Army (minus one corps
which Conrad decided to leave in Serbia) had arrived in the area
just south of Lvov. Conrad ordered the Third Army to halt and
make a stand about twenty miles west of the city, with the Second
on its right. The Fourth Army, having been victorious over the
Russian Fifth at Komarow, was also available to assist the hard-
pressed Third. Conrad ordered Von Auffenberg to wheel com-

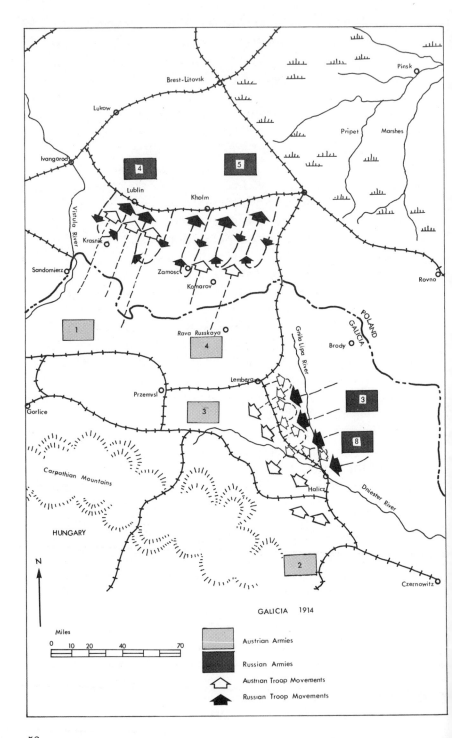

GALICIA   1914

Austrian Armies

Russian Armies

Austrian Troop Movements

Russian Troop Movements

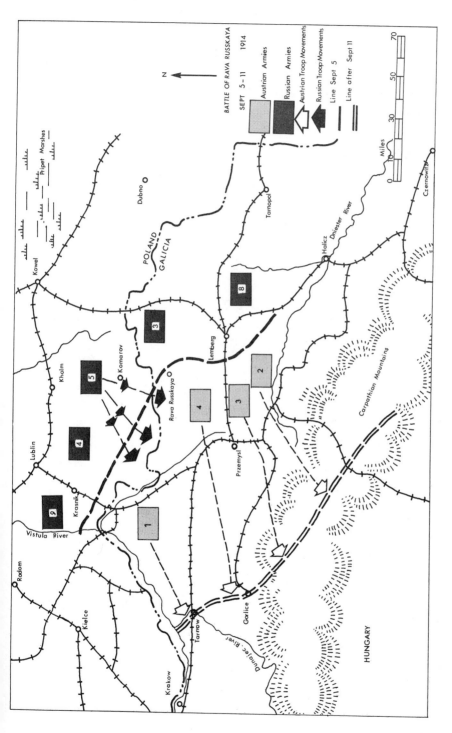

BATTLE OF RAVA RUSSKAYA
SEPT 5 – 11   1914

Austrian Armies

Russian Armies

Austrian Troop Movements

Russian Troop Movements

Line Sept 5

Line after Sept 11

Miles
0   30   50   70

Pripet Marshes

POLAND
GALICIA

Dubno

Kowel

Kholm

Lublin

Krasnik

Radom

Kielce

Krakow

Tarnow

Golice

Dunajec River

Przemysl

Rava Russkaya

Komarov

Lemberg

Halicz

Tarnopol

Dniester River

Czernowitz

Carpathian Mountains

HUNGARY

Vistula River

N

pletely around and head south to form on the left wing of the
Austrian line. The plan was for the Fourth and the Second Armies to attack the flanks of the Russian Third and Eighth Armies
while the Third held the center, creating a double envelopment of
the Russian forces. Conrad assumed that the Russian Fourth and
Fifth Armies were out of action.

Ivanov, however, had ideas of his own. He also had reinforcements. The Ninth Army, commanded by General Platon A. Lech-
itski, had arrived from eastern Poland and entered the line west
of the Fourth Army, between it and the Vistula River. Ivanov decided to order the Ninth and Fourth Armies to advance along the
Vistula to cut the Austrian communications lines west of Lvov.
To relieve pressure on the Fifth Army—which at this time was
still being driven back by the Austrian Fourth—Ivanov ordered
the Third and Eighth Armies to advance to the northwest. Thus
they would continue their drive past Lvov, but the Third Army
would then strike the right flank and rear of the Austrian
Fourth.

On September 3 the Austrian Fourth Army, just beginning to
move in its new direction, unexpectedly found itself face to face
with the Russian Third Army in the vicinity of Rava Russkaya.
Both army commanders were stunned, for each had expected to
come upon the other's flank and at a different location. Fighting
was intense for several days and approached a stalemate, as the
Austrian Fourth Army moved into a north-south line beside the
Third, which had reassembled and was attacking toward Lvov.

On the right wing of the Austrian line, the Second Army,
weary after almost thirty days of travel by train from Belgrade,
completely failed in the attempt to envelop the Russian left flank.
Consequently, all along the front the two forces were locked in an
inconclusive struggle.

Meanwhile the Russian Ninth and Fourth Armies were slowly
pushing back the Austrian First. The shifting of the Austrian
Fourth Army had opened a gap between it and the First Army
fifty miles wide. Although Conrad realized this, he discounted its
importance, judging that the badly mauled Russian Fifth Army
could not take advantage of it. Besides, he had left three divisions
there to cover the gap. But Von Auffenberg had hardly begun to
move south when Plehve halted the retreat of the Russian Fifth

Army, reformed a line, and ordered his troops to advance southward again. Sweeping aside the feeble covering force, Plehve marched through the gap and on into Galicia, behind the Austrian Fourth Army.

In the confusion of the battle at Rava Russkaya neither Ivanov nor Conrad realized for several days what was happening. Ivanov was not really aware of the opportunity which Plehve's advance had given him, while Conrad was unaware of his deadly peril. On September 11 an intercepted Russian message informed Conrad of Plehve's position. With disaster staring him in the face, Conrad ordered a general retreat. During the next two weeks the Austrians withdrew about one hundred miles, until they reached a strong position in the Carpathian Mountains. They had abandoned most of Galicia, except for the fortress of Przemysl, where about 100,000 men remained.

The casualties in these battles in Galicia had been enormous. Of the 900,000 Austro-Hungarians initially committed, almost 250,000 were dead, wounded, or missing. Russian losses, not recorded, must have been over 200,000. Unlike their opponents, however, the Russians had vast numbers of potential replacements.

FIRST BATTLE OF THE MASURIAN LAKES

After the Battle of Tannenberg the Austro-Hungarians urged Von Hindenburg and Ludendorff to undertake an offensive against Warsaw to relieve Russian pressure in Galicia. But with Rennenkampf's First Army still 150 miles into East Prussia and closer to Danzig than any German unit, the Germans refused to go farther south. To deal with the Russians, Von Hindenburg by this time had six corps, about three hundred thousand men, for the reinforcements from Von Moltke had arrived.

After Rennenkampf learned of Samsonov's defeat, he hastily withdrew to the Insterburg Gap and entrenched with his three hundred thousand troops on a line with the right flank resting on the Baltic Sea and the left extending to the Masurian Lakes. A corps on the left covered the gap in the line of lakes at Lötzen through which ran a railroad line. Only two divisions were held in reserve.

The reorganized German Eighth Army began to advance east-

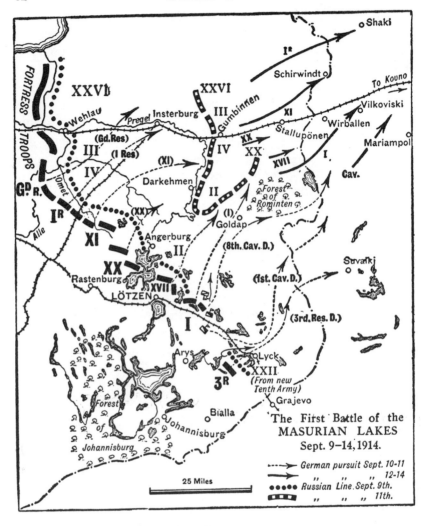

The First Battle of the
MASURIAN LAKES
Sept. 9–14, 1914.

25 Miles

German pursuit Sept. 10-11
           ,,   ,,   ,,   12-14
Russian Line Sept. 9th.
       ,,   ,,   ,,   11th.

ward on September 4. Four corps were to attack the Russian center at the Insterburg Gap, while the XVII and the I Corps, plus
two cavalry divisions, infiltrated through the Masurian Lakes region to envelop the Russian left flank. At the extreme German
right the 3rd Reserve Division covered the southern end of the
lakes.

On September 8 Von François attacked first, securing the
southern flank in the vicinity of Lyck and then pushing the Russian II Corps, on the left flank, northeast toward Gumbinnen. The

XVII Corps made no headway in the Lötzen Gap, although the attack was strong enough to cause Rennenkampf to commit his reserves. Nor did the rest of the Eighth Army make progress against the Russian positions in the Insterburg Gap.

The next day the German XVII Corps broke through, and with the I Corps drove toward Vilkoviszki just east of the frontier. Rennenkampf was threatened with encirclement, and he ordered his army to withdraw. To protect the retreat, however, on September 10 he counterattacked along the line between Nordenburg and Angerburg, driving back the German XX Corps. This alarmed Ludendorff, who ordered the German right wing to slow down and to swing closer, thus cutting off only a portion of the Russian force. By September 13 Rennenkampf managed to escape with the bulk of his army, most of the units intact and retaining their heavy equipment and artillery. However, about 125,000 Russian soldiers were lost, the majority of them prisoners.

9

From the Oise to the Sea

After the Battle of the Marne, Von Moltke ordered his retreating right wing to stop on the ridge line north of the Aisne River. The German Seventh Army was to move northwest by rail, and by reorganizing along the Chemin des Dames Ridge close the gap that still existed between the First and Second Armies. By September 14, the day Von Moltke was relieved, the main German units were on the ridge north of the Aisne, having destroyed the bridges behind them, and were entrenching and fortifying their already strong position. The German right flank rested on the Oise River.

FIRST BATTLE OF THE AISNE

Allied units were not far behind the retreating Germans. When Joffre learned that the enemy had stopped, he assumed that they had decided to stand and fight. So he ordered his forces to attack them frontally on September 14, unaware of the defensive strength of the hastily organized German field fortifications. The British, who had seen less action at the Marne, were to carry the main burden. For the first time, at the Aisne the Allies encountered an enemy dug into the ground, with machine guns and artillery strategically placed to defend the front lines. The Allied attacks were repeatedly thrown back by this strong defense, with heavy losses. Yet they continued until Joffre called them off on September 18. The line had changed but little from its position four days before.

BATTLES OF PICARDY AND ARTOIS

Although the German armies were in a strong defensive position, there were two weaknesses. The fortress of Antwerp, still in Belgian hands, was behind the German line, and the right flank of the German line was unprotected. The Allied left flank also was "in the air," but Joffre planned to rush up reinforcements, and with these he expected to envelop the German right. Von Falkenhayn was aware of the situation and was also rushing reinforcements east of the Oise. With them he was planning to envelop the Allied left.

As each side was extending its own open flank, while trying to turn the other's, they clashed in a series of actions that gradually, through late September and early October, stretched the lines

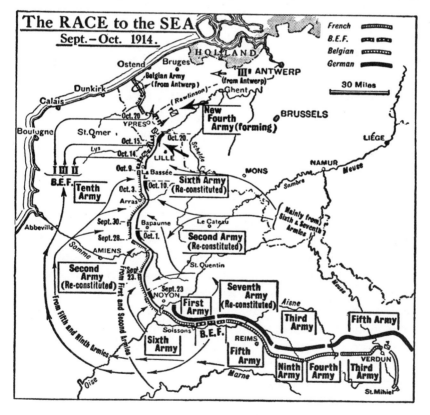

north toward the North Sea. This series of encounters and abortive attempts at envelopment has long been known as "the Race to the Sea." In reality, in the beginning neither commander was eager to reach the sea. Their attempts to maneuver and outwit each other put them on the path that eventually took them close to the coast.

In order to extend the Allied front to the left, Joffre moved De Castelnau and part of the Second Army (the remainder became part of Dubail's command) from Nancy to a position on the left of Maunoury's Sixth Army, which had been reconstituted after the beating it took at the Marne. At the same time the Germans were strengthening their right. Von Kluck remained where he was, at the angle of the Oise and the Aisne, where the front line turned and ran almost due north. On Von Kluck's right Von Falkenhayn placed Von Bülow's Second Army. The Third Army stretched out to cover the front the Second had been occupying.

De Castelnau attacked on September 22, and fierce fighting continued until the twenty-sixth, as each side tried to circle above the other. Joffre took units from the far right of his line and formed a Tenth Army, under General Louis Maud'huy, which he placed on De Castelnau's left. Von Falkenhayn also extended his line by moving Rupprecht's Sixth Army, which had been east of Nancy, to the right of Von Bülow, near Arras and Lille. Attacks and counterattacks went on until October 10, when the flanks of the two armies had reached the Lys River, near the Belgian frontier.

At the other end of the line, meanwhile, there had also been activity. The French forces had entrenched after the Battle of the Marne, on a front stretching from the Oise to the Swiss border opposite the positions the Germans had already fortified. German forces tried twice to outflank the fortified area at Verdun, without success. Farther south, however, they pushed a wedge into the Allied line, taking St. Mihiel and a section of the west bank of the Meuse River before the French halted the attack. This salient remained in German hands until 1918.

Elsewhere along the line relatively small attacks and counterattacks continued, but neither side penetrated far into the other's position. One event during this period received great publicity, horrifying the western world and adding to the propaganda picture of the Terrible Hun. For ten days German heavy artillery shells were poured on the city of Reims. They destroyed much of it and reduced the world-renowned cathedral to a shell, but achieved nothing.

By mid-October both Joffre and Von Falkenhayn were well aware of the importance of extending the line to the seacoast, but each wished to include as much territory as possible on his side of the line. Von Falkenhayn hoped to gain control of the French Channel ports of Calais, Dunkirk, and Boulogne, taking Antwerp in passing. Joffre was anxious to push farther east and join the Belgians, who were still defending Antwerp, before the Germans could succeed in capturing it. But Antwerp's condition was already critical.

ANTWERP

King Albert and his field army of approximately seventy-five thousand men had been based on the fortress of Antwerp since mid-August. Another sixty thousand men garrisoned the ring of forts around the city. The Belgians were held there by a reinforced German Corps of sixty thousand men from the German First Army, commanded by General Hans von Beseler. Until German artillery at Liège demonstrated the vulnerability of nineteenth-century fortifications, Antwerp had been considered virtually impregnable. Von Beseler, outnumbered, had a defensive, blocking mission. He made no attempt to attack and had not even tried to isolate the Antwerp area from Belgium's allies.

The Allies, in truth, had given Albert and his men little but moral support, partly because they had enough problems supplying their own forces, and partly because Antwerp was not easily accessible. Although situated on the east bank of the navigable Scheldt River, the city could not be supplied by this obvious water route, because the Netherlands refused to risk violating her neutral status by permitting the Allies access to the mouth of the Scheldt, which is in Dutch territory. Consequently anything going to Antwerp had to be landed at Ostend or Zeebrugge and moved by road or rail, always risking attack from the Germans, who controlled central and southern Belgium.

As the battles in France moved toward the coast, the security of the Channel ports seemed precarious. The British, to whom control of the coastal area was particularly important, became greatly concerned about the importance of holding Antwerp. At the end of September Sir John French asked and received permission from Joffre to move his British Expeditionary Force from its position on the Aisne to Flanders at the northern end of the front. There he hoped to use his troops to protect the ports and keep them as close as possible to his lines of support from England. In London fears were felt for the Belgian Army, which, although small, was well trained and had proved itself in battle, as well as for Belgium herself, whose defense the British had undertaken to support.

King Albert had not stayed quietly in camp at Antwerp during August and the early days of September, but had tried to help the Allies. When the British and French were hard pressed at Mons and the Sambre, on August 24, Albert attacked Von Beseler, hoping to draw troops away from the Allied front. The Allies withdrew from their position two days later, and Albert halted his operations. On September 9, having learned that some of the German troops had been rushed from Antwerp to the Marne, he attacked again. This time he almost broke through the weakened German line, but his supplies were insufficient to sustain a long campaign. He gave up after four days of fighting. That same day the Kaiser gave orders that Antwerp must be taken.

The first Allied realization of the impending German attack came on September 28, when forty-two-centimeter shells were hurled at Antwerp's defenses. The Belgian government asked for help, and both Britain and France tried to send it. It was a race against time, for the German howitzers were knocking out the forts at Antwerp at the rate of one a day, just as they had done at Liège and Namur. German field guns were destroying the shallow trenches with which the Belgians had tried to strengthen their defenses in this water-logged land where deep entrenchments were impossible. Without help the Belgians could not hold for long.

The British Cabinet received word on October 2 that the Belgian king and his field armies planned to withdraw from Antwerp west to the coast the following day. Quick decision was made to rush help to the area. Prime Minister Herbert Asquith decided to send Winston Churchill, First Lord of the Admiralty, to survey the situation. Word was sent to the king not to move until Churchill's arrival. The British Marine Brigade, which had been at Dunkirk, was rushed to Antwerp and went into the line beside the Belgians on October 4. The French agreed to rush two reserve divisions to Dunkirk by October 7.

Churchill, a former soldier, hurried to Antwerp and flung himself into the midst of the activity, obviously enjoying playing an active role under fire. On October 6 he welcomed two British Naval Brigades, outfits which he had formed but which were not yet fully trained. The same day a British infantry division and a cavalry division, forming the IV Corps under General Sir Henry Rawlinson, landed at Ostend and Zeebrugge. Rawlinson was put in command of all British military forces in the Antwerp area, although Churchill had hoped to have the job himself.

Despite these efforts to help the Belgians, German pressure continued, and the king decided his men must withdraw. As the defenders began to move to the left bank of the river, Churchill returned to England, deciding he could do no more. The three British brigades helped a Belgian division and the garrison troops hold the inner line of forts as long as they could. Two days later, when the main Belgian Army had completed its evacuation, the defenders left the city, crossing the river and following the other Belgian forces, who were heading for Ghent and Ostend. The first German patrols entered Antwerp on October 9, receiving a formal surrender the following day. Although Antwerp was lost, the Germans had been held up there for five precious days. Now fresh Allied troops were available to cover the Belgian withdrawal to Ghent. The Germans pursued to the Ghent area, then halted temporarily, awaiting reinforcements.

THE FIRST BATTLE OF YPRES

Field Marshal French reached Flanders on October 10, as the Belgians were making their withdrawal to Ghent. During the next few days, the remainder of the BEF arrived from the Aisne. The British moved into position on the left of the French Tenth Army near La Bassée, their line stretching north to link up with Rawlinson's IV Corps. The two French divisions, which had arrived too late to assist at Antwerp, moved in between Rawlinson and the Belgians. With the Belgians still holding northwest Belgium from Ghent to the border with the Netherlands near the coast, the Allied line, though somewhat shaky, was forming all the way from La Bassée to the sea. There still were gaps in it, however, when major action began.

The British II Corps, under Smith-Dorrien, was in position near La Bassée by October 10, and promptly attacked eastward against a thinly held German line. North of the II Corps, the British III, commanded by General William Pulteney, and the Cavalry Corps under General Edmund Allenby assembled on October 12 and 13 and advanced against increasing resistance near Armentières and Messines. Haig's I Corps was due to arrive in the next few days to take its place north of Allenby. Sir John French, who thought he would have numerical superiority when the I Corps arrived, planned to launch a full-scale offensive to take Menin and Lille, cut off any German troops farther north, and push back the German right flank, firming up the line with Rawlinson and the Belgians.

Von Falkenhayn, however, was also planning an offensive, a massive drive to take the Channel ports. He assumed that the weakened Belgians would not hold and that the rest of the Allied line was not strong enough to prevent his getting through. He had for the attack a new Fourth Army, with four new corps, a mixture of trained young volunteers and veterans, in addition to the III Reserve Corps which had taken Antwerp. The German Sixth Army also had been shifted north to Flanders. With these formidable forces, on October 12 Von Falkenhayn launched an attack toward the Strait of Dover, along a front extending generally from Lille to Ghent.

The German offensive started slowly. British communications were not operating well, and it was three days before Sir John French realized that his troops, who were supposedly attacking, were actually on the defensive. Joffre, grasping the situation more rapidly, rushed General Foch and some units of his Ninth Army to the area, with orders to coordinate Allied operations in Flanders. Foch was the right man at the right time for many reasons, not the least of which was that he had amicable relations with Sir John French. Foch succeeded, where few others could have, in getting the Belgians, French, and British to work together in a situation that rapidly became desperate.

The outnumbered Belgians and the British IV Corps in the north were pushed back by the advancing Germans as far as the

Yser River, giving the Germans a firm foothold on the North Sea coast from the Dutch border to the river mouth. British monitors came as close as they could to shore and used their guns with telling effect to support the Belgians. Although the Belgians fought bravely, they were close to exhaustion and could not hope to withstand the much more powerful force for long. Driven back across the river, they withdrew on October 24 to the railroad causeway between Dixmude and Nieuport.

This part of Belgian Flanders is an area of marshy land, much of it below the level of the sea, kept dry only by dikes that hold back the seawater. In this critical hour Nature was called to the aid of the weary Belgians. King Albert ordered the sluice gates of the dikes opened, and the sea poured in shoulder-deep, flooding the area between the Yser River and the causeway for two miles. The German attackers, unable to fight the sea, were forced to withdraw.

Haig's I Corps was committed to battle on October 19 and ordered to counterattack east of Ypres. Some of its units were still arriving from the Aisne and detrained under long-range German artillery fire. By the end of the second day the Allies had taken the initiative away from the Germans in this area. Foch and French, underestimating the German capacity, thought the time was propitious for another attempt to turn the German flank, take the pressure off the Belgians, and drive the Germans from the coast. They ordered a renewed attack. The Germans, however, held excellent defensive positions on the high ground east of Ypres. They easily threw back the Allied attacks, aided by heavy rains which turned the already messy battlefield into a quagmire. The Allies continued to attack until October 28, when Foch called off the offensive.

Meanwhile Von Falkenhayn had concentrated most of the newly arrived German troops on the right flank of the German Sixth Army. With six additional divisions, his forces now outnumbered the Allies by a ratio of better than two to one in men, and about five to one in artillery. On October 29 Von Falkenhayn resumed his offensive. The Germans moved slowly forward for three days, while Foch and French shifted reserves back and forth to bolster the desperately fighting Allied troops. On October 31 the line was broken at Gheluvelt, five miles east of Ypres, but the British were able to halt the Germans before they could exploit the breakthrough. More German gains in the next two days were followed by a three-day pause in which both sides added reinforcements to their lines, the Germans bringing down some of the troops that had been opposing the Belgians. By this time the Allied line was well scrambled, with British and French units holding sectors alternately from the Lys River to the Belgian sector near the coast.

The pause was ended by a new German attack on both sides of the Ypres salient. Despite fierce resistance and heavy losses, the Germans drove slowly ahead on November 7, 8, and 9. On the tenth Dixmude fell, after a long and bloody defense by the Belgians. A full-strength German attack on November 11 all along the front accomplished little. The crisis had passed. Snow began to fall on the battleground the following day, hampering operations. Although German attacks continued until November 22, the height of the fighting was over.

The Battle of Ypres was inconclusive as a tactical battle. Neither side gained or lost much territory. Neither force was defeated decisively and neither succeeded in gaining its objectives. But the failure of the more powerful Germans to achieve theirs, an objective that might have had very serious strategic results, was the most significant outcome. Consequently, the battle was a strategic success for the Allies. Although French forces made an important contribution and without Foch's leadership the outcome might have been quite different, the British Expeditionary Force deserves the credit for this defensive victory. Unfortunately the BEF was also the loser. The British Regulars, highly trained, expert marksmen, grimly determined, had paid a high price. More than half of those who had landed in France less than three months before were dead or wounded, and from the Battle of Ypres to the end of the war Britain would have to depend almost entirely on Territorials, volunteers, and finally conscripts. Spirit they would have, but spirit is no substitute for training.

When the lines stabilized east of Ypres, open warfare was ended on the Western Front until 1918. On both sides of the line more trenches were being dug, barbed wire installed, guns emplaced. A stalemate with its own brand of horror had begun. The men on both sides of the line would spend long, weary, miserable months in the ground, the pattern broken only by futile, bloody attacks that were more horrible still.

10

Offensives and Counteroffensives in the East

POLAND IN OCTOBER

The Russian victories over the Austrians in Galicia opened the door to the mineral-rich, industrial German province of Silesia. Von Hindenburg and Ludendorff, well aware of the gravity of the situation for them, knew that they had to act, to help the weary Austrians and to prevent a Russian invasion into the heart of Germany. They also knew that they could expect no reinforcements from the west, where the German armies had just been defeated at the Battle of the Marne and Von Moltke had been replaced by Von Falkenhayn. In these circumstances they drew up a new plan and had it in motion by September 17.

A new army, the Ninth, was formed by detaching four of the six corps (XX, XVII, XI, and Guard Reserve) from the Eighth Army. Von Hindenburg assumed command of this new army, in addition to retaining command of the Eighth. On September 17 the troops and equipment of the new army, accompanied by Von Hindenburg and Ludendorff, began entraining for a trip through Silesia to Cracow (then in Austria-Hungary) and southwestern Poland, to take positions on the left wing of the demoralized Austrian First Army. It was a major logistics achievement to move almost two hundred thousand men, horses, artillery, equipment, ammunition, food, fuel, and the numerous other items that an army needs six hundred miles, even on the efficient railroad system the Germans had developed. By September 28 the army was in position and Von Hindenburg ordered it into action.

The Russians at this time were also reorganizing their armies. Communications and supply problems in Galicia had become so

difficult that they decided to abandon the drive there and concentrate on preparing to attack Silesia and on establishing a defense
against attack from the Germans in East Prussia. General Nikolai Russki was put in command of the Northwest Army Group,
replacing Zhilinsky.

The Russian Tenth Army, which had relieved the First after
the defeat at the Masurian Lakes, was ordered to hold positions
along the East Prussian frontier. Southwest of it would be the reorganized First and the reconstituted Second. The left flank of
the Northwest Group was to be screened by Plehve's Fifth Army,
just east of the Vistula River. The Fourth and Ninth Armies of
the Southwest Army Group were to be in the bend of the Vistula
River, with the Third and Eighth on the left flank. The invasion
of Silesia was set for early October, but the German Ninth Army
changed the schedule.

As soon as the German forces were assembled, Von Hindenburg ordered the advance from the Galician border northeast toward Warsaw to begin. The Ninth Army moved out on September 28, slowly and deliberately. Engineers improved the condition
of the roads and railroads as the army advanced and planted
charges of dynamite in bridges and tunnels in anticipation of the
possibility of having to retreat. The German commanders knew
that the Russians greatly outnumbered them, and they had little
faith in the ability of their Austro-Hungarian allies on their
right.

Two days after the German advance started, the Russian High
Command (known as the Stavka) finally realized that the Ninth
Army was advancing toward Warsaw. Promptly Grand Duke Ni-
cholas changed the orders to his assembling armies. With the
First and Second Armies concentrated north of Warsaw and the
Fifth, Fourth, and Ninth on the line of the Vistula River south of
the city, Nicholas hoped to repay the Germans for Tannenberg
and the Masurian Lakes. He would envelop the left flank of the
German Ninth Army with his two armies north of Warsaw while
hammering at the center and the right wing with the others.

On October 9 the Germans reached the Vistula. Having received the usual uncoded Russian messages and read captured
Russian documents, Von Hindenburg and Ludendorff were aware
of the trap the Grand Duke had set. So confident were they of

their army's ability, however, that they advanced in spite of the dangers. In the face of strong Russian resistance the Germans penetrated to within twelve miles of Warsaw, where the pressure on their left flank began to increase. The Austrian armies on the right of the Germans were faltering in the face of Russian attacks.

Von Hindenburg, realizing that he could not withstand the stronger Russian forces (sixty divisions to his eighteen), ordered his army to withdraw. The earlier preparations paid off. The Germans fired their explosives behind them, destroying bridges and blocking defiles, holding up the Russian pursuit. By November 1 the Germans and Austrians were back in their starting positions. The German offensive had not resulted in any territorial gains. It had, however, completely achieved the objectives of Von Hindenburg and Ludendorff: to rescue the Austrian armies and upset the Russian plans.

BATTLE OF LODZ

Von Hindenburg and Ludendorff next decided to deal directly with the continuing Russian threat to Silesia, by striking at the Russian right flank from positions east of Posen before the already delayed Russian invasion could get under way. On November 4 the Ninth Army again entrained, starting north for the border region between Thorn and Posen. There it was joined by new units from the Eighth Army, which had received newly mobilized reserve units since the Ninth's departure. General von Mackensen was put in command of the Ninth Army, organized in five corps of infantry and two of cavalry, and General von Below commanded the Eighth. Von Hindenburg was commander of the army group they formed.

On November 10 a message from Von Falkenhayn informed the German commanders in the east that the armies on the Western Front were on the verge of a major victory and that he would be able to send four additional corps to the Eastern Front within ten days. But Von Hindenburg knew that the Russian offensive was scheduled to begin on November 14. In ten days Russian troops might already be on Silesian soil. So, even though still greatly outnumbered, he ordered the offensive to proceed the fol-

SERBIA
Situation at end of
August 1914.

Serbian
Austrian

30 Miles

lowing day. It was well that he did not wait, for no reinforcements actually came from the west until December.

While the Germans were assembling, Russian armies had advanced into western Poland. In the center were the four which
were to participate in the invasion, the Second, Fifth, Fourth, and
Ninth from north to south. Covering the right flank along the
lower Vistula, north of Kutno, was the First Army, while the
Third protected the left flank south of Kielce.

On November 12 General Rennenkampf's Russian First Army
was advancing along a seventy-mile front, with two corps north
and two corps south of the Vistula River. Suddenly his lead corps,
the V Siberian, south of the river, was unexpectedly struck by
spearheads of four German corps, the XXV Reserve, the I Reserve, the I Cavalry, and the XX Corps. Despite the experience of
the Tannenberg campaign, the Russians had no covering screen
of advance cavalry scouts. Taken by surprise, the V Siberian
Corps fell back under the attack, pursued by the German I Reserve Corps. Rennenkampf, unaware that he was facing most of
the Ninth Army, ordered his corps to halt and dig in. To reinforce it he moved his two northern corps south of the Vistula
River, leaving only a small force on the northern bank.

By this time, November 14, the German XX and XVII Corps
had hit Rennenkampf's left flank corps, the II, driving it back to

Kutno. The Germans pursued it for three days, beyond Kutno, then headed southeast toward Lodz, joined by the I Cavalry and the XVII Corps.

Meanwhile, to the south, the Russian Second Army had begun its advance toward Silesia when its right-flank corps, the XXIII, was struck by the German XI Corps. The Russians fled southward in great disorder, closely pursued by the Germans. By November 15 a thirty- to thirty-five-mile gap had been opened up between the Russian First and Second Armies, and four German corps—the XXV Reserve, the XX, the XVII, and the XI—were streaming through. Von Mackensen ordered them to hasten south and southwest, hoping to encircle the whole Russian Second Army.

On the morning of November 16 the Russian Stavka began to take steps to rescue its threatened armies. Halting the plans for invading Silesia, Grand Duke Nicholas ordered the Fifth Army to hurry north to fill the gap between the First and Second Armies. The Second he ordered to fall back to Lodz, while the Fourth moved north to cover the line formerly held by the Fifth. To the north the VI Corps and VI Siberian Corps of the First Army, called the Lowicz Force, were to exert pressure on the left flank of the advancing Germans. Recovering from the original shock of surprise, the Russian units quickly and competently changed their directions of advance and hastened to carry out the new orders. By November 19 the four corps of the Russian Second Army were concentrated around Lodz, and the German advance from the west and north had been halted. Two corps of the Russian Fifth Army, coming up from the west, had attacked the left of the German XI Corps and driven it back almost five miles.

North and east of Lodz, however, the German I Cavalry Corps and the XXV Reserve Corps (with the 3rd Guards Division attached) had swung far to the east of the city. On November 19 General Reinhard von Scheffer-Boyadel, commanding the XXV Reserve Corps, pivoted his troops west and attacked the rear of the Russian Second Army. Except for a narrow passage to the southwest that was held by elements of the Fifth Army, the Russians in Lodz were encircled.

The Germans could not complete the encirclement, however. As the Russians well knew, their Fifth Army was in a firm position to support the left flank of their Second. On November 20 the

Fifth Army's V Corps struck at the left (south) flank of Von Scheffer's troops southeast of Lodz. At the same time, north of Lodz, the Lowicz Force hit the left wing and rear of the German XX Corps and other units struck the XXV Corps from the rear. By the following day Von Scheffer's troops were being encircled. While the Russians ordered special trains to carry off the prisoners they anticipated, the threatened Germans continued to fight in all directions. On the evening of November 22 Von Mackensen radioed Von Scheffer to withdraw by the best route available. The bitter cold which had invaded the area added to the misery of the Germans. Von Scheffer kept his head, however, and started to withdraw in good order the next morning, not toward the rest of the Ninth Army, but southeast toward Karpin, in order to gain room to maneuver. This move was completely unexpected by the Russians.

From Karpin, Von Scheffer turned north, holding the Russian Second and Fifth Armies at bay with determined rearguard actions. Just west of Koluszki he ran into the 6th Division of the VI Siberian Corps. Slipping his 3rd Guards Division north through a gap in the Russian line between Koluszki and Lodz in order to keep an escape route open, with the rest of his corps Von Scheffer attacked the 6th Division on the night of November 23-24. Only fifteen hundred Siberians escaped in the slaughter that followed. Only two divisions of the Lowicz Force remained, and they had to withdraw to escape destruction from coordinated attacks by the German XXV Reserve and XX Corps on their flanks. Marching west through the area the Russians had evacuated, Von Scheffer joined the other Germans, taking up his position between the XX and the I Reserve Corps.

In five days of intense fighting in the bone-chilling cold of an Eastern European winter, Von Scheffer had completed one of the outstanding feats of military history. While sustaining only 4,300 casualties, he had rescued his forces from threatened annihilation and retreated in good order with 2,800 wounded men, 16,000 Russian prisoners, and sixty-four captured artillery pieces.

The Battle of Lodz has to be considered a tactical victory for the Russians, for they had defended Lodz and had foiled Von Mackensen's effort to exploit his initial success. Strategically, however, the German purpose had been accomplished. The threat of a Russian invasion of Silesia was removed, and the Russians never again seriously considered undertaking one. Two Russian armies had been badly beaten. Although the Germans suffered almost thirty-five thousand casualties themselves, the Russian losses were much greater. On December 6 the Russians evacuated their forces from Lodz eastward to a better defensive position between Lodz and Warsaw. Having by this time received some of Von Falkenhayn's reinforcements, Von Hindenburg moved his line eastward also. Plans were already being made for a new offensive early in 1915.

SERBIA

Having failed twice to knock out Serbia, Austrian General Potiorek was determined to do it on the third try. During September and October, 1914, he strengthened his forces, preparing about three hundred thousand well-equipped and -trained men for the invasion. The Serbs could do little more than wait for the inevitable attack. Their supplies were low, particularly ammunition, which reached them only over the mountain trails of Montenegro, carried by sturdy pack mules. More had been promised by the Allies, but when the Austrian invasion began, on November 5, nothing had arrived.

Despite miserably rainy weather the Austrians advanced, one column near the Jadar, another seventy miles to the south, toward the western Morava River. A third crossed the Danube at Semendria and advanced southward down the railroad. Almost without opposition they came on, some units penetrating as much as forty miles into Serbia. Putnik withdrew before them, ordering a retreat across the Kolubara River. The Serbian government had left Belgrade in mid-August for greater security and had gone to Nish. On November 30 the troops also abandoned Belgrade without a fight. Putnik finally stopped on a new line, running between the lower Morava River, on the right, and the western Morava, on the left. Since the Austrians' attack had slowed almost to a halt because of logistical problems and muddy roads, Putnik set about preparing to counterattack.

At this point the much needed ammunition arrived, by way of Salonika, and helped greatly to raise the sagging morale of the

Serbs. The thing that really bucked them up, however, was a visit by old, ailing King Peter I to the battlefield. Telling the men they might go home if they liked, the old monarch said, "But I and my sons stay here." This appeal to patriotism made the difference Putnik needed.

On December 3 the Serbian armies launched their counterattack. The Austrians, taken by surprise, panicked. The battle continued for three days. Then the Austrian line broke and began to withdraw. The Serbs seized the opportunity to divide the enemy and drive them into the hills. Potiorek ordered a withdrawal on December 9, although most of his troops were already headed back to Austria. For six days the Serbs pursued them mercilessly, until the last Austrian crossed the border on about December 15. Belgrade was once again in Serb control. The tiny country had gained a long respite from invasion. About sixty thousand Austrians had been killed or wounded in the abortive invasion, and forty-two thousand were in Serbian hands. The Serbians had suffered about thirty thousand casualties.

11

Naval Action and Inaction

While British soldiers in the Expeditionary Force were fighting and dying in France and Belgium, the sailors of the Royal Navy were playing a vital but less dramatic role in this first year of war. Britain in 1914 controlled the seas as she had for centuries, to the farthest colonies of the Empire. But since the first requisite in wartime was defense of the British Isles, the biggest and best of the British warships were never far from home.

It was customary each summer for the Royal Navy to hold fleet maneuvers as a training exercise. In the spring of 1914, however, the First Lord of the Admiralty, red-headed, young, energetic Winston Churchill, had decided to alter the custom and run a test mobilization of all units of the Home Fleet, active and reserve, in mid-July. On July 15 all reserves were activated, and soon assembled off Spithead were the ships of all three fleets—the First or Grand Fleet, which included all the dreadnoughts and their accompanying smaller ships; the Second or Channel Fleet, part of whose crews were stationed ashore; and the Third Fleet, composed of reserves. Two days later, the entire armada put to sea for exercises, reviewed by King George on his royal yacht. The parade of ships passed in a mighty procession, about fourteen miles long, which lasted for six hours.

Exercises completed, demobilization began on July 23, the same day Austria's ultimatum was delivered to Serbia. The ships of the Third Fleet returned to their home ports, and their reserve crews were released. However, when it appeared that Austria would not accept the Serbian response, the First Sea Lord, Prince Louis of Battenberg, called a halt to further demobilization. He ordered the First Fleet not to disperse to its several bases and the ships of the Second to remain in their home ports. This order was officially reported to the press, in the vain hope that it might have a restraining effect on the Central Powers.

By July 28 the situation was so tense that Churchill, with the approval of Prime Minister Asquith, secretly ordered the Grand Fleet to leave Portland in the morning of the twenty-ninth and, steaming without lights through the narrow Straits of Dover the following night, speed north to the base at Scapa Flow. The Second Fleet was to assemble in Portland. Thus, when Britain's ultimatum to Germany expired on August 4, the ships of the Royal Navy were at their battle stations.

Across the North Sea, the German High Seas Fleet was concentrated at Wilhelmshaven in Jade Bay, where it was protected by the defenses on the island of Heligoland and by a system of minefields. Since 1900 the German government had been rapidly building ships, fast, well-armored, and armed with heavy, modern guns. In the summer of 1914 the German Navy still was smaller than that of Great Britain, but it was a formidable force nonetheless and would be no pushover in an all-out sea battle.

With the German Army command confident of a quick victory on land, and the Kaiser intent on retaining the fleet as a bargaining factor at the peace settlement, Admiral Friedrich von Ingenohl, commander of the High Seas Fleet, had orders not to risk loss of any ships and to concentrate on defense against possible attempted landings. This precluded any planning for offensive action by the German Navy.

The Germans expected that the British would immediately establish a close blockade of German ports, and that the Royal Navy would appear in force to challenge the High Seas Fleet. The British, for their part, expected the German fleet to come out and attack the convoys carrying troops to France, or perhaps try to provoke a major sea battle. Both were mistaken. The High Seas Fleet remained in Jade Bay, and the Grand Fleet stayed close to Scapa Flow.

The idea of a close blockade of Germany had been abandoned by British naval planners a few years before, for the marine mine and the submarine had rendered it impractical to try to keep naval vessels close to enemy ports. Moreover, German ports were so far from British bases that even the Royal Navy could not maintain enough ships at that distance. Instead the British planned to try to bottle the Germans up in the North Sea, by blocking the Straits of Dover and the English Channel and the northern edge of the North Sea, to prevent ships from traveling to or from Germany with vital matériel for the German Army. This distant blockade was established soon after the declaration of war. Effective but dull for those who participated in it, it was maintained by patrolling ships of the Royal Navy day after day, week after week, month after month until the war was over.

THE *KÖNIGIN LUISE* AND *THE AMPHION*

German minelayers put to sea as soon as war was declared, to plant deadly mines at strategic points in the North Sea. On August 5 one of these small ships, a converted passenger vessel named *Königin Luise,* was discovered at her task by a British light cruiser, the *Amphion,* and her three escorting destroyers. Giving chase for about thirty miles, the warships finally found the range and sank the German vessel. But revenge came swiftly. On the return trip to England the *Amphion* struck one of the newly planted mines and followed her victim to the bottom of the sea.

HELIGOLAND BIGHT

As day after day passed with no sign of a German warship, impatience in Britain grew. Was there no way to entice the German ships out to fight? Finally, on August 23, intelligence reports from submarine and destroyer patrols indicated that the Germans were making a practice of sending destroyers each night to patrol north and west of Heligoland. A light cruiser or two escorted them about twenty miles to sea and met them again at daylight with more destroyers to relieve them.

The British commander of the submarines based at Harwich, Commodore Roger Keyes, and the commander of the light cruisers and destroyers of the Harwich Striking Force, Commodore Reginald Tyrwhitt, soon worked up a plan to send some British submarines into the area west of Heligoland just before dawn and try to lure the German destroyers and cruisers out into the open sea to attack them. As soon as the Germans were out, Tyrwhitt's force, swooping down from the north, would attack them from behind. The date was set for August 28. Admiral Sir John Jellicoe, commander in chief of the Grand Fleet, sent Admiral David Beatty with three battle cruisers and Commodore William E. Goodenough with six light cruisers to rendezvous with Keyes's force. Unfortunately neither Keyes nor Tyrwhitt was told that these ships were coming, and when Goodenough showed up he came close to being attacked as an enemy.

Rumors that something was going on in British naval headquarters reached the German naval command, and nineteen German destroyers, with the cruisers *Stettin* and *Frauenlob*, were sent out toward Heligoland, with five more cruisers close behind. Behind the Jade Bay bar the German Battle Cruiser Squadron was available if needed, but unable to cross the bar until the afternoon tide.

At 7 A.M. the British sighted a German destroyer, and Tyrwhitt in the *Arethusa* followed her into the Heligoland Bight, where he soon found himself trading fire with the two German cruisers. When the British cruiser *Fearless* came up, the Germans divided their attention. Tyrwhitt, despite suffering severe damage to the *Arethusa*, inflicted worse than he got, and only with difficulty did the *Frauenlob* limp back to Wilhelmshaven.

Action continued into the afternoon as British and German ships haphazardly encountered one another, with no effective coordination of effort on either side. Admiral Beatty finally swept into the Bight with his battle cruisers to rescue Tyrwhitt, whose force had been taking the brunt of the attack of the German cruisers. The big guns of Beatty's ships were more than a match for the Germans. Goodenough's ships had already sunk the *Mainz*, and Beatty sent two more cruisers, the *Köln* and the *Ariadne*, to the bottom. Then the British withdrew, unwilling to venture further into the mine-strewn Bight and unaware that the German battle cruisers, having finally crossed the bar, were on their way out.

For the German Navy this action was of great significance. Over twelve hundred officers and men had been killed, wounded, or rescued by the British and so made prisoners. Three cruisers and a destroyer were gone and three other cruisers had significant damage. The Kaiser promptly gave orders that there should be no further risking of ships, but that the navy should stay inside the Bight, except with special permission from him. The combined effect of the ship losses and the Kaiser's restrictions was disastrous to naval morale.

The British for their part seized on this victory and magnified it for popular delight. Only the *Arethusa* and three destroyers had suffered much damage; thirty-five British sailors had died and about forty more were wounded. The Royal Navy had lived up to its traditions and had taken the war to the Germans' own sea. At a time when the Germans were plunging ahead in France, this action gave a needed boost to British morale. Within a month, however, it was the British who were on the losing side.

U-BOAT AT THE BROAD FOURTEENS

As part of the defense of the English Channel and the approaches to the British coast, the Admiralty had established a regular patrol of the area known as the Broad Fourteens, off the coast of Holland. The patrol was maintained by two destroyer flotillas, supported by five old cruisers which had been reconditioned and manned by reservists. Unfortunately the old ships were poorly armored and slow.

On September 17 the weather on the eastern North Sea became so bad that the British destroyers returned to port, leaving three cruisers, the *Aboukir, Hogue,* and *Cressy,* unprotected, to patrol a narrow and dangerous area. The weather continued bad until September 22, when Tyrwhitt, with eight destroyers, started off for the Broad Fourteens to relieve the three British cruisers. It was too late.

At 6:30 A.M. on September 22, the three cruisers were steaming north at ten knots, making no attempt to zigzag or otherwise evade attack. Suddenly a torpedo, fired by the German submarine *U–9,* struck the *Aboukir.* Within a half-hour she capsized and sank. The two other cruisers, unwilling to leave British sailors in the sea, moved in close and lowered their boats to save them. In no time at all, the German skipper, Kapitänleutnant Otto Weddigen, had scored two more hits, and the *Hogue* and the *Cressy* followed their sister. Over fourteen hundred men went down with their ships. It was the Germans' turn to cheer.

MERCHANT RAIDERS

The German High Command was well aware that its few war-ships at sea in 1914 could not accomplish a great deal and probably could not stay in action very long. To add to the trouble they could cause the Allies, however, the Germans turned loose a few armed merchant ships to prey on the rich trade route from South America to Europe. One of these was the *Kaiser Wilhelm der Grosse,* once the fastest liner on the North Atlantic. Despite her speed, however, she succeeded in sinking only ten thousand tons of shipping before she encountered the British cruiser *Highflyer* on August 26, off Spanish Morocco. Old but well-armed, the *Highflyer* quickly caused such damage to the German ship that her crew scuttled her.

Even less successful than the *Kaiser Wilhelm der Grosse* was the *Cap Trafalgar.* Her skipper, Commodore Julius Wirth, after carefully camouflaging her as a vessel of the British Union Castle Line, took her out to prowl the South Atlantic sea lanes. He had had no luck when, on September 13, he rendezvoused with three colliers off rocky, isolated Trindade Island.

At nine-thirty the following morning, the former Cunard Line ship *Carmania,* en route to join Rear Admiral Sir Christopher Cradock's squadron in the South Atlantic, approached Trindade. German radio operators on the *Cap Trafalgar* had detected the wireless signals of the *Carmania* at seven o'clock, but the island screened the ships from each other, and it was eleven before lookouts on either ship sighted the other.

Aboard the *Cap Trafalgar,* coaling was abruptly halted, battle stations were manned, the anchor weighed. While Wirth tried to identify the approaching vessel, he ordered his ship to put to sea. When at last he could make out the Union Jack and distinguish the outline of a merchant vessel like his own, he turned and headed toward her.

Just after twelve noon, the *Carmania*'s gunnery officer, Lieutenant Lockyer, reading the closing distance at 8,500 yards, called out, "In range, sir!" From Captain Grant came the order, "Port No. 1, load blank. Fire across his bow! . . . fire!" From the forepeak of the *Cap Trafalgar,* battle flags were broken out.

For about an hour the firing went on, both sides giving their utmost and both receiving damaging hits. On both vessels fires were raging. Finally the *Cap Trafalgar,* listing badly to starboard, turned and headed for the beach.

Commodore Wirth, though badly wounded, was still commanding his ship, his hopes buoyed by a message from the German raider *Kronprinz Wilhelm,* only ten miles away and hastening toward Trindade. But the *Cap Trafalgar* could not wait. Lifeboats were lowered, and "Abandon ship!" was ordered. Explosions shook the dying vessel. Then, bow first, her flags still flying, she slipped beneath the waves.

Although still afloat, the *Carmania* was in bad shape. Her bridge had been destroyed, and 304 holes had been made in her hull and superstructure by the German shells. With a makeshift bridge, and navigating by compass and sextant without a chart, she headed south, an easy prey for the *Kronprinz Wilhelm,* which arrived on the scene shortly after the action. The German skipper passed up the opportunity, however. Having assured himself that the colliers were caring for the *Cap Trafalgar* survivors, he headed back to the shipping lanes, neither then nor later explaining why he let the *Carmania* go.

The *Kronprinz Wilhelm* continued to prey on shipping until April, 1915, when, having sunk fifteen ships for a total of fifty-eight thousand tons, she came to the end of her resources of fuel and ammunition and turned in to internment at Newport News. The *Carmania* sailed on to Pernambuco, where she found sanctuary for repairs.

WAITING

Britons who had been brought up with the idea that the Royal Navy was the best in the world grew increasingly unhappy as the first months of the war brought nothing but bad news from the army in France and no news at all of the great battleships they had looked on with pride for so many years. What sort of war was this, with those lovely dreadnoughts swinging at anchor in Scapa Flow, and the battle cruisers sitting idly at Cromarty? Why didn't they lure that German High Seas Fleet out into the North Sea and have it out? Germans, who had for years been told that their High Seas Fleet was going to be strong enough to challenge Britain's control of the seas, wondered why it was staying so quietly behind the defenses of Heligoland. Actually it was not yet that strong, having only thirteen dreadnoughts to the British twenty. On October 27, 1914, Britain lost one, the *Audacious,* to a mine north of Ireland, but she had more being built, and more than Germany did.

The British had an additional advantage over the Germans. In August, 1914, the Russian Navy sank the German light cruiser *Magdeburg* in the Gulf of Finland. Unbeknownst to the German Naval Staff, the Russians salvaged the ship's naval code books, and in October they turned them over to the British Admiralty. The codes used in World War I were relatively simple and seldom changed unless it was known that they had been compromised. Hence it was not difficult for the cryptanalysts in the Admiralty to use these books and decipher any coded messages their radiomen intercepted. The combination of this fact and the existence of a series of radio direction-finding stations on the coasts of the British Isles and France, plus a variety of intelligence sources, made the British naval leaders confident that the German High Seas Fleet could not emerge without being detected. Yet somehow, in November, four German battle cruisers got close enough to England to bombard the port of Yarmouth. Although there was little damage, faces were red in the Admiralty, only a little relieved by word that an escorting cruiser, the *Yorck,* had hit a mine on the way back and gone down with half her crew.

HIDE AND SEEK IN THE NORTH SEA

This success, and the realization that the British battle cruisers *Invincible* and *Inflexible* were off at the Falkland Islands, led the German naval planners to try a larger operation. Admiral Franz von Hipper would take four battle cruisers and the armored cruiser *Blücher* in close enough to the British coast to fire on the ports of Hartlepool and Scarborough. Meanwhile Admiral von Ingenohl would start out with the High Seas Fleet—fourteen dreadnoughts by this time and eight older battleships—and wait in the North Sea about two hundred miles to the east in case the British fleet came out to attack.

British intelligence detected activity on December 14, 1914, indicating that some German battle cruisers, light cruisers, and destroyers were planning to put to sea the next day, probably on another expedition against the British coast. But there was no indication that the High Seas Fleet would be involved. Consequently it was decided to send only part of the Grand Fleet to intercept the Germans. Six dreadnoughts under Vice Admiral Sir George Warrender, four battle cruisers under Admiral Beatty, and cruiser and destroyer escorts would go out to the Dogger Bank, while Commodore Tyrwhitt, with some cruisers and destroyers, waited off Yarmouth, and eight British submarines took station off Terschelling.

At 5:15 A.M. Warrender and Von Ingenohl were within ten miles of each other, when British destroyers encountered German destroyers and cruisers, approaching from the east. Unaware that the High Seas Fleet was coming on behind them, Warrender's force engaged the smaller ships, which soon withdrew, followed by Warrender. Von Ingenohl, thinking that he was about to clash with the entire Grand Fleet, decided he should not risk his ships. He ordered course reversed, and headed home as fast as he could go.

Meanwhile, Von Hipper, unaware of what was going on, continued to the British coast, fired his heavy guns at Hartlepool, Scarborough, and Whitby from 8:30 to 9:00 A.M., and started back. Warrender, still not knowing that he was pursuing the whole High Seas Fleet, upon hearing of these attacks turned his whole force about and hurried over to try to intercept Von Hipper.

In the Admiralty War Room the two forces were plotted as reports of their whereabouts came in. Interception seemed inevitable and the outcome predictable as the much heavier British force spread across Von Hipper's homeward route. Eager officers estimated that the two would meet at about noon. But they didn't reckon on Nature, which decided the outcome by brewing up a thick fog interspersed with rain squalls over the North Sea. First Beatty's, then Warrender's light cruisers made contact with the German screening forces. Destroyers and cruisers exchanged fire but soon lost sight of each other again in a ghostly game of peekaboo on the high seas. Von Hipper had no desire to tangle with whatever was coming behind these British vessels. So he changed course, circled north of the whole fleet, and escaped to the safety of Heligoland.

At the time, of course, no one knew the whole picture. The High Seas Fleet was first detected in the early afternoon, already well on its way back. Neither the British nor the Germans knew what forces had been so close together in the early morning. The citizens in the British coastal towns where five hundred had been killed or wounded knew only that somehow the German battle cruisers had been able to approach that close, unhindered by the Royal Navy. And the Admiralty could not reveal how close those ships had been to destruction without revealing how they knew the Germans were coming. It was all a tremendous frustration.

DOGGER BANK

Profiting from this experience, the Admiralty was determined not to let any other German force that turned up escape. So when it was learned, on January 23, 1915, that Admiral von Hipper was about to go out to the Dogger Bank with the large armored cruiser *Blücher,* three battle cruisers—the *Seydlitz, Moltke,* and *Derfflinger*—and some light cruisers and destroyers, everyone was ordered out to intercept them.

Admiral Beatty, with five battle cruisers—the *Indomitable, New Zealand, Princess Royal, Tiger,* and *Lion*—was to join Commodore Sir William Goodenough and the 1st Light Cruiser Squadron, and Tyrwhitt with three more light cruisers and some thirty destroyers, about thirty miles north of the Dogger Bank at 7 A.M. on January 24. Meanwhile Admiral Jellicoe was to bring the entire Grand Fleet, plus seven old battleships from Rosyth, down from Scapa Flow.

As Von Hipper steamed out of the Heligoland Bight and turned west and then northwest, some of his ships were spotted by Goodenough's cruisers. Their report to Admiral Beatty, who was coming up, and to Admiral Jellicoe, who was still far from the area, was intercepted in the Admiralty. Once again the Map Room was filled with officers eagerly awaiting what seemed certain to be the long-awaited major engagement at sea. The atmosphere grew tense with anticipation.

From a distance of about twenty-five thousand yards, Von Hipper could see the masts of the approaching British ships and decided they were cruisers and destroyers, which he could handle or outdistance. So he turned back toward home at comfortable speed. Beatty, however, had increased his speed to the maximum, twenty-eight or twenty-nine knots, and Von Hipper soon became aware that he had met up with some battle cruisers. He knew that they could outdistance him, since the top speed of the *Blücher* was but twenty-three knots. The two fleets ploughed along through the sea on parallel courses, with Beatty's battle cruisers gradually gaining on the Germans. At the unprecedented range of twenty thousand yards, Beatty, in the lead ship, *Lion,* opened fire on the lagging *Blücher* at about 9 A.M. As the *Tiger* and *Princess Royal* came up, they too joined and almost at once found the target. Behind them came the *New Zealand,* and then the *Indomitable,* while in order ahead of the *Blücher* raced the *Derfflinger, Moltke,* and *Seydlitz.* The Germans were firing back by this time, as both columns rushed through the water at top speed. When Beatty's ships had all come up he ordered each to fire on her opposite number in the German line, his own *Lion* taking on the *Seydlitz.* Unfortunately the captain of the *Tiger* misunderstood the order and attacked the *Seydlitz* also. He compounded his error by mistakenly correcting his range by observing the *Lion*'s fire. This left the *Moltke* with no attacker, free to concentrate on the *Lion,* at which the other German battle cruisers also were firing.

The *Lion*'s accurate fire had shattered the *Seydlitz*'s stern, destroying the two after-turrets and their crews. But still she was able to keep up, and soon after ten o'clock she herself knocked out two of the *Lion*'s dynamos. The *Lion* had already sustained about fourteen hits when the *Derfflinger* pierced her armor below the waterline, stopping the port engine so that she could no longer keep up. The *Blücher*'s wounds were worse, however. Seeing her afire and listing, Beatty dispatched the *Indomitable* to finish her off, while ordering his other ships to pursue the rest of the fleeing Germans. They misunderstood his signal, however, and left the chase to assist the *Indomitable.* Von Hipper, two of his ships afire, continued on his way back to the safety of Heligoland, while the *Blücher* went down to the bottom of the North Sea. Except for the return, with the *Indomitable* towing the limping *Lion,* the battle was over. Again the Germans had escaped. But this time at least there was the *Blücher* to report as a victim. And there had been numerous casualties and damage to the other ships as well. Von Ingenohl too was a victim, for the Kaiser was irate at the loss of the *Blücher*. Admiral Hugo von Pohl was ordered to relieve the man who had lost her.

BLOCKADE AND COUNTERBLOCKADE IN 1915

As month after month of war dragged on, the pattern of Britain's naval blockade became more clearly defined, although no more exciting. At the southern entrance to the North Sea, carefully planted minefields in the Straits of Dover left only a narrow, easily controlled channel through which ships could pass, but the broad expanse of sea between Scotland and Norway could hardly be closed. Even if it had been possible to close it, ships from the Atlantic could still pass north of Scotland or between Iceland and Greenland to the coast of Norway and then sail down the Norwegian coast inside Norwegian territorial waters, protected by international law from seizure and search. Only by constantly patrolling the northern waters could the British hope to interfere with this traffic. By March of 1915 a small fleet of twenty-four armed merchant ships and eight old armored cruisers was ploughing back and forth in this cold, rough, miserable area, stopping as many as three hundred merchant ships a month to be thoroughly searched for contraband, while they themselves hoped not to be stopped and perhaps sunk by a German U-boat.

The British definition of contraband changed as the war went on. At first they followed the Declaration of London of 1909, defining absolute contraband as instruments of warfare, like guns and ammunition, and conditional contraband as food, clothing, and fuel for the belligerent's army or navy. They also included a list of free items which were neither. But on March 11, 1915, the British government announced that it considered anything at all bound for Germany contraband. No ship headed there would be allowed to continue, no matter what its cargo. The results of this policy would be felt by everyone in Germany, for soon food, clothing, and raw materials grew scarce. As the years passed, the shortages caused more and more distress among the German people.

The German Navy could not hope to break the British blockade, but it could fight back with a different weapon, the U-boat *(Untersee-boot)* or submarine. In the first months, before firing at a merchant ship the U-boat captain gave warning, so that passengers and crew could take to the lifeboats. But on February 4, 1915, the German government announced:

> All the waters surrounding Great Britain and Ireland, including the whole of the English Channel, are hereby declared a war zone. . . . Every enemy merchant ship found within this war zone will be destroyed without it being always possible to avoid danger to the crews and passengers. . . . It is impossible to avoid attacks being made on neutral vessels in mistake for those of the enemy.

This was clearly a challenge to the United States. Her reaction was prompt: She would hold Germany responsible for any American lives or ships lost to U-boats.

The number of ships sunk under this new policy rose sharply —thirty-nine by the end of April, 1915, forty-two in August alone. The first American victim was a passenger aboard the British steamer *Falaba,* sunk in March, 1915. Three more Americans died on May 1, aboard the American tanker *Gulflight.* The ship herself survived. She was towed ashore and later repaired.

Less than a week after the attack on the *Gulflight* another U-boat hit a larger target. Despite warnings published by the German embassy in *The New York Times* and other papers not to travel to England on the great Cunard liner *Lusitania,* when the ship sailed from New York on May 1, 1915, there was a full complement of passengers aboard, many of them Americans. In the hold was artillery ammunition for the British Army.

As the *Lusitania* steamed along within sight of the Irish coast in the early afternoon of May 7, she made a perfect target for the *U-20,* cruising in the area. The German skipper fired two torpedoes that hit their mark. Twenty minutes after they hit, the ship went down, taking with her 1,198 people, 128 of them Americans.

The sinking of the *Lusitania* aroused public opinion as nothing else had. In Germany it was hailed as a great victory, and medals were struck to commemorate it. But the people of the United States were angry. President Wilson protested to Germany, and the German ambassador expressed his "deep regrets." But although the country was pushed farther from her position of neutrality, as Germany had correctly estimated, she was not incensed enough to declare war. So the U-boat attacks continued, and in August more Americans died on the British liner *Arabic*. President Wilson's protest brought forth a German announcement on August 30 that thereafter passenger ships would be given a warning and the passengers allowed to leave before the ships were torpedoed.

U-boats did not operate unchallenged, and the British soon had a great variety of things with which to fight them. Nets, moored or towed; depth charges; towed explosive devices; all were used with some success. Small coastal vessels, private yachts, and whatever else could be found were pressed into service to patrol the British coast, searching for U-boats. In July, 1915, the Western Approaches Command was set up, with the job of keeping U-boats from the vital approaches to the British Isles. Still they took a toll of shipping. Although no serious shortages resulted, each ship that sank took with her supplies that would be missed.

12

The Odyssey of Admiral von Spee

In addition to the *Goeben* and the *Breslau*, two German armored cruisers, the *Scharnhorst* and the *Gneisenau*, and six light cruisers, the *Leipzig, Nürnberg, Emden, Dresden, Königsberg,* and *Karlsruhe*, were on foreign stations in 1914 when war began. The two armored cruisers, and the *Leipzig, Nürnberg,* and *Emden*, were based at Tsingtao, on the Shantung Peninsula of Northeast China, under command of Admiral Graf Maximilian von Spee. Only the *Emden* was actually there, however, since Von Spee had taken the *Scharnhorst* and the *Gneisenau* on a training cruise to the South Pacific and was at Ponape when word of the outbreak of war reached him. The *Leipzig* was on the west coast of Mexico, and the *Nürnberg* was returning from San Francisco. The *Königsberg* was in the Indian Ocean, and the *Dresden* was in the Atlantic.

On August 6 the *Nürnberg* joined Von Spee's squadron, and the ships put to sea, disappearing temporarily from Allied view. The *Emden* left Tsingtao the same day and met up with the squadron on August 12. Von Spee at once sent her off to the Indian Ocean to raid Allied shipping.

As long as these German ships were loose on the oceans, the British Admiralty could not relax its efforts to hunt them down. Never sure where they might strike next, the Royal Navy had to assign some of its ships to searching them out and to protecting the vital shipping lanes that must be kept open to deliver the essential supplies of food and matériel to the British Isles.

THE *EMDEN*

In early September the *Emden*'s presence in the Indian Ocean began to be felt. Within a week she sank four ships and captured two more. Allied merchant ships sailing from ports on the Bay of Bengal were halted, and cargoes that were sorely needed in Britain lay on the Indian docks. Convoys of troops from Australia and New Zealand were delayed.

The *Emden*'s raids continued. On September 22 she set fire to oil tanks at Madras. Then she steamed out of the Bay of Bengal, south of Ceylon, and captured seven ships, including one loaded with the coal she needed, and sank six more. Withdrawing southward into the Indian Ocean to the distant island of Diego Garcia, a British colony, the *Emden* found a warm welcome from its inhabitants, who had heard nothing of the war. From them she received coal and a necessary overhaul before putting to sea again and sinking seven more ships on the shipping lanes of the northern Indian Ocean. Next she sank a warship, the Russian light cruiser *Zemchung*, which she surprised in the harbor of Penang. Then the *Emden* took another merchant vessel and a small French destroyer.

But the *Emden*'s days were numbered. By this time British, French, Japanese, and Russian war vessels were combing the waters around Sumatra and Malaya looking for her. She was in fact heading for Cocos Island, through which passed the communications cables that connected Australia, South Africa, and the Dutch East Indies. As she approached the island harbor on November 9, an alert radio operator broadcast word of her arrival.

Only about fifty miles from Cocos that morning a convoy of Australian and New Zealand troops was steaming west toward Europe, escorted by the Japanese armored cruiser *Ibuki,* the British armored cruiser *Minotaur,* and two Australian light cruisers, the *Sydney* and the *Melbourne.* Although the Japanese commander begged to go after the *Emden,* the convoy commander sent the light cruiser *Sydney,* instead, not caring to risk losing the heavier ship.

The unsuspecting *Emden* was taken by surprise, when the *Sydney* appeared and fired on her as she lay at anchor. The 4.1-inch guns of the German vessel were no match for the 6-inch guns of the Australian; the *Emden's* gunners could not even find the range. In an hour and a half she was a flaming wreck. The Royal Australian Navy hailed its first naval victory.

THE *KÖNIGSBERG*

Farther west in the Indian Ocean the German cruiser *Königsberg*, at sea in the area when war began, had been a constant threat to all shipping near the approaches to the Suez Canal. She was little more than a threat, however. Although she sank the British light cruiser *Pegasus* near Zanzibar on September 20, she could claim only one merchant ship before her captain yielded to the problems of supply and maintenance without adequate bases and sailed her into the Rufiji River in German East Africa. The British finally discovered her there and bottled her in with an old ship, sunk across the mouth of the river. There the *Königsberg* remained, bombarded periodically by British cruisers, aircraft, and monitors, until their gunfire finally destroyed her in July, 1915. Even after the *Königsberg* had settled on the river bottom, however, her guns were taken off and used by Colonel Paul von Lettow-Vorbeck in his brilliant defense of German East Africa.

THE *KARLSRUHE*

At the outbreak of war the *Karlsruhe* was in the West Indies, a strategic spot from which to harass shipping between Brazil and England. After a trip into the Middle Atlantic, where she sank three ships, the *Karlsruhe* moved down to richer hunting grounds off Natal, Brazil. Between August 31 and October 14, she sank or captured fourteen British ships. The British Navy was kept busy following clues to her whereabouts, hoping to meet her and send her to the bottom. The chance never came. On November 4, 1914, while the crew was listening to a concert by the ship's band, an unexplained explosion blew the ship apart, killing most of the crew, including her captain. A few survivors landed in the West Indies. But the secret of the *Karlsruhe's* end was well kept. Until March, 1915, the British continued to look for her and to guard their merchant ships against attacks she would never make.

VON SPEE SAILS EAST

After leaving Ponape in August, Von Spee, with the *Scharn-horst, Gneisenau,* and *Nürnberg,* had headed east, stopping occasionally to attack Allied island installations or take on coal. On October 2 he was at Easter Island, where the *Dresden,* which had been off the coast of Brazil, joined his squadron. The *Leipzig* also arrived. After a week at Easter Island Von Spee moved to Mas Afuera, in the Juan Fernandez Islands, where he picked up a converted merchant ship, the *Prinz Eitel Friedrich.* After a few days, however, he sent her off to raid independently.

Meanwhile the British Admiralty had been receiving occasional reports of Von Spee's whereabouts and correctly concluded that he was heading for the west coast of South America. Not being sure whether he planned to stay there or round the Horn and move into the South Atlantic, the Admiralty directed the British commander of the South Atlantic Station, Rear Admiral Sir Christopher Cradock, to prepare for both possibilities.

Cradock had been following the *Dresden*'s movements in the South Atlantic closely but had been unable to catch her. As she headed for Cape Horn he had followed in his flagship, the armored cruiser *Good Hope,* accompanied by the armored cruiser *Monmouth;* a newer light cruiser, the *Glasgow;* and the armed merchant ship *Otranto.* When Cradock learned that the *Dresden* had eluded him and gone into the Pacific Ocean, he sent Captain John Luce, commander of the *Glasgow,* up the west coast with the other ships, while he returned in the *Good Hope* to the Falkland Islands for coal. He was there when word came from the Admiralty that Von Spee was apparently heading for South America. Cradock was ordered to look for him and was sent an old battleship, the *Canopus,* to help in tracking him down. Slow and antiquated, the *Canopus* carried four twelve-inch guns, which would give Cradock an advantage over the German cruisers, if she could get within range. However, she would not do much better than twelve knots, and Cradock decided that her only value to him was as a guard for his colliers. Since his request for the fast new cruiser *Defence,* which was just arriving on the South American Station, was denied, he started from the Falklands on October 22 with a distinct disadvantage in firepower over the ships he hoped to find.

BATTLE OF CORONEL

Cradock, having joined his other ships on the west coast of South America, on October 27 sent the *Glasgow* north to Coronel, to pick up messages from the Admiralty, relayed from Montevideo. As the *Glasgow* approached Coronel two days later her wireless operators intercepted a large number of coded messages that appeared to be German. This was reported to Admiral Cradock, who decided to head for Coronel with his other ships to search for the Germans.

At this point the Admiralty ordered the *Defence* to join Cradock, but it was already too late. Von Spee had heard that the British were in the Pacific. As Cradock steamed north on October 30, Von Spee was fifty miles west of Valparaiso. He received word of the *Glasgow*'s presence at Coronel, but she had disappeared by the time he got there the following day.

The *Glasgow* joined the rest of the British squadron on November 1, about fifty miles west of Coronel. By this time all the British ships were intercepting German signals, and Cradock had concluded that the *Leipzig* must be in the area. Accordingly he

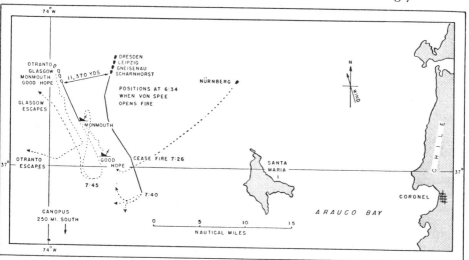

Battle of Coronel, November 1, 1914

spread out his ships, fifteen miles apart, and ordered them to look for her. At the same time the Germans, unaware that more than one British ship was close by, had started a search for the *Glasgow*.

In the late afternoon the two forces sighted one another, and their commanders squared off for a fight. Both were on a southerly course, the Germans in toward the land and the British to the west, with the sun descending the sky behind them. Admiral Cradock tried to force the Germans to fight while the sun was still above the horizon so that it would blind the eyes of the Germans who would have to fire into it. But Von Spee reversed the advantage by remaining out of range until after sunset, when the British ships were silhouetted against the western sky and the outlines of the Germans dimmed against the darkening land. He then opened fire at extreme range, with only the *Good Hope*'s two 9.2-inch guns able to engage the sixteen 8.2-inch guide firing guns of the *Scharnhorst* and *Gneisenau*.

Within minutes after the battle began the *Good Hope*'s forward gun was out of action and the ship was afire. As the Germans concentrated their long-range fire on the *Good Hope* and the *Monmouth,* their firepower advantage soon began to tell. Although the British tried to close the range, high waves made many of their guns unusable. The *Good Hope,* almost consumed in flames, dropped behind the other British ships. At about 8 P.M. she exploded and sank. The *Monmouth* fared no better. She was damaged badly at the water line, but for a time it appeared she might escape. However, at about 9 P.M. the *Nürnberg* came upon her in the darkness. When the British captain refused to surrender, the *Nürnberg* poured shells into her until she sank, taking her entire crew with her. Meanwhile the *Otranto,* no match for any of the Germans, had withdrawn early in the battle. The *Glasgow* had been the target of about six hundred German shells and had fired many of her own with some effect. But, following Cradock's orders, she escaped without serious damage and disappeared in the darkness. The Germans withdrew. Only three German sailors had been wounded.

BRITISH REORGANIZATION

Two days before this catastrophe at Coronel a change in personnel had taken place at the British Admiralty. Prince Louis of

Battenberg had been a target for criticism since the beginning of the war, because of his German ancestry and Austrian birth. Although he had been a British subject and Royal Navy officer for more than forty years, and was completely loyal to his adopted country, it seemed best to remove him from his sensitive post. Prince Louis was replaced by a former First Sea Lord, Admiral Lord John Fisher, who had retired from the Navy shortly before the war. Fisher had been responsible for development of the superbattleships known as dreadnoughts. A confident, professionally competent, dynamic man, Fisher at once took a firm hold on the helm, and the change in command was felt throughout the Royal Navy.

Greeted almost at once by the news of Coronel, Fisher set about planning measures to dispose of the German cruisers. Clearly the Germans could make several different moves with their ships, and until they struck again it would not be known which way they were going, for British intelligence sources from the west coast of South America were not very good. Fisher concluded that the most likely place for the *Scharnhorst* and the *Gneisenau* to go was the South Atlantic, where they could do the most damage to the Allies by attacking the vital supply lines from Rio de Janeiro to London. So, while he took measures in anticipation of other moves, he concentrated primarily on building up naval strength in the South Atlantic.

When Admiral Cradock went to the west coast of South America, by order of the Admiralty he had left half of his squadron on the east coast, under command of Admiral Archibald Stoddart. After the battle at Coronel, the *Canopus*, the *Glasgow,* and the *Otranto* returned to the Atlantic to rejoin Stoddart's command. Admiral Fisher promptly ordered the *Canopus* to remain at Port Stanley in the Falkland Islands. She was to be grounded or moored in a position where her guns could serve as a permanent defense of the harbor.

Stoddart was off the River Plate with the *Defence*—which had arrived at Montevideo on November 3—plus the armored cruisers *Carnarvon* and *Cornwall,* and the merchant cruiser *Orama*. There he awaited the arrival of the *Otranto* and the *Glasgow*. To strengthen the force in the South Atlantic, Admiral Fisher, with Churchill's approval, took the bold step of sending two powerful battle cruisers from the Grand Fleet, the *Invincible* and the *Inflexible*. To command them and a newly established regional

command for the South Atlantic and the South Pacific, he sent
Vice Admiral Sir Doveton Sturdee. Sturdee was a competent
sailor, but he had been serving without great success as Chief of
the War Staff in the Admiralty; Fisher was glad to replace him
as a staff officer, and to use him as a fighting commander at sea.
Removal of the two battle cruisers from Admiral Jellicoe and the
Grand Fleet gave the Germans a temporary numerical advantage
of one battle cruiser in their High Seas Fleet. But Fisher considered that the possibility of destroying the formidable *Scharnhorst* and *Gneisenau* was worth this risk.

Sturdee and his two cruisers joined Stoddart at Abrolhos
Rocks, about seventy miles off the coast of Brazil, on November
26. Also there by this time were the armored cruiser *Kent,* the armored cruiser *Macedonia,* which had been operating in Central
American waters, and the light cruiser *Bristol.* Sturdee and his
formidable squadron hurried on to Port Stanley, where they arrived on December 7 and at once started coaling, preparatory to
rounding the Horn to look for the German warships.

BATTLE OF THE FALKLAND ISLANDS

Von Spee, in the meantime, had gone into Valparaiso after the
Battle of Coronel. There the German Admiral was acclaimed as a
great victor. He left Valparaiso after one day and stayed in the
Juan Fernandez Islands until the very day that Sturdee arrived
at Abrolhos Rocks. Having received orders to take his ships back
to Germany, Von Spee left on November 26 for Cape Horn
and the South Atlantic. As he moved north along the coast of Ar-
gentina, he decided to stop at the Falkland Islands, destroy the
few ships he believed to be coaling there, and demolish the wireless station.

Just before 8 A.M. on December 8, a British lookout at Port
Stanley sighted two unknown warships approaching from the
south. The British ships were all in the process of coaling or
being repaired, having planned to leave the following day for
Cape Horn. The *Carnarvon* and the *Glasgow* alone had finished
coaling. The *Inflexible* had started coaling only a half-hour before. The rest had not yet started. However, Sturdee ordered the
entire squadron to get up steam and prepare for action. In thirty
minutes the armored cruiser *Kent* was steaming out to investigate.

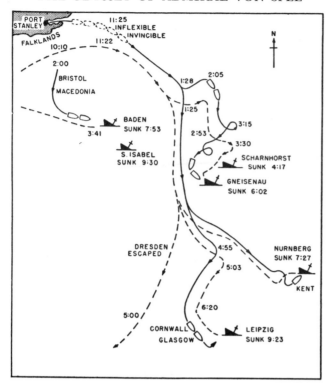

Battle of the Falkland Islands, December 8, 1914

Von Spee, approaching the Falklands after three days spent transferring coal from a captured British four-masted sailing vessel that had been headed for San Francisco with a load of anthracite, sent the *Gneisenau* and the *Nürnberg* ahead to scout the islands and to shell the wireless station. While the British ships were hustling to get steam up and get to sea, Von Spee, with the *Scharnhorst*, the *Leipzig*, and the *Dresden*, was following behind his two scouts, entirely unaware of the presence of British battle cruisers in the area. By 9:15 the *Kent* was approaching within range of the German lead ships when the *Canopus* opened fire. Although the shots fell short, the *Gneisenau* and the *Nürnberg* first turned away, then turned back as the firing ceased and the *Kent* approached. By this time the British had sighted the remaining German ships, but it was not until 9:40 that German lookouts on the *Gneisenau* made out the tripod masts of the British battle cruisers and realized the size and power of the force they had come upon. The captain of the *Gneisenau* turned at once to report to Von Spee.

By ten o'clock all the British ships were under way. The Germans, well aware that their chances against battle cruisers were poor, had turned away and were hastening off to the southeast, pursued by the *Glasgow* and the *Kent,* with the rest of the British ships rapidly moving up. Except for the heavy smoke of the coal-burning ships, visibility was perfect, and the sea was calm as the two squadrons raced along on nearly parallel courses. Just before 1 P.M. the *Inflexible* opened fire on the *Leipzig,* which had fallen behind the faster ships of the German squadron.

Von Spee then made an important decision. His light cruisers were of greater potential value for disrupting British trade with South America. So he ordered the three to head west for the coast of South America while he stood with his armored cruisers to fight as best he could, although there was little chance that he or his two ships would survive the battle.

A fierce fight followed, as Von Spee boldly tried to maneuver close enough to bring his secondary guns to bear, and Sturdee tried to remain out of range of all the German armament but within range of his battle cruisers' twelve-inchers. From time to time the targets disappeared entirely in the dense clouds of smoke. At length the *Scharnhorst,* having received numerous damaging hits and having been set afire in several places, at 4:17 turned on her beam ends and disappeared beneath the water, taking her entire crew, including Admiral von Spee, with her. The *Invincible,* the *Inflexible,* and the *Carnarvon* then concentrated on the *Gneisenau.* Despite the constant pounding from three directions, her skipper gallantly but stubbornly refused to surrender. It was about six o'clock when she finally turned over and sank. With no other ship to engage their attention, the British then stopped and rescued about two hundred of her crew.

In the meantime, Admiral Sturdee, having anticipated Von Spee's order to his light cruisers to flee, sent his own *Kent, Cornwall,* and *Glasgow* in pursuit. The three British cruisers strained their boilers to the maximum to maintain their top speed and gradually closed to within effective range. The *Kent* finally finished off the *Nürnberg,* after a fierce battle, watching her go to the bottom at about seven-thirty. Both the *Glasgow* and the *Cornwall* attacked the *Leipzig* and sank her an hour later. The swift *Dresden,* however, escaped. Although Sturdee searched for her the following day, she was not to be found. She subsequently turned up at Punta Arenas and then fled to the Juan Fernandez Islands. In March, 1915, she was found by the *Glasgow*. The *Dresden*'s captain tried to scuttle her, but she was finally sunk by the *Glasgow*'s guns.

The action at the Falklands more than avenged the losses at Coronel. The formidable German squadron had been all but annihilated. Even two of three German colliers were sunk. British casualties had been very light and the British ships had suffered little damage. Fisher's gamble with the battle cruisers had paid off, and they could now return to their stations. British morale, which had been very low since Coronel, soared when news of the victory was published in England. In Germany the reverse was true. The last hope of effective naval action overseas had been destroyed.

13

Turkey Joins the Central Powers

Turkey was still a nonbelligerent in late October, 1914, when the erstwhile German ships *Goeben* and *Breslau,* accompanied by a Turkish cruiser and a division of destroyers, steamed northward into the Black Sea. There they sank two Russian ships and shelled four Russian ports before returning to Constantinople. The incensed Russians declared war on Turkey on November 1. Declarations by France and Britain followed on November 5.

Turkey could hardly be expected to help the Central Powers by sending troops to fight in Europe. Her main contribution would clearly be made toward disrupting the Russian war effort and attacking British possessions on her southern and eastern borders. Under the close direction of the head of the German military mission, General Otto Liman von Sanders, the Turk military leaders had set three objectives: to cut off Russia from the oil fields of Persia and Mesopotamia by attacking in the Caucasus, to try to gain control of the Suez Canal, and to attack the oil fields around the Persian Gulf. To accomplish these purposes Turkey had already mobilized thirty-six divisions, under Commander-in-Chief Enver Pasha, one of the "Young Turks" who had overthrown Sultan Abdul Hamid in 1908.

THE CAUCASUS

Russia's border with Turkey, in the Caucasus, is in a mountainous, almost impassable area, where even existence is difficult. Yet in November, 1914, with the bitter cold of winter coming on, both Turkey and Russia were preparing to fight there.

The main Russian base in this region was at Kars; that of the Turks was at Erzerum. Promptly after the declaration of war, Russian troops under Myshlayevski moved south into the area where Russia, Turkey, and Persia met. With little or no opposition they crossed the frontier and occupied Bayazid, near Mount Ararat, penetrated through Kurdistan toward Van, and advanced from Erivan toward Kara Kilisse.

On November 20 a stronger Russian force crossed the frontier farther west and occupied Koprikeui, on their way to attack Erzerum. Unwittingly they had cooperated nicely with Enver, who was planning to draw the Russians across the border in the area of Sarikamish, hold them with part of his army, and send the rest of his troops around behind to cut the Russians off from their base at Kars and attack them from the rear. Having annihilated this force, he would invade Russian Georgia. Now that the Russians had crossed the border, Enver assigned to the Turkish XI Corps the task of occupying the Russians on the front, while the X Corps went around to cut the road between Sarikamish and Kars, and the IX Corps prepared to move in between the other two. The Turkish I Corps at the same time would land at Trebizond and work its way inland to Ardahan, Alexandropol, and Kars.

On December 14 the XI Corps attacked at Koprikeui and drove the Russians back about two miles. The IX and X Corps, struggling through snow, high winds, and freezing cold, reached the Kars-Sarikamish road by Christmas Day, exhausted and short of guns and ammunition. The I Corps had pushed up the Choruk Valley, across an eight-thousand-foot pass, in a raging blizzard. They reached Ardahan and captured it on January 1, 1915. But they were too exhausted to proceed further.

On December 28 the Russian General Vorontsov attacked the X Corps near Kars and defeated the Turks in a battle that lasted for four cold and miserable days. Then he turned on the IX Corps near Sarikamish and nearly wiped it out completely, while his right wing drove the I Corps and the fleeing X back down the Choruk Valley toward the Black Sea. The Turkish XI Corps, meanwhile, had been gaining in a struggle with the Russian left, but Vorontsov, seeing what was happening, shifted some of the troops that had been pursuing the X Corps to help against the XI and soon drove the Turks back on Erzerum.

The operation was a costly fiasco for the Turks. Their losses were estimated at over sixty thousand men, many of them victims of the weather. The first of Turkey's plans had gone sadly awry at the hands of the Russians. Meanwhile in Mesopotamia other Turk soldiers had encountered the British.

MESOPOTAMIA

Britain's chief source of oil in 1914 was the oil fields on Abadan Island, at the head of the Persian Gulf. In October, 1914, a force of British and Indian troops was sent from India to the area, to protect the oil fields and to strengthen support for them in the neighboring sheikhdoms. The Turks, for their part, sent troops down from Baghdad to forestall a possible British invasion of Mesopotamia.

When the Turk troops reached Basra, just after the declaration of war, they found the British already landing on the Turk side of the Shatt-al-Arab, the estuary formed by the Tigris and Euphrates Rivers where they join before flowing into the Persian Gulf. The British objective was Basra, but they dug in at Saniyeh to await the arrival of their commander, Sir Arthur Barrett, with more men. Turkish reaction to the British presence was slow, but at length about fifteen hundred men set out from Basra. At Sahil they lined up to await the approaching British, their left flank on the Shatt-al-Arab and their artillery on the right in a grove of date palms.

Gunboats had advanced close by the British as they advanced overland toward Basra. The vessels proved useful, for from the Shatt-al-Arab they could enfilade the Turkish trenches from the left. Across a muddy field and under heavy but ineffective artillery fire, the British attacked.

When the advancing British reached the Turks' front lines, the defenders broke and fled, losing a large percentage of their numbers and leaving the road to Basra open. Some of the British boarded steamers, to continue north by water while the rest pursued the Turks by land. On November 22 the water-borne contingent arrived at Basra, where they were soon joined by the rest. There they established a base camp.

The next town up the Tigris River was Al Qurna, where the Turks had encamped. On December 3 a detachment of British

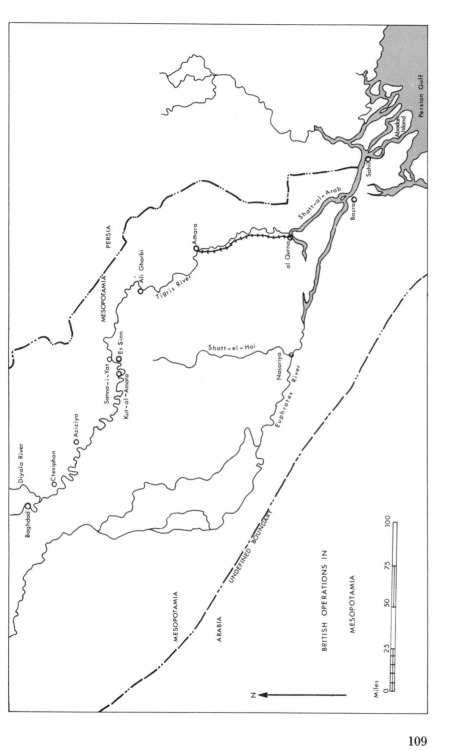

BRITISH OPERATIONS IN

MESOPOTAMIA

Persian Gulf

Abadan Island

Shatt-al-Arab

Sahil

Basra

al Qurna

Amara

Tigris River

Ali Gharbi

PERSIA

MESOPOTAMIA

Samna-i-Yat

Es Sinn

Kut-al-Amara

Shatt-el-Hai

Nasariya

Euphrates River

Aziziya

Ctesiphon

Diyala River

Baghdad

MESOPOTAMIA

ARABIA

UNDEFINED BOUNDARY

Miles

0   25   50   75   100

N

troops was taken by water to within four miles of the Turkish camp. While gunboats shelled the city the troops advanced on the shore under heavy fire. Unable to accomplish their objective, however, they finally abandoned the attack and sent to Basra for reinforcements. On December 7 the new troops arrived and captured Mezera on the opposite bank of the river. The British were preparing a strong attack on Al Qurna when the Turks surrendered, about twelve hundred of them, with nine guns.

With Basra and Al Qurna in British hands, British planners looked longingly at the rest of Mesopotamia. Responsibility for action there lay with the Indian government, with the approval of the British Secretary of State for India in London. In practice it was in London that decisions were made. There was no real strategic reason for taking Mesopotamia, but the ball had started rolling and no one tried very hard to stop it. There seems not to have been a definite decision to proceed. As soon as one objective was gained another was approved, and the British became involved in a meaningless campaign.

THE SUEZ CANAL

Executing an attack on the third Turk objective, the British-controlled Suez Canal, was by no means easy. Since Britain controlled the sea, the only way to reach the canal from Turkish territory was across miles of desert, with inadequate or nonexistent roads and no water supply. In January, 1915, about twenty thousand men under the command of German Colonel Baron Friedrich Kress von Kressenstein marched across the desert, dragging their guns and pontons which they hoped to use to construct a bridge across the canal. Their hope of surprising the British on the west bank of the canal was frustrated by British planes that saw them as they approached.

On February 2, 1915, the Turks reached the eastern bank of the canal, near Ismailia, and deployed along the shore between Lake Timsah and the Great Bitter Lake, facing the British at Toussoum. The Turks waited for darkness and then tried to launch some pontons and rafts made of empty cans, but British machine guns sank their primitive craft and killed many of the Turkish soldiers. The following day they tried again, under fire from British artillery supported by three gunboats, an armed transport, and a French guardship. Three boatloads of Turkish troops managed to cross the canal, only to be pounded mercilessly by the guns of the British defenders.

Finally Sir John Maxwell, the British commander, sent two columns of Indian troops across and drove off the Turks, who were already retreating. The remnants of the hot and weary Turkish force made their way back across the desert to Beersheba. The British made no attempt to pursue them.

14

Stalemate on the Western Front

After the Battle of Ypres in 1914, Joffre ordered attacks near Arras in Artois and in Champagne, where he thought the German defense was weak enough to break through. Although the French in Artois outnumbered the Germans, they were quickly beaten off by machine-gun and artillery fire. In Champagne they made small gains, but nowhere did they advance as much as a mile.

Shocked by the high casualties, Joffre abandoned the offensives, and the Allies as well as the Germans settled into a defensive position, the Germans usually in the best strategic position available, the Allies on the line of farthest advance. Trench warfare, in a pattern that was to be followed with little deviation for the next three years, had begun. The whole front became two systems of ditches, separated by thirty to eight hundred yards of no-man's-land.

The first trenches were crude, three or four feet deep, with the earth piled in front to conceal men walking erect. Here and there rough caves in the trench walls provided shelter, where men could huddle for sleep or for protection from the elements, while remaining available to join the firing line if necessary. Gradually the trenches were deepened, and the shelters were enlarged and improved. Thickets of barbed wire were stretched along the front line to hold off attackers. In such holes in the ground millions of men on both sides of the line lived for month after month and year after year.

At first the trenches were plotted in two lines—the front line and the support line—separated by about two hundred to three hundred yards. Then a third line was added in depth, and a network of communicating trenches was dug to tie the system together. Well behind the front lines, more elaborate dugouts sheltered those off duty, and in still more complex caverns command headquarters functioned deep underground. Telephone lines and electric light wires were strung everywhere.

Within these warrens lived the infantrymen, in constant discomfort and frequent misery. Rains turned the "floor" into mud that swallowed up boards put down to provide a dry passage. Cold weather turned the ground hard with frost, and no heating system could compete with the open-air ventilation. Rats and lice abounded and thrived. And always, through the boredom of idle waiting, there was the haunting prospect of an artillery barrage that would wipe out whole sections of the trench system, burying those occupants who survived the blasts of high explosives, or of a sudden rush of enemy infantrymen, rifles blazing and bayonets fixed. Attack though they might, however, neither side could break through the lines of trenches. Hundreds of thousands of lives were sacrificed in repeated attempts to do so.

The year 1915 had its share of futile attacks from the trenches, with their chief result long lists of battle casualties posted in London, Paris, and Berlin. Only a few of the attempts made enough difference to discuss.

CHAMPAGNE

The front line at the beginning of 1915 ran south from Nieuwpoort in Belgium to Noyon, the point of deepest German penetration into France. Then it swung a little south of east and ran well into Lorraine, to Verdun, before bending southeast toward Switzerland. Joffre based his strategic planning in 1915 on attempts to straighten out the bulges in the line, the so-called Noyon salient, and the St. Mihiel salient farther south. In the early months of 1915 he ordered attacks on both.

In Champagne the French attack came on February 16, preceded by an intense artillery bombardment that announced to the Germans that an attack was coming. Six weeks later Joffre called a halt. The French had suffered about ninety thousand casualties and the Germans about the same number. The attackers had not even reached the railroad five miles behind the original German front.

THE WOËVRE

Farther south, the St. Mihiel salient bulged to the west across the Meuse River below Verdun, threatening the fortifications there. East of the river, just south of St. Mihiel, in the muddy plateau of the Woëvre, the French First Army under General Auguste Dubail attacked on April 6, in an attempt to eliminate this salient. The attackers failed to break through the German line, however, and Dubail abandoned the attempt on April 24.

NEUVE CHAPPELLE

After the Battle of Ypres, Sir John French received some Territorial units and a Canadian division, and he organized his forces in France in two armies, the First commanded by General Sir Douglas Haig, the Second under General Sir Horace Smith-Dorrien. The First Army held the southern part of the British sector, opposite Neuve Chappelle, an area where the Germans were known to have only about fifteen hundred men. Haig was anxious to attack there, for he knew his men outnumbered the enemy. Although Joffre was trying to assemble forces farther south for an attack at Arras, French decided to undertake an offensive.

The operation began on March 10, 1915, with a heavy half-hour artillery barrage on the German trenches in front of the town of Neuve Chappelle. Then the range was extended to the town itself, while First Army infantrymen advanced on a front of 3,500 yards. Having gained the front line of German trenches, they halted to reorganize. The artillery again extended the range, to lay down a curtain of fire beyond the town. The British infantrymen moved out once more, this time advancing into the town. A gap well over a mile wide and nearly a mile deep had been torn in the German lines. As more British troops moved into the gap, preparing to advance again, German units on either flank, having recovered from the original surprise of the attack, raked the advancing lines with machine-gun and artillery fire. The element of surprise had not been exploited by the British, for they had no reserves ready to move in behind the advancing and expanding front line. Consequently, the Germans were able to rush reinforcements to the area and hold the British gains to a minimum. On the night of March 12-13, Field Marshal French ordered his troops to dig in where they were and halt the attack.

SECOND BATTLE OF YPRES

Next turn for a major attack was the Germans', and they used it to introduce a new and formidable weapon. For two days artillery shells had been fired at the sector held by the British Second Army in Flanders. Then, at 5 P.M. on April 22, Allied lookouts noticed a sort of yellow-green mist, carried on the northeast wind from the German front lines toward the Allied trenches. On a front of about four miles, highly poisonous chlorine gas bore down upon the French Colonial Corps and the Second and Third Brigades of the Canadian Division. Taken completely by surprise, many men died where they were; others ran from this new horror. But the sanctuary they sought was downwind, and the gas traveled with them as they ran. The Canadians, on the left flank of the attack, received a lighter dose than the French and held their ground. Beside them, however, a gap over four miles wide was opened in the Allied line.

German preparations had not included troops to exploit such an opportunity. By the following morning Field Marshal French had sent up five British battalions and two Canadian reserve battalions to close the gap. A second gas attack found the Canadians at least prepared with wet handkerchiefs to cover their faces. It was harder to withstand the attacks of the German infantry, who followed close—but not too close—behind the wave of gas. Finally, despite reinforcements, General Smith-Dorrien decided he must withdraw to the outskirts of Ypres. French was furious at this and ordered Smith-Dorrien relieved at once by Lieutenant General Sir Herbert Plumer. Plumer promptly ordered the same withdrawal, and this time French accepted it. The battle smoldered until May 24, when the Germans again attacked in force, behind a gas barrage. But by this time the men had been supplied with crude protective masks; the British held, and the battle finally died out.

In this second Battle of Ypres, the British lost sixty thousand men; the French lost ten thousand and the Germans about thirty-five thousand. Although the Germans advanced closer to Ypres, they missed a great opportunity to exploit their new, illegal weapon. It was not long before the Allies too were using gas, and the gas mask became an item of regular issue to the front-line troops on both sides of no-man's-land.

SECOND BATTLE OF ARTOIS

The battles at Neuve Chappelle and Ypres had postponed until May the offensive Joffre wanted in Artois. By that time it had become a dual offensive. The British First Army under Haig was to try to capture Aubers Ridge, near Festubert, while the French Tenth Army under General Henri Philippe Pétain attacked on a ten-mile front about ten miles to the south toward Vimy Ridge, between Lens and Arras.

General Haig was short of high-explosive artillery shells by this time, for enormous quantities had been expended at Ypres, and the urgent demands of the Gallipoli Peninsula campaign had further depleted the British supply. Haig limited his bombardment to forty minutes, and fired mostly shrapnel, which was of little use for breaking up barbed wire and concrete. The French, on the other hand, preceded their attack by five days of heavy firing. It was not entirely an asset, however, for it gave the Germans ample warning of an impending attack. They moved three divisions to the area to meet it.

The British attacked on the morning of May 9, 1915, fought fiercely, and got nowhere. The offensive was halted the same day it began. On Joffre's urging, Haig renewed it the following week and kept attacking sporadically until May 27. By then about ten thousand men had been lost, and the greatest gain was less than a mile.

The French artillery barrage had so effectively smashed the German defenses that the French troops, also attacking on May 9, in some places penetrated two and a half miles into German-held territory; but the Germans had fortified the area with an intricate system of trenches, so interconnected that the destruction of one part didn't impair the defensive strength of the rest. There were always more trenches beyond or beside the ones that were taken, as well as underground passages that permitted the defenders to move undetected from one trench line to the next. A complex of machine-gun emplacements covered the area, and the attackers had to knock them out one by one.

Perhaps the outcome would have been different if sufficient reserves had been ready to move up behind the first line before the Germans could bring up reinforcements. Rugged fighting continued until May 15 and flared up again a month later for four more bloody days. But Vimy Ridge remained in German hands. This futile slaughter had cost the French one hundred thousand casualties. Only by comparison could the Germans' loss of seventy-five thousand seem preferable.

15

A New Venture—The Dardanelles and Gallipoli

EAST? OR WEST?

Prewar planners had not foreseen the stalemate that had developed on the Western Front as both sides dug down into trenches and began to realize that they had seen only the beginning of a long war. The lightning victory both sides had anticipated had vanished in bloody clashes that had cost Britain and France close to a million casualties in a few months and the Germans almost as many. Surely there must be another way to fight this war?

British, French, and German leaders spent many hours debating the question of what should be done next. Neither side had an adequate stockpile of weapons and ammunition or sufficient trained men to force a breakthrough on the Western Front or continue the costly battles of the opening war months. On the Eastern Front both sides had problems, but the Allies' problems were greater. Russia was almost entirely cut off from the west and could neither send the wheat her allies badly needed nor receive the weapons and ammunition her industry could not supply. To the Germans, Russian resistance had proved stronger than anticipated, and it was clear that the Eastern Front was going to need a larger share of German resources than had been planned.

British options as the year ended were greater than those of any other belligerent. Although British manpower was limited, training programs had been intensified by Lord Kitchener and were already producing more and better troops. Trained men also were beginning to arrive from Canada, Australia, and New Zealand. These troops were free to move, for they had the Royal

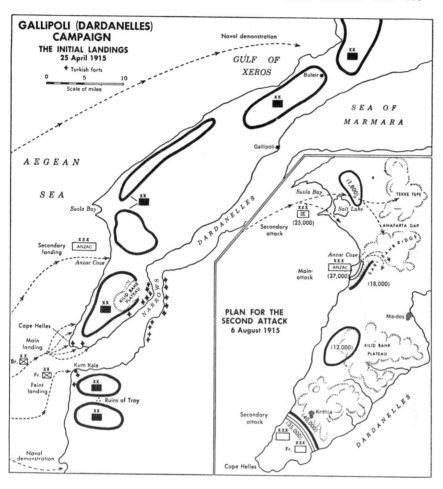

GALLIPOLI (DARDANELLES) CAMPAIGN
THE INITIAL LANDINGS
25 April 1915
+ Turkish forts
Scale of miles
0   5   10

Naval demonstration

GULF OF XEROS

Bulair

SEA OF MARMARA

Gallipoli

AEGEAN SEA

Suvla Bay

Secondary landing   ANZAC

Anzac Cove

KILID BAHR PLATEAU

NARROWS

Cape Helles

Main landing

Br.

Fr.

Feint landing

Kum Kale

Ruins of Troy

Naval demonstration

DARDANELLES

Suvla Bay

Salt Lake

(25,000)

Secondary attack

Main attack

(37,000)

(18,000)

Anzac Cove   ANZAC

(1,800)

TEKKE TEPE

ANAFARTA GAP

H B RIDGE

Maidos

KILID BAHR PLATEAU

(12,000)

PLAN FOR THE SECOND ATTACK
6 August 1915

Secondary attack

(35,000)

(40,000)

Krithia

Fr.

Cape Helles

DARDANELLES

Navy to transport them. The question was, should they be sent to France to build up the great machine that would be required to break through the German line, or was there somewhere else where they could find a weak spot in the enemy's flanks and achieve something significant, cheaply and fast?

There was disagreement about what should be done among the military leaders and the members of the British War Council—the Prime Minister (Herbert Asquith), Lord Chancellor (Richard Burdow, Lord Haldane), Secretary of State for War (Lord Kitchener), Chancellor of the Exchequer (David Lloyd George), Foreign Minister (Sir Edward Grey), Secretary of State for

India (Robert Crewe-Milnes, Lord Crewe) , and First Lord of the Admiralty (Winston Churchill). One group believed that the Western Front was and must be the decisive theater of the war and that nothing should be done to reduce the supply of men and equipment available for it. No matter where else fronts might be developed, only on the Western Front could the war be won or lost. Even the collapse of Russia would not be decisive. Britain and France could continue to fight without her. But the collapse of the Western Front would mean defeat for Britain, as well as for France. Therefore, these Western Front advocates argued, all available manpower must be used to build up a force strong enough to hold in France and finally win a smashing victory.

While not necessarily disagreeing that the Western Front was decisive, another group, led by Winston Churchill and the dynamic Chancellor of the Exchequer, David Lloyd George, deplored the heavy casualties that had already been suffered there. They thought that until enormous strength in men and equipment was accumulated in France the cost of further offensive operations would be exorbitant. For the present, they argued, the Allies should remain on the defensive in the West and use some of the force that was becoming available to strike somewhere else.

Churchill at first favored a move into the Baltic to try to open a northern route to Russia. When this operation was judged impracticable, he turned toward the East, where Russia's isolation was making it seem desirable to open the sea lane to the Black Sea, through the Strait of the Dardanelles, the Sea of Marmara, and the Bosporus, controlled by Turkey. If Turkey could be knocked out of the war, it would also be easier to get at Austria, and undoubtedly Italy and the Balkan States could be persuaded to join the Allied cause. Churchill's view won, in a limited way, and because of the limitations the results were disastrous.

THE DARDANELLES OPERATION

In January, 1915, Grand Duke Nicholas, uncertain whether the Turks were planning more operations in the Caucasus after their defeat by Russian forces, appealed to Lord Kitchener to make some kind of demonstration to draw the Turks away from the area. The request found Kitchener sympathetic but unwilling to spare any troops for that area. To the Grand Duke he sent word that Britain would do something, but it was unlikely that she could divert many Turks from the Caucasus.

Thus began what became probably the most controversial operation of World War I, an operation that promised much and delivered little but disaster, haunting those involved in its planning for the rest of their lives. Churchill in particular always remembered it vividly, and there is no doubt that it strongly influenced his strategic thinking in World War II.

On January 3, 1915, Sir John Fisher, First Sea Lord, in a memorandum to Churchill recommended a large-scale attack on Turkey. He proposed landing a strong British force south of the Dardanelles and a Greek force on the Gallipoli Peninsula, while a naval force pushed through the Dardanelles. Churchill realized that no such operation would be approved by the British War Council. But the naval-attack part of it might. He decided to pursue the idea.

The first move was to ask the man who would be responsible for such a naval attack. That same afternoon, with Fisher's approval, Churchill sent a cable to the commander at the Dardanelles, Vice Admiral Sir Sackville Carden, asking whether he thought the Strait could be forced by ships alone. With little enthusiasm Carden said he thought the Dardanelles could not be "rushed," but "they might be forced by extended operations with [a] large number of ships." He then submitted a plan calling for reduction of the Turkish force (1) at the entrance from the Aegean, (2) along the banks of the Strait, and (3) at the Narrows, while battleships bombed the coast at Bulair and the battery near Baba Tepe. Carden's plan also included clearing a passage through the minefields, and the advance of the naval force through the Narrows. When the forts above the Narrows had been silenced, the warships would proceed into the Sea of Marmara.

Carden's plan was more than Churchill had contemplated, and he was delighted to find verbal support for it on all sides in the government. Kitchener was enthusiastic, although he said he could not supply troops for any supporting action. The Navy was confident the Strait could be forced without Army help. When the War Staff proposed that the brand-new dreadnought *Queen Eliza-*

beth with her fifteen-inch guns, already under orders to the Mediterranean for trials, be sent to support the operation, approval of the plan by the War Council was practically assured. The approval was general: "That the Admiralty should . . . prepare for a naval expedition in February to bombard and take the Gallipoli Peninsula with Constantinople as its objective."

Churchill's enthusiasm for the plan grew rapidly as it was studied in detail in the Admiralty. But as his increased, Sir John Fisher's practically disappeared. Where previously the admiral had been bold in his plans for the Navy, he suddenly became conservative almost to the point of timidity. "Being already in possession of all that a powerful fleet can give a country," he said, "we should continue quietly to enjoy the advantage without dissipating our strength in operations that cannot improve the position." Like the librarian who is happiest when all the books are in their places on the shelves, Fisher did not wish to risk any losses of ships or men. This attitude led him also to oppose another operation that was currently under consideration, an attack on coastal installations at Zeebrugge, where the Germans were building up what became their chief U-boat base.

Finally Asquith ruled out Zeebrugge, but like the rest he supported the Dardanelles, and Fisher was left with the choice of going along or resigning. Kitchener appealed to his duty to his country, and Churchill plied him with figures and facts to prove that the operation would work and would not endanger the strength of the Grand Fleet. After a long day of discussion, Fisher agreed on January 28 to go along with the plan.

Up to this point this was being contemplated as a purely naval operation, mainly because of Kitchener's earlier refusal to contribute ground forces. But Kitchener was coming to realize that he could give some military support. The 29th Division, which was approaching combat readiness in England, was not vitally needed in France. Nor was the Australian and New Zealand Corps (ANZAC), which was in Egypt. The advantages of having troops at hand near the Dardanelles if needed were apparent, and the War Council agreed to provide them. On February 16 it was decided that the 29th Division should go to Lemnos, where the Greeks offered a base at Mudros, that the troops in Egypt should be made available, and that small craft should be assembled for a possible landing. But three days later Kitchener had again changed his mind. Transports were to be prepared in case the 29th was sent, but there would be no immediate decision to send it. The next day even the transports were not to be assembled. By then the naval attack had begun.

THE NAVAL ATTACK

The Strait of the Dardanelles is four thousand yards wide at the western entrance, widens to eight thousand yards, then closes again to sixteen hundred yards at the Narrows. Beyond the Narrows lies the Sea of Marmara, from which the narrow Strait of the Bosporus leads into the Black Sea. There were seventy-eight Turkish guns in the forts at the Narrows in January, 1915, and twenty-four at the western entrance. Between them were a few scattered forts and some mobile German howitzers, added by the Turks after the British bombarded the outer forts on November 3. Distributed among the fortifications on both sides of the Strait was a division of Turkish troops. In addition and, as it proved, crucially, the waters were well planted with mines. No warships could push confidently through the Dardanelles unless the mines were swept. With no regular minesweepers available, the Admiralty provided Admiral Carden with fishing trawlers from the North Sea with their crews to sweep them.

Just before ten o'clock on the morning of February 19, 1915, the British fleet approached to attack the outer forts.

Besides the *Queen Elizabeth* Admiral Carden had the large battleships *Agamemnon* and *Lord Nelson* and the battle cruiser *Inflexible* in the first division; the battleships *Vengeance, Albion, Cornwallis, Irresistible,* and *Triumph* in the second division; and the French battleships *Suffren, Bouvet, Charlemagne,* and *Gaulois* in the third. Until 2 P.M. they fired their heavy guns at long range at the Turkish forts. Then they moved to six thousand yards. It was not until almost five o'clock, when three ships had moved in still closer, that the Turkish guns replied, revealing that the shelling had not been very effective. Whether not wishing to risk his ships or anxious to get away before darkness fell, Admiral Carden ordered the fleet to retire.

Next day the weather turned bad and continued so until February 25, when the fleet returned. With greater accuracy the British gunners succeeded in destroying a large proportion of the Turk-

ish guns in the outer forts and forcing the Turks to withdraw
their garrisons. The *Agamemnon* took a half-dozen hits, three of
her men were killed and seven wounded, but the price was low for
the damage inflicted. Mines were cleared from the entrance that
night, and the following day three battleships went in a little way
and finished destruction of the forts from the inside. During the
next few days landing parties of sailors and marines went ashore
and destroyed whatever they could find on both sides of the
Strait.

Reports of all this were greeted with pleasure in London and
exerted some influence on Kitchener, who indicated that perhaps
the 29th Division could be sent out after all. He ordered General
W. R. Birdwood up from Egypt to observe the naval operation.
Birdwood's report came on March 5. "I am very doubtful," he
said, "if the Navy can force the passage unassisted." Not until
March 10 was the decision made to send the 29th Division. By
then the transports had been dispersed and there was no plan for
loading the men and the equipment. No one knew what they
would be used for when they arrived. In view of the unsystematic
way in which the whole thing had been handled, it is remarkable
that the 29th Division actually sailed for the Mediterranean on
March 16.

Ahead of the troops went General Sir Ian Hamilton, whom
Kitchener had appointed to command the army forces allocated to
the Dardanelles operation—the 29th, two ANZAC divisions from
Egypt (hereafter called Anzacs), and a French division. Hamilton had no operation orders. His men were to be used in a major
attack "only . . . in the event of the Fleet failing to get through
after every effort has been exhausted."

At about this stage Admiral Carden's health broke under the
strain and he was relieved by his second in command, Vice Admiral John M. de Robeck. Under De Robeck's command the fleet returned to the attack on March 18. At a distance of 14,400 yards
from the Narrows the *Queen Elizabeth, Agamemnon, Lord Nelson,* and *Inflexible* opened fire on the forts in that area. Immediately the howitzers along the shore, and then the guns in the
forts, replied.

After the four French battleships moved up and opened fire at
closer range, one by one the forts ceased firing, until about 1:30,

when most had been silenced. Ordered back by De Robeck, the French vessels were moving along near the southern shore when the *Bouvet* was suddenly torn apart by an explosion. In two minutes she went to the bottom, taking all but sixty-six of her crew of six hundred. About two hours later, the *Inflexible, Irresistible,* and *Ocean* in quick succession hit mines. The *Inflexible* dragged herself back to Tenedos, but the other two sank where they were hit, their crews first having been removed. This experience, unexpected because the area was thought to have been swept free of mines, was unnerving, and Admiral de Robeck decided to withdraw the rest of his ships. One more, the *Gaulois,* had been hit so effectively that she had to be beached on Drepano Island.

Unbeknownst to De Robeck, the Turks were in worse shape than he at the end of the day, for they had fired almost all of their ammunition. Had the British returned the next day, there could hardly have been any response from the Turks. But there was to be no attack the next day.

Before De Robeck would risk his warships again, he decided that the mines must be removed, but the untrained civilian trawler crews balked at sweeping under fire from the shore. So De Robeck improvised, equipping destroyers, torpedo boats, and the picket boats with various sweeping devices, while the Admiralty staff eagerly awaited news that the attack had been resumed.

In the meantime General Hamilton had arrived in the area and had witnessed the attack on March 18. His presence and the expectation of having military forces available convinced De Robeck that the ships should not be sent through the Strait until the Allies controlled the beach of the Gallipoli Peninsula. Unfortunately, even had the forces been assembled they could not have been put ashore immediately.

No one at this time had any experience with amphibious landings such as was to be developed in World War II. The 29th Division had sailed with no thought of unloading men and equipment together and landing them on the beach. There were no amphibious craft to ferry them ashore, and no detailed plans for the operation had been developed when Hamilton and De Robeck decided to undertake it. So Hamilton went to Alexandria, where facilities were adequate for unloading and reloading the troops and where he could assemble a planning staff and work out details. The target date for a landing was set for April 14, and until that time the battleships did not return to the attack.

The Turks did not sit by and wait for the landing that by this time they expected. German General Liman von Sanders, who had previously been an adviser, was put in command of all the Turkish forces on the Gallipoli Peninsula. He had six divisions with which to defend it, two on the Asiatic side of the Strait, two at the tip of Gallipoli, and two at Bulair.

Working from very scanty and often inaccurate information, Hamilton's planners decided to land the 29th Division on five beaches around Cape Helles, at the tip of the peninsula, and to send them inland to converge on the highest point, known as Achi Baba Hill. Reading counterclockwise the beaches were identified as Y, X, W, V, and S. In addition, the Anzacs were to land about twelve miles above Y, on the outside of the peninsula. The two forces were to join as soon as possible and together to attack the Kilid Bahr Plateau, from which they could look down on the Narrows and support the naval drive through to the Sea of Marmara. The French, meanwhile, were to land at Kum Kale, on the Asiatic shore, as a diversion.

It was not until April 23 that the transports, having assembled at Mudros, were ready to sail. Early on the morning of April 25 the ships' boats and an assortment of other small craft headed for the beaches. The Anzacs, fifteen thousand of them, landed first, a mile north of where they were supposed to be, on a narrow beach edged by steep cliffs. The troops worked their way up the cliffs and part way up the Sari Bair Ridge beyond. There they were halted by the Turks' 19th Division, commanded by Lieutenant Colonel Mustapha Kemal, later to become famous as Atatürk. The Turk defenders drove the Anzacs back to their beachhead, inflicting casualties. General Birdwood would have taken his men off, had Hamilton not ordered him to stay.

At S, X, and Y Beaches, meanwhile, the troops had met no resistance as they went ashore. But W Beach was well defended with barbed wire, and three platoons of Turk soldiers greeted the British invaders with rifle and machine-gun fire. Although over five hundred British were killed or wounded, the Turks were soon driven off.

V Beach was a different story. In an attempt to land men on

the beach more rapidly, an old coaling steamer, the *River Clyde*, was run in close to the beach and grounded, and a bridge of barges was strung from her to the shore. Through large openings in her side some men were to walk ashore, while others, as at the other beaches, went in in small boats. Unfortunately for the British, three Turkish platoons were strategically placed at V and picked off the men as they tried to walk ashore from the *River Clyde* or land from the boats. The result was slaughter. The British died in droves; only a few reached shelter on the beach. As darkness fell they were at last able to move freely in the area. More men were safely landed, and the dead and wounded were evacuated by the hundreds.

General Sir Aylmer Hunter-Weston, commander of the British 29th Division, was embarked in the *Euryalus* at this time and had no clear picture of what was going on. He did not realize that the troops who had landed without opposition on both sides of V and W were simply sitting where they landed. Hence he did not order them to fall on the Turks who were defending the two beaches. General Hamilton apparently understood more of the situation, but he did not want to interfere with his subordinate, and so he also did nothing.

General Liman von Sanders was asleep when the first attack began. Learning that troops were landing on the tip of the peninsula and that a large force—actually a decoy—was off Bulair, where he very much feared an attempt to cut the peninsula in two, he concluded that the Bulair danger was greater, and he concentrated his major forces in that area. Later, however, when no landings were made there, he turned his men around and sent them down to the invasion area. So it was that by late afternoon the troops at Y Beach were under heavy attack. The next morning, through a confusion of orders, the troops at Y Beach were all taken off. The French too were evacuated from Kum Kale, taking with them 450 prisoners. The next day the French troops were sent ashore at V.

The beachhead units gradually pushed inland during the next few days and joined forces in a continuous front. By April 28, however, progress had slowed and both sides dug in, adopting the trench stance of the Western Front. The Anzacs, too, had dug in at their beach. Thus, within a few days of the landing, the situation was stabilized, with little to show for the many who had died (three thousand) or been wounded (six thousand) in the first three days.

If progress was to be made, Lord Kitchener decided, there would have to be reinforcements. Consequently he ordered the 42nd Division and a Gurkha brigade from Egypt to proceed to the Dardanelles. The French also sent another division to the area.

The weary soldiers ashore on Gallipoli did not have long to rest. On May 1 the reinforced Turks attacked with fixed bayonets. Three days of tough fighting changed the positions hardly at all. The British reinforcements were already beginning to arrive, however, and on May 6 General Hamilton ordered an attack. Poorly planned and coordinated, it petered out two days later, adding to the casualties, which by then exceeded twenty thousand.

The leaders in London were appalled at the punishment the troops had suffered. Reports were being received also of the horrible conditions ashore—interminable heat, dirt, dysentery, inadequate supplies of food and ammunition, combined with the misery of living in trenches. Had it all been a great mistake? And if so, what could be done about it?

The Navy, during the landings and the following days, had been giving support from a distance and then closer in, bombarding the shore and beyond the front lines of the Allies on the beach. Naval firing was not coordinated with the Army's needs, however, and hence its effectiveness was limited. The plan to move into the Strait had been shelved. Eager to make use of the naval power available, Commodore Roger Keyes, De Robeck's chief of staff, urged that the fleet proceed at least to attack the Narrows in order to lend support to the hard-pressed Army. De Robeck was reluctant, but after a conference with his staff he agreed to try. On May 10 he cabled the Admiralty for an opinion as to whether the forcing of the Narrows and entrance into the Sea of Marmara would be of real help to the Army. De Robeck expressed the view that in itself it would not be decisive and the fleet might well find itself closed in, with the Strait blocked behind it.

De Robeck's cable found deeply divided opinion at the Admiralty. Churchill, while not favoring an immediate attempt to force passage through to the Sea of Marmara, at least wanted the operation to proceed to the point of sweeping the mines in the Strait so that ships could go up close enough to attack the forts at the Narrows. Lord Fisher was firmly opposed to trying to push through and believed that even the minesweeping was impossible until the Army controlled the land on both sides. There followed an exchange of memoranda as each tried to convince the other of his position and neither budged. Then came word that a Turkish destroyer had sneaked out of the Strait in the darkness of the morning of May 12 and sunk the old battleship *Goliath* with three torpedoes.

For Lord Fisher this was enough. He determined to take a positive step and call the *Queen Elizabeth* back home before she too fell prey to a mine or a torpedo. This brought down on Fisher the wrath of Lord Kitchener. In vain did Fisher and Churchill point out to Kitchener that naval replacements would be sent at once. He remained opposed to the whole idea. Nevertheless Fisher and Churchill proceeded to plan on the ships to be sent in place of the *Queen Elizabeth*. When Churchill decided independently to add two E-class submarines, Lord Fisher's pent-up wrath exploded. He resigned. Nothing would persuade him to change his mind, and in his frustration he called on the opposition Conservative Party to insist that Churchill be fired. Prime Minister Asquith yielded. Churchill left the Admiralty, replaced by Arthur Balfour. Admiral Sir Henry Jackson replaced Lord Fisher, whose fears seemed to be vindicated on May 25, when the German *U–21* sank the battleship *Triumph* off Gallipoli. Two days later the *Majestic* too went down, victim of a German torpedo.

Gallipoli by this time had become a lost cause, although the fact was not to be accepted for some time. Three times in June the Allies tried in vain to push out of their line on Cape Helles. Five more British divisions were sent to the area in July, and General Hamilton made a new plan. He would send part of the new troops ashore to reinforce the Anzacs, who were still immobilized not far from the beach, and land the others at Suvla Bay, farther north. The two units would then join and push together across the peninsula to cut it off close to the Narrows.

Lieutenant General Sir Frederick Stopford commanded the IX Corps, which landed at Suvla Bay on August 7, with scarcely a

shot fired. The whole corps could have pushed ahead with no resistance had Stopford been on the spot and imaginative enough to
send his men ahead. Instead, with only junior officers ashore, the
troops stayed where they landed for two precious days. General
Liman von Sanders was not asleep. Two days gave him ample
time to move two divisions onto the high ground behind Suvla
Bay, where they met the British when the attack finally got under
way on August 9. Two more British divisions joined the fight on
August 21, but the picture was the same as everywhere else—no
progress.

The operation continued with little change, a series of futile attacks and counterattacks, for the next few months. Gradually
opinion grew that the whole operation should be abandoned. General Hamilton was relieved by General Sir Charles Monro in October, when the intense heat had given way to piercing cold. In
November a terrible blizzard added to the misery. After Lord
Kitchener went to Gallipoli to see for himself what the situation
was, it was finally decided that there should be no more. Ultimate success was by no means certain, and if it were achieved
there was no certainty that the total effect on the war would be of
great significance.

The one perfectly executed maneuver of the whole Gallipoli
campaign was the evacuation of the troops. Thirty-five thousand
men were taken off the beaches at Suvla Bay and Anzac Cove in
two nights (December 18 and 19) without the Turks realizing what
was going on. The same thing was accomplished at Cape Helles,
where the Turks in the early hours of January 9, 1916, first realized what was going on when they saw ammunition and supplies
go up in flames on the beaches. Not an Allied soldier remained.

The "ifs" of Gallipoli have been discussed to a fare-thee-well
since that January morning, and inevitably blame has been liberally scattered among the participants. The fact is that it proved
an enormously costly failure. How costly no one knows—perhaps
two hundred thousand casualties for the Allies and at least as
many for the Turks. It accomplished little or nothing—but who
knows what might have been, with competent planning and direction?

16

Italy Enters the War

Although Italy had been a partner with Austria and Germany in the Triple Alliance before World War I, when war began she refused to join, using as an excuse that Austria had violated an article of the treaty by not consulting her before making demands on Serbia. On August 3, 1914, the Italian government declared itself neutral.

Italy's public statements of neutrality did not hinder either the Central Powers or the Allies from trying to persuade her to join them. For months the Italian government listened with interest to the promises and arguments of both sides. Finally on April 26, 1915, Italy signed a secret treaty with the Allies, the so-called Treaty of London. The Allies had promised her the Trentino area of the Cisalpine Tyrol, Istria, including Trieste, and Dalmatia—all parts of Austria-Hungary; part of Asia Minor if Turkey were partitioned; and some of Germany's African colonies if they were parceled out to the victors after the war. But of course at the time the treaty's terms were not published.

When the Italian Prime Minister, Antonio Salandra, announced on May 3, 1915, that he was denouncing the Triple Alliance, a Cabinet crisis developed. But war was declared on Austria-Hungary at midnight, May 23. Not until August 27, 1916, did Italy declare war on Germany.

Italy's declaration was eagerly welcomed by the Allies, for nothing was going well for them at the end of May, 1915. All six nations were hopeful that Italy's activity would improve matters. France and Britain did not expect direct help on the Western Front. Since Italy had a common border with Austria, her part would be to draw off some of the Austrian forces from the Eastern Front and so add to the demands on German manpower.

THE ITALIAN FLEET

As part of the agreement with the Allies, Italy promised to operate her fleet primarily in the Adriatic, where the presence of Austria's fleet had forced the British to maintain some ships to prevent it from emerging into the Mediterranean. The British continued to keep four battleships and four cruisers in the area. There was no combined naval command, however, and French, British, and Italians had little success at coordinating their operations at sea.

Within four months Austrian ships, with the aid of some German submarines, had sunk two Italian cruisers, one destroyer, two torpedo boats, and three submarines and damaged a British cruiser. The Austrians had also shot down two Italian dirigibles. The British installed submarine nets across the Strait of Otranto in an effort to prevent German submarines from passing into the Adriatic and heading for the Austrian base at Cattaro. The nets were only partially successful, however, and German submarines continued to ply the Adriatic.

THE ITALIAN FRONT

Most of the Italian boundary with Austria-Hungary in 1915 was at the foot of heights that had long been fortified by the Austrians. In the west the Trentino jutted into northern Italy, threatening the northern Italian plain and affording a base for an offensive toward Venice that could cut off northeastern Italy. The Austrians were limited in their exploitation of this position, however, by the inadequacies of the single railroad line from central Austria that supplied the area. It would never suffice for the needs of a large military force.

East of the Trentino the Dolomites and the Carnic and Julian Alps could be crossed only by specially trained troops and during a few months of the summer. Italy had eight Alpine regiments, but they were not enough to penetrate the combination of natural and Austrian-built defenses in the area. Between the Alps and the Adriatic is a hilly, rough region marked by three rocky plateaus, the Bainsizza, the Selva di Tornova, and the Carso. West of them the Isonzo River flows south to the Gulf of Panzano. All of its crossings were controlled by Austro-Hungarian soldiers, and the higher land beyond the river was sown with Austrian artillery.

PRELIMINARY OPERATIONS

Austria struck the first blow in this new area of war, sending planes high over Venice to drop bombs at 3:30 A.M. on May 24. There was great excitement in Venice, but little damage. This was the only Austrian activity for a while, for the Austrians were busy in Galicia.

As soon as the Italian Chief of the General Staff, General Count Luigi Cadorna, could get his armies in motion, Italian troops crossed the Austrian frontier in three areas. The First and Fourth Armies moved into the Trentino to keep the Austrians from moving down into Italy. They made good progress, and by June 2 they controlled some important mountain passes. Two Italian Alpine groups pushed into the Carnic Alps, and action began in two sections of the Isonzo River area.

THE ISONZO

In the first series of Italian offensives, troops crossed the northern end of the river and ascended Monte Nero, north of Tolmino. Farther south, the Second and Third Italian Armies, under the command of Lieutenant General Pietro Frugoni and the Duke of Aosta, were also attacking east. The Third Army took Monfalcone on June 9 and Gradisca two days later, both on the west side of the river. The Second Army had approached close to Gorizia by June 16, when they halted to rest and reorganize and prepare to make a major attack.

Cadorna's main objective was Trieste. To take it he would first have to take Gorizia, a heavily fortified position that guarded the route across the Carso Plateau. On June 23 he launched the first of a series of eleven battles, all known as Battles of the Isonzo. The Second and Third Armies struck against the Austrian Fifth Army under General Baron Svetozan Borojević von Bojna.

The First Battle of the Isonzo ended on July 7; the Second lasted from July 18 to August 3, the Third from October 18 to

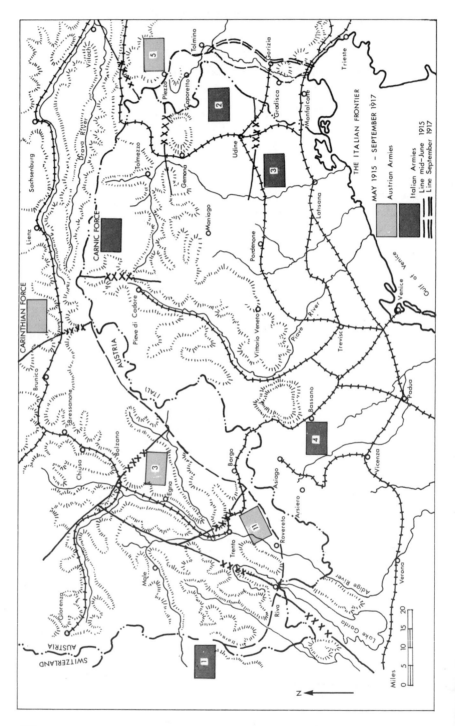

THE ITALIAN FRONTIER
MAY 1915 – SEPTEMBER 1917

Austrian Armies

Italian Armies
Line mid–June 1915
Line September 1917

November 3, and the Fourth from November 10 to December 2. For all the effort and cost in men and matériel that went into these four battles, gains were very small and of little strategic value.

The Italians were short on artillery and low on ammunition, but they had to face strong, well-placed defenses, adequately supported by artillery. Shells exploding on the ground sent sharp, deadly fragments of rock flying in all directions. Heavy rains and bitter cold in late November added to the misery. Then a heavy fog moved in and reduced visibility to practically zero. Reluctantly, the Italians called off the offensive on December 2.

The Isonzo battles had contributed the major portion of Italian casualties by the end of the year. They amounted to 66,000 dead, 190,000 wounded, 22,500 missing. The Austrians had suffered 165,000 casualties, of whom 30,000 were prisoners. The Italians had captured five artillery pieces, sixty-five machine guns, a number of mortars, thousands of rifles, and a good supply of ammunition. But they had advanced only a short distance from their original position.

17

More Offensives in the East

Among leaders of the Central Powers there was divided opinion at the beginning of 1915 as to how the available military strength had best be used. Since the Western Front had settled into a stalemate, some said, might it not be better to concentrate more forces in the east, where Russia was clearly feeling the impact of the 1914 campaigns?

The Austrian Chief of Staff, Field Marshal Franz Conrad von Hötzendorf, concerned about the possibility that Italy might join the war on the side of the Entente, proposed a large-scale offensive in Galicia to discourage the Italians and bring Russia closer to submission. The Chief of the German Army General Staff, General Erich von Falkenhayn, however, still believed that the war had to be won in the west, and that one more major offensive would defeat the French and British there. For this reason he refused to spare any troops from the Western Front to help the proposed Austrian offensive, and he hinted that the only way for Austria to keep Italy out of the war was to cede her the Austrian frontier territory that was largely inhabited by Italians. This was unacceptable to the Austrians.

Von Hindenburg also disagreed with Von Falkenhayn. Since Von Hindenburg had been given command of all German forces in the east, he unilaterally promised Conrad the support of several German divisions. This challenge to Von Falkenhayn's authority as Chief of the General Staff forced the Kaiser to decide which strategy Germany would follow. Von Hindenburg's won out, and on January 8, 1915, Kaiser Wilhelm announced support for a joint German-Austrian offensive.

Von Hindenburg at once implemented his decision by ordering

formation of a Southern Army under General Alexander von Linsingen, to work directly with the Austrians.

The rivalry that had long existed between Von Falkenhayn and Von Hindenburg was now clearly revealed, as Von Falkenhayn obtained the Kaiser's consent to transfer Ludendorff from Von Hindenburg's headquarters to be chief of staff to Linsingen. Enraged, Von Hindenburg fired off a note to the Kaiser asking for the return of Ludendorff and for four more corps for his command. He went on to suggest that Von Falkenhayn was impeding the chance of German victory and should be removed as Chief of the General Staff. Again Kaiser Wilhelm listened to Von Hindenburg. On January 11 he agreed that four corps would be sent to the east, that Ludendorff would return to Von Hindenburg as soon as the Southern Army was organized, and that Von Falkenhayn would resign as Minister of War, though not as Chief of the General Staff.

SECOND BATTLE OF THE MASURIAN LAKES

Von Hindenburg by this time had two armies and part of a third in East Prussia. From north to south were the newly organized Tenth, under General Hermann von Eichhorn, the Eighth, commanded by General Otto von Below, and the Ninth, which extended across the border to Lodz, under General August von Mackensen. Southeast from Lodz were the Austro-Hungarian armies, the Second, First, Fourth, and Third, backed by the forming German Southern Army.

Von Hindenburg was planning a double envelopment of the Russian Tenth Army, which was still deployed along the eastern frontier of East Prussia, with the new Twelfth Army on its left. The German Tenth Army was to swing around north of the Masurian Lakes while the Eighth went around to the south. After encircling the Russian Tenth Army, the two German armies would advance eastward to cut the Warsaw-Petrograd railroad. The Ninth Army, meanwhile, would make a feint toward Warsaw in the vicinity of Bolimov.

The feint came first, in a blinding snowstorm on January 31, 1915. Artillery fire softened up the area on the east bank of the Rawka and Bzura Rivers. Chlorine-gas shells were mixed with

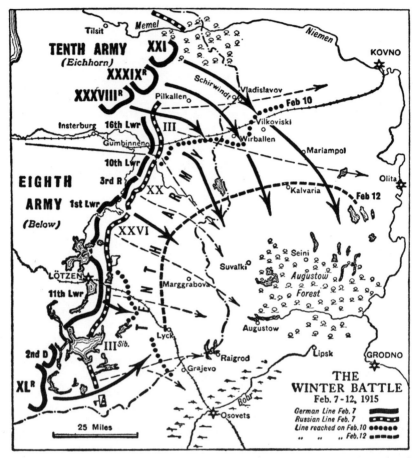

THE
WINTER BATTLE
Feb. 7-12, 1915

German Line Feb. 7
Russian Line Feb. 7
Line reached on Feb.10
  "   "   " Feb.12

25 Miles

the high explosives, but the cold kept the gas from spreading, and
this first use of gas went almost unnoticed. Russian artillery and
machine guns raked the men of the German Ninth Army as they
advanced, seven divisions of them. The Germans took the first
line of Russian trenches, but by February 4 their advance had
been halted by reinforcements rushed to the aid of the Russian
defenders. It was just such a shift of reinforcements that Von
Hindenburg and Ludendorff had hoped for.

Meanwhile the major German offensive had been in preparation farther north. On February 5 and 6 blizzards swept across
East Prussia, piling snow in great drifts that made movement
difficult. Nevertheless on the seventh the German Eighth Army
began its advance somewhat south of east between Johannisburg

and Lötzen. On February 8 the German Tenth Army, of whose existence the Russians were completely unaware, advanced through the Insterburg Gap. Taken completely by surprise, the Russians withdrew through the Angustów Forest, the XX Corps fighting a delaying action. Although warmer weather on February 14 turned the area into an ocean of mud, the Germans struggled on through it and four days later had trapped two Russian corps in the forest. After trying for three days to break out, the thirty thousand Russian survivors there surrendered.

The Russian Tenth Army, having lost over two hundred thousand men (one hundred thousand killed and wounded and another one hundred thousand taken prisoner) and three hundred artillery pieces, had virtually ceased to exist. The two surviving corps retreated to the Niemen and Biebrza Rivers, closely pursued by the German Eighth and Tenth Armies. There the retreat halted, for the Grand Duke rushed up reinforcements to aid his battered army. With these fresh troops the Russians rallied and counterattacked all along the front, halting the German advance and driving the Germans back almost to the East Prussian border. To the extent that the German offensive had caused Russian casualties, it was successful. But it had made little difference in the strategic positions of the two forces.

In the south, the Russian Eighth Army, commanded by General Aleksei Brusilov, was preparing for an offensive into Galicia to capture the mountain passes from Dukla to Turka, when the Austrians, with the help of the German Southern Army, struck out toward Przemysl and Lvov. The Austrians were anxious to relieve the siege at Przemysl, where some two hundred thousand Austrians, soldiers and civilians, were surrounded. The fortress lay at a crossroad of the main rail line from Cracow to Lvov, which made it necessary, as long as Przemysl was in Austrian hands, for the Russians to send their supplies by a longer and slower route.

Holding firm, the Russians repulsed every effort of the Austrians to break through the Carpathian Mountain passes. In Bukovina, however, defending elements of the Russian Eleventh Army were driven back, in the only Austrian victory of the campaign. Przemysl finally fell to the Russians on March 18. With the troops released by its fall, Brusilov was able to make small-scale attacks on the Austrians, but he did not have the strength to attempt an invasion of Austria-Hungary. By mid-April even these small actions had to be called off because of the utter weariness of the Russian troops.

THE GORLICE-TARNOW OFFENSIVE

Despite the failure of the Austrian campaign in the Carpathians and the less than satisfactory victory of Von Hindenburg's forces in East Prussia, military leaders of the Central Powers still believed that another, bigger offensive could succeed in knocking Russia out of the war. Reports of food shortages and war weariness behind the Russian lines and lack of clothing and ammunition on the fighting fronts lent strength to this position.

Von Hindenburg proposed a major spring offensive for 1915, using the German armies in a sweep down from East Prussia behind Warsaw. Conrad wanted an attack from the Carpathian foothills east of Cracow, along the Dunajec River, to break up the Russian forces that were harassing him. And now Von Falkenhayn too advocated action on the Eastern Front. With the Allies attacking at the Dardanelles, his idea was to make a major attack on Serbia and open a direct line of communications with Turkey. Conrad proved unwilling to divert units from the Carpathian front to fight in Serbia, however, and Von Falkenhayn abandoned that idea and supported Conrad's.

Von Falkenhayn was reluctant to transfer sizable forces to the east, for he still insisted that the major victory must be won on the Western Front. But he sent four corps to bolster the Austro-Hungarian armies. A new German army, the Eleventh, was formed, with Von Mackensen in command. It comprised eight German divisions, two Austrian, and one division of Hungarian cavalry. Although Von Mackensen was nominally under Conrad's overall command, his orders were actually to be approved first by Von Falkenhayn.

The line of departure for the offensive was along the Dunajec River between Gorlice and Tarnow. From left to right on the line were the Austrian First (Von Dankl) and Fourth (Archduke Joseph Ferdinand) Armies, the German Eleventh (Von Mackensen), the Austrian Third (Borojević von Bojna) and Second

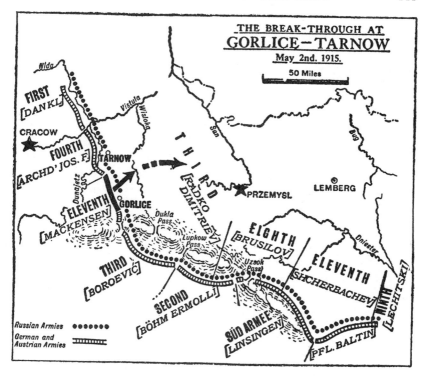

THE BREAK-THROUGH AT
GORLICE—TARNOW
May 2nd. 1915.
50 Miles

(Baron Eduard von Bohm-Ermolli), the German Southern Army
(Von Linsingen) and the Seventh (Baron Karl von Pflanzer-
Blatin). Von Mackensen was given control of the Fourth Army
(three corps and a cavalry division) as well as his own, and it
was these two that were to carry out the attack.

To meet the impending attack the Russians had only two corps
of the Third Army, for the remainder of the army had been
spread thin over a hundred-mile front to the south in order to
support Brusilov in the Carpathian operation. Not only were the
Russians greatly outnumbered, but their defenses were poorly designed, although they were about five miles deep and had three
lines of trenches.

On May 1 some of the more than nine hundred artillery pieces
that Von Mackensen had in his command commenced firing at
various points along the front. This was but the beginning. The
following morning, from 6 to 10 A.M., German artillery blasted
the Russian positions, driving those of the Russians who survived
out of the front-line trenches. The German infantry moved out

when the artillery had done its work. By the end of the day the second line of trenches had been taken and a number of weak Russian counterattacks smashed. The third line of trenches was captured on May 3, assuring a complete breakthrough on the following day. The Russian Third Army was in headlong retreat.

All along the front the other Austro-German units began to advance as the Russian Eighth and Eleventh Armies fell back. Little was left of General Radko Dimitriev's Third Army. Thousands had been killed and other thousands were willing prisoners of the triumphant foe. Brusilov withdrew his Eighth Army in orderly fashion, guarding the left flank of the retreat. Grand Duke Nicholas rushed reinforcements to the Third Army area. Despite the rapid pursuit the army managed to maintain a line unbroken. Gradually the combination of Russian delaying actions and German transportation difficulties slowed the advance. By the end of May the Russians had retreated to the high ground in the upper San and Dniester valleys, in the vicinity of Przemysl. There they were able to hold the Germans long enough to evacuate their supplies and rolling stock from the fortress before abandoning it on June 3 and moving back toward Lvov.

On the same day the Kaiser, Conrad, Von Falkenhayn, Ludendorff, Von Hindenburg, Hoffman, and Von Mackensen met at Pless to discuss what should be done next. Von Falkenhayn, noting that despite the overwhelming tactical success the Russian armies had not been destroyed, proposed breaking off the offensive and returning four divisions to the Western Front. Von Hindenburg and Ludendorff urged an enveloping movement through Kovno to Vilna and Minsk, to trap the Russian forces in Poland. Conrad, nervous about the newly belligerent Italy, was anxious to divert some of his forces to the southern front. Kaiser Wilhelm, desirous of maintaining the impetus of the successful operation, decided that Von Mackensen should continue his drive in Galicia, and Conrad should transfer the Third Army to the Italian front.

Reinforced by four and a half divisions, Von Mackensen's force again attacked. On June 22 they were in Lvov, and shortly thereafter they had taken Rava Russkaya. By the end of the month most of Galicia and a sizable portion of southern Poland had been occupied. But the Germans had slowed down again, for supplying their forces so far from their bases was becoming a major problem.

The German commanders met at Posen on July 1 for another discussion of what should be done. Von Hindenburg still urged the attempt at encirclement from the north which Von Falkenhayn opposed. He feared that it might so overextend the Germans that more and more troops would have to be transferred from the Western Front, dangerously weakening their position there. The Kaiser, sharing Von Falkenhayn's concern, again decided not to order the full-scale Von Hindenburg plan. Instead, the new Twelfth Army, under General Max von Gallwitz, would undertake an attack across the Narev River; the Ninth Army and a force under General Remus von Woyrsch would strike eastward across the Vistula; and Von Mackensen would turn and attack north into the area between the Vistula and the Bug, where the Russian forces were concentrated. This would in effect result in a smaller encirclement than that desired by Von Hindenburg and Ludendorff. Elsewhere along the front, pressure would be maintained in order to prevent the Russians from shifting reinforcements to the area of main attack.

The new German attacks began on July 13, 1915, and met with success in all sectors. The Twelfth Army pushed the Russians back across the Narev, while the Ninth advanced toward the Vistula. Von Mackensen, although slowed by marshy terrain and extended lines of supply and communications, reached Lublin on July 30 and continued on toward Brest Litovsk. Grand Duke Nicholas, having already removed a large percentage of his supplies from the area and made plans for an orderly withdrawal, finally decided that Warsaw must be abandoned. On August 5 his troops left the city and retreated to the east. Reserve troops, almost one hundred thousand of them, were left in the fortress of Novogeorgievsk to cover the withdrawal and to prevent the Germans from transporting supplies on the Vistula River. The garrison held out until August 20, when the troops finally surrendered under the incessant pounding of heavy German guns. By then most of the Russian troops had retired. Shortly thereafter Brest Litovsk fell, and the Germans were still advancing. By the end of September, however, progress had slowed almost to a halt.

Meanwhile, farther north, Von Hindenburg and Ludendorff at last had their chance to strike toward Vilna, although without the force they had desired. Their first objective was the loop of the Niemen River north and south of Grodno, where the Russian line formed a salient that invited envelopment. The German Tenth Army attacked from the north, while the Eighth struck east from the region of the Masurian Lakes. Grodno fell on September 1, but for almost a week stubborn Russian resistance prevented the Germans from taking the rail lines that extended eastward from the city.

Next the Germans moved on to attack the area around Vilna. Again the Tenth Army attacked from the north and west while the Eighth, with the Twelfth on its right flank, attacked from the south. German cavalry units also moved in behind the Russians to seize the railroads. Encirclement seemed to be complete, and Vilna fell. But the Russians succeeded in driving the German cavalry troops out of an important rail junction, enabling their Tenth Army to retreat along the Minsk railroad toward Vileika.

Except for an abortive attack on Russian positions around Riga, and unsuccessful and costly attacks by Conrad in Galicia in late September and October, the operation died down as winter came on. Von Falkenhayn by this time could see no justification for continuing an inconclusive offensive against Russia when Turkey was under attack at the Dardanelles and the Allies on the Western Front were likely to attack at any time. In August and September, 1915, eleven German divisions were withdrawn from the Eastern Front and sent to the Danube and to France. When Von Hindenburg was told on September 17 that several more would be taken from his command, at first he refused to send them. But the Kaiser supported Von Falkenhayn and the divisions were transferred.

The 1915 campaign had cost Russia approximately two million men, of whom one million were prisoners of war. Battered though the Russian armies were, they still had not been destroyed as an effective fighting force. They held a line six hundred miles long, stretching from Riga on the Baltic Sea to Czernowitz on the Rumanian frontier. On this line they prepared defenses and shelter from the approaching winter weather.

CHANGE IN THE RUSSIAN COMMAND

On September 5, 1915, Grand Duke Nicholas, who had commanded the Russian armies since the war began, was relieved by his nephew, Czar Nicholas II, and sent to the Caucausus as Viceroy and commander in chief of the Russian forces in the area. Not only had he led the army in a disastrous defeat, but also, and perhaps more importantly, he had incurred the wrath of the Czarina by expressing his contempt for the monk Rasputin, who had gained her confidence and worked his way into a position where he exerted great influence on her and the Czar. The Czar assumed personal command of Russian armies on the fighting front in western Russia. The change was not a happy one, for while the Grand Duke was a capable military man and an effective leader, the Czar was neither. Actual military decisions were thenceforth made by the Chief of Staff, General Mikhail Vasilievich Alekseev, who unfortunately did not have the competence or self-confidence to make them.

18

Knockout in Serbia

During the third Austrian invasion of Serbia, in the fall of 1914, the troops were struck by an epidemic of typhus, which spread to the Serbs as they reclaimed their occupied territory. Through the winter and early spring of 1915 they fought this new enemy, and when it was finally overcome in April over seventy thousand Serbian soldiers and civilians had died. Fortunately the Austrians were fully occupied with the Russians in Galicia during this time, and for many months they made no further attacks on Serbia.

The British attack on Gallipoli in April, 1915, and an announcement by Rumania in June that she would no longer permit the shipment of munitions across her territory, caused Von Falkenhayn to urge a new attempt to knock Serbia out of the war. The only remaining route by which Germany could send ammunition and matériel to Turkey was via the Oriten railroad, which followed the valley of the Morava River across Serbia. To Von Falkenhayn it seemed more important to secure this route and so to bolster Turkey than to continue with the offensive that Von Hindenburg and Conrad were advocating in Poland. His views were not accepted by the Kaiser, however, who set them aside temporarily.

Von Falkenhayn's plans for Serbia were both military and diplomatic. He favored the combination of an attack from neutral Bulgaria, which bordered Serbia to the east, with whatever Austria and Germany could mount from the north and west. But first it would be necessary to secure the support of Bulgaria.

The Bulgarian government had been playing both sides in the war for months, encouraging both the Central Powers and the Allies to talk, and waiting for an offer from one or the other that

warranted going to war. From the beginning the Central Powers
had an advantage. The Bulgarians harbored a bitter hatred for
the Serbs as a result of the Balkan Wars of 1912 and 1913, when
Serbia acquired parts of Macedonia which the Bulgarians
thought should be theirs. These and other areas Bulgaria coveted

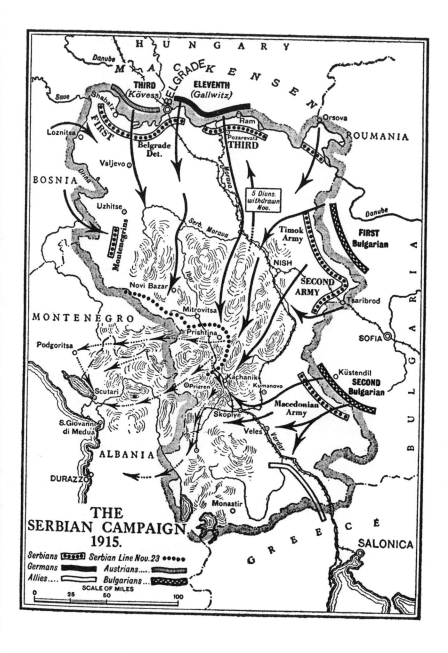

THE
SERBIAN CAMPAIGN
1915.

Serbians ▢▢▢ Serbian Line Nov. 23 •••••
Germans ▆▆▆ Austrians....
Allies....▭▭▭ Bulgarians...▆▆▆
SCALE OF MILES
0   25   50   100

could readily be promised her by the Central Powers as part of the postwar settlement. Still Bulgaria waited and encouraged both sides to think she might move in their direction, until it became clear that the British were not going to have immediate success at Gallipoli. On September 6 Bulgaria finally signed a secret agreement with Germany and Austria-Hungary to join an attack on Serbia in October, and began to mobilize.

The Serbian government, well aware of Bulgarian sentiment, viewed with alarm the assembling of troops across the eastern border, and begged the Allies for help in attacking the Bulgarians before they could get ready to strike. But the Allies did not understand the significance of Bulgaria's mobilization. They refused, not wishing to stir up more trouble in the Balkans. Misguided through their reasoning was, their advice was probably good, for the final outcome by this time was inevitable.

Throughout the spring and summer the Germans and Austrians assembled matériel along the Serbian border and prepared forces for the attack. The Austro-Hungarian Third Army, now commanded by General Hermann Kövess von Kövessháza, was transferred from the Galician front in June. The German Eleventh, under General Max von Gallwitz, followed about a month later. The plan was for these two armies to strike south from positions west and east of Belgrade, while the Bulgarian First Army attacked Serbia from the east. Overall command of the three would be under newly promoted German Field Marshal August von Mackensen. At the same time the Bulgarian Second Army would attack the vital railroad line to Salonika, the only route by which Serbia's allies could possibly support her. Together the four attacking armies numbered about four hundred thousand men. Only about half as many Serbs awaited the attack, their chief strength being their determination to defend their homeland.

The attack started with an artillery bombardment by the Austrian Third Army on October 6, three days after Bulgaria had finally declared her support for the Central Powers, and one day after the first British and French troops evacuated from Gallipoli landed at Salonika and headed up the Vardar valley to try to assist the Serbs. The Austrian and German armies started crossing the Sava and the Danube Rivers on October 7, and the Serbs withdrew before them. Belgrade fell on October 9. A fierce

Serb counterattack was beaten off, and the Serbian withdrawal continued. On October 11 the Bulgarians marched across the border, to add their weight to the Austrian attack. The Bulgarian Second Army reached Veles on October 23 and cut the railroad from Salonika.

ALLIES IN SALONIKA

The British and French, meanwhile, had been having problems with Greece. The Greek government was divided, for the King, Constantine, was pro-German, and the Prime Minister, Eleutherios Venizelos, favored the Allies. Greece had a treaty of mutual aid with Serbia, by which she had agreed to go to the assistance of Serbia in the event of an attack by Bulgaria. It stipulated, however, that Serbia must first assemble 150,000 men on the Bulgarian border. With a coincident attack from Austria, however, the Serbs obviously could not spare any such force from the northern sector. A solution seemed to have been found when, after much negotiation, it was agreed that the Allies could land troops taken from Gallipoli at Salonika, which would give them access to southern Serbia. It appeared that Greece might join the Allies, but on October 5, when the first Allied troops landed at Salonika, Venizelos resigned under pressure. Greece remained neutral, but unofficially the British and French were allowed to build up their forces at Salonika.

There was no unified command of the Allied troops in Greece, although General Maurice Sarrail was nominally in command. The British were free to do as they liked with their troops, and they did not hurry to order them forward. The French advanced as soon as they landed, but they arrived at Veles too late to be of help to the Serbs. Confronted by a much larger Bulgarian force, they were driven back. The British finally moved into the mountainous area near Lake Doiran, but they too were forced to retreat. Although the Allies had done nothing to hold back disaster, they contributed to the larger picture by preventing the Bulgarians from throwing their entire weight against the Serbs.

CONQUEST OF SERBIA

Putnik's main forces in the north were pushed farther and farther south by the invading armies, closer to the Bulgarian Second

Army, which was preparing to crush them from the south and southeast. Refusing to surrender, the Serbs headed across their southwestern borders into the rugged mountains of Montenegro and neutral Albania, following a large proportion of the civilian population, who had fled before the invaders.

The pursuit halted at the frontier, for Germany and Austria did not want Bulgaria to gain a port on the Adriatic. Nature was enough of an opponent for the miserable refugees, however. Cold, hungry, mostly on foot, they struggled across the mountains. With them went the aged, nearly blind King Peter. In December they finally emerged on the Adriatic coast, bedraggled, sick, homeless. Italian, British, and French naval vessels carried them to the island of Corfu. There the soldiers were refitted and reorganized, then landed in Salonika to participate in the recapture of their own country.

General Kövess von Kövessháza, meanwhile, had invaded tiny Montenegro, which surrendered on January 17, 1916.

19

Autumn Offensives on the Western Front

The summer of 1915 in France was a time for building up strength. Both the Allies and the Central Powers had greatly depleted their stocks of ammunition and sustained enormous troop losses in the first year of fighting. Industry was working at full steam to produce the bullets and shells, the guns and other equipment that were badly needed. Troop replacements were bringing armies up to strength. In England Lord Kitchener had instituted an intensive campaign to recruit volunteers to fight for Britain. The eager young men who responded were put through a rapid training program that produced soldiers unequaled in spirit although far from the expert professionals of the BEF. The first three hundred thousand of these were organized in ten divisions, the New Army, and began to arrive in France in the summer of 1915.

The Western Front saw no major action for months, while the armies were being built up and defenses were being elaborated. A number of small actions followed the pattern that would be maintained in larger or smaller dimensions until 1918. An artillery barrage would sweep the front line area; an infantry charge would seize a portion of the devastated line of trenches; then a counterattack would halt the advance. In the ensuing bloody struggle the attackers would either retain the few yards they had gained or be pushed back. In either event the results were the same: almost nothing gained and thousands more wounded or dead.

As soon as stockpiles of weapons and ammunition permitted and sufficient reserves were available, General Joffre planned to use them in another attempt to reduce the Noyon salient. This time an offensive in Champagne would be combined with another in Artois and a supporting attack by British forces farther north, near Loos. Loos is in an area of coal mines, a flat region of Flanders, where a slight elevation became a towering observation post and where German defenses were strong. Sir John French was not eager to undertake an operation there, but Joffre was planning to attack Vimy Ridge, and he and Foch wanted British support as close as possible to that area. So Lord Kitchener agreed that the British would go into action at Loos, and their attack was launched on the same day as that of the French, September 25, 1915.

General Haig attacked on a four-mile front with six divisions of the British First Army, three divisions of regulars, one Territorial division, and two Scottish divisions of Kitchener's New Army. After the usual artillery preparation, the infantry moved out, seizing the first and second German defense lines all along the front. The Scottish 15th Division pushed on and occupied the town of Loos and Hill 70, which commanded the neighboring town of Lens. Unfortunately Haig had no reserves to send in behind his Scotsmen. Eight miles behind the front Sir John French had three reserve divisions which he belatedly made available to Haig. They were tired troops, however, having just arrived after three night marches. Another march at night took them to the front, weary and hungry, for logistics arrangements were poor. They were in no condition to be sent in to the front line the next morning. A German counterattack broke them up almost as soon as they moved out. Although another infantry division and a cavalry division were then rushed up, the British were gradually pushed back during another month and a half of bloody thrust and counterthrust, until the front finally stabilized on November 4, with the British two miles ahead of where they had started. French's ineptitude in handling his reserves led the British government to replace him with Haig on December 15.

The French Tenth Army, commanded by General Foch, attacked at Vimy Ridge on September 25, on a six-mile front. Although the artillery bombardment had destroyed much of the first line of German trenches, machine guns blasted the advancing infantrymen. German reinforcements were rushed to the area, but the French fought their way foot by foot to the western side of Vimy Ridge by September 28. There they dug in, for the IX Corps had to be withdrawn to assist the British, and a spell of bad weather put an end ot the action.

In Champagne, meanwhile, the French Eastern Group of Armies, commanded by General de Castelnau, and comprising the Second Army under General Henri Philippe Pétain and the Fourth under General Fernand de Langle de Cary, had attacked on a fifteen-mile front. A two-day artillery bombardment had demolished the front lines of the complicated network of German trenches. These had been only lightly held; the defenders were concentrated in the much stronger second defense line, beyond the range of Allied artillery. German artillery had the range on the space between, however, and as the French poured through the first line, to the tune of the "Marseillaise" and the "Carmagnole," bursting shells and machine-gun bullets fell upon them. So high were their spirits, however, that those who escaped the rain of fire continued and swarmed upon the German defenses, advancing almost two miles in one area. The local German commanders were considering withdrawal when General von Falkenhayn arrived at the front and ordered them to hold. German reserves came up and soon halted the French advance. After battering at the line until October 8, the French gave up and dug in, having gained a mile or two, taken 25,000 prisoners, and suffered about 130,000 casualties.

Once again both sides settled down to the dreary life of the trenches as 1915 moved to its end and 1916 began. Here and there small actions were tried and resisted, but there were no more large operations for months, until the Germans perfected their plans for an assault on one of France's strongest points, Verdun.

20

Germany's Colonies

Germany did not become a political entity until 1871 and was late in joining the game of acquiring colonial possessions, which had long been played by most of the other European powers and smaller maritime nations. By 1914, however, Germany had many colonies, ranging from a naval base at Tsingtao to thousands of square miles in Africa. Some of her colonies had potential strategic value; some were sources of raw materials; some had sizable military garrisons close to the Allies' possessions; all contributed to German influence and prestige. Whatever their importance, the Allies could not afford to overlook the opportunity the war offered to detach the colonies from German control.

TSINGTAO

Tsingtao, on the southeast coast of China's Shantung Peninsula, the base for the fleet commanded by Admiral von Spee when war began, had long been coveted by Japan. It was a major reason for Japan's declaration of war against Germany, and she lost no time in demanding, by an ultimatum on August 15, 1914, that Tsingtao be surrendered to her. Germany refused, for the fortifications were strong and well placed, and there were four thousand German marines to defend them.

The Japanese declared war when the ultimatum expired on August 23 and promptly moved to attack Tsingtao, putting some troops ashore on small islands near the mouth of the harbor and bringing up some well-armed ships to bombard the fort. When it became apparent that the Germans would not give in easily, the Japanese landed troops north of the base and proceeded to fight their way down the peninsula. Two months later they were still at it. By then there were 23,000 Japanese troops and 1,350 British ashore, and the Japanese had lost one cruiser, one destroyer, and three minesweepers to German gunfire and mines. Slowly they had pushed ahead through the outer rings of fortifications, however, and on November 6 the weary Germans finally surrendered.

PACIFIC ISLANDS

Many of the German colonies were taken over by the Allies with little trouble. Australians, New Zealanders, British, or Japanese occupied the most important German possessions in the Marianas, the Carolines, the Marshalls, the Palaus, Samoa, the Solomons, and New Guinea by the end of 1914. Strategically this made little difference to Germany, who in any case could not have used the bases, supplied their needs, or transported their products, since she no longer had warships in the Pacific.

CAMEROONS, TOGOLAND, AND SOUTHWEST AFRICA

In Africa the problem was different. The colonies were larger, closer to Germany, and garrisoned with German troops. On the northeast corner of the Gulf of Guinea, the German Cameroons was bordered by British and French possessions. From both sides invasion attempts were made by land in 1914, only to be driven back by German and African soldiers and a most inhospitable climate. The next attempt, by sea, resulted in capture of the port of Duala by the British on September 27. French troops also landed on the coast, and the two forces, almost twenty thousand strong, very slowly worked their way in through the jungles, opposed by guerrillas, the tropical climate, disease, and an almost impassable terrain. It was not until January 1, 1916, that they finally captured the German headquarters at Yaunde, only 100 miles from Duala. The German and African troops, about eight thousand when it all started, never surrendered. Wise to the ways of the jungle, they left Yaunde as the Allies entered, and disappeared into the jungle, to emerge 125 miles away, safe in Spanish Guinea, where they were interned.

Togoland, west of the Cameroons, was an easier target for the Allies. A single British cruiser took the capital, Lomé, on August

8, 1914. British and French troops streamed ashore and pursued the German defenders inland to Atakpamé, where the Germans surrendered, having first carefully destroyed the powerful radio station the Allies had hoped to capture.

Troops from the recently established Union of South Africa took care of German Southwest Africa. Faced by three mounted battalions of Germans and about two thousand Africans in rifle companies, the South African troops invaded their neighbor in January, 1915. The combination of stubborn defense and difficult terrain made progress slow, but superior numbers won out. The German commander surrendered on July 9.

EAST AFRICA

German East Africa promised to be no greater problem to the Allies than any of the other German colonies. It lay south of British East Africa, and could readily be invaded from there, the British thought. South and west, moreover, lay British colonies of Rhodesia and Nyasaland. To insure a large enough force to occupy German East Africa, the British transferred two brigades from India to East Africa, bringing the strength of the invading force to about eleven thousand men.

The British had planned without realizing the capacity of their enemy, however. The garrison in German East Africa was commanded by a very able lieutenant colonel, Paul von Lettow-Vorbeck. He had in his command a small contingent of German officers and noncommissioned officers and about three thousand native troops whom he had trained himself. They were armed with rifles, some machine guns, and a few small cannon. Besides these he had a ready reserve in the German settlers, many of whom were retired soldiers and all of whom were loyal to the Fatherland and ready to fight for the colony.

There was activity on both sides of the border in 1914, for Von Lettow-Vorbeck had ideas of conquering British territory and not just waiting to defend his own. Small German units raided successfully across the border into British East Africa in several places in the first weeks of war, and at the end of September a larger operation was launched. With support from the guns of the cruiser *Königsberg,* a force moved up the coast to attack Mombasa, but the British halted it and drove it back into German territory.

Next was the British turn. Their objective was Tanga on the northern coast of the colony. On November 2 troopships carrying Indian units, which had been sent directly from Mombasa without being allowed ashore after their four-week voyage from India, appeared off the coast and anchored, warning Von Lettow-Vorbeck that something was coming. He was ready when the first troops landed that night about a mile from Tanga. As the British advanced up the coast the next morning, they immediately met German fire from front and left, for the defenders made good use of the covering trees. Panic resulted, and for a while all was confusion, but the British clung to their beachhead.

The next morning the British commander, Major General A. E. Aitken, sent four battalions marching toward Tanga. Again they ran into German fire, and the battalions on the left broke and ran. Confusion was increased by swarms of vicious wild bees that descended on Indian and German alike. Two Indian battalions managed to get through to Tanga, only to be driven out again by Von Lettow-Vorbeck's men.

Realizing that his troops' morale was shattered, General Aitken made no attempt to regroup, but sought a truce in order to remove the wounded and reembark his men. Back he went to British East Africa, having suffered 817 casualties, killed, wounded, or missing. The victorious defenders eagerly took possession of a number of machine guns, several hundred rifles, and six hundred thousand rounds of ammunition.

In 1915 German East Africa was the scene of a fantastic naval action. Part of the western border, between the German colony and the Belgian Congo, was formed by Lake Tanganyika, four hundred miles long and thirty to forty-five miles wide. Early in the war Von Lettow-Vorbeck had assured naval control of the lake for the Germans by putting Lieutenant Commander Zimmer in command of a fleet of three armed steamers and an assortment of small craft, with a crew of four hundred. Unchallenged they roamed the lake, raiding Belgian ports and protecting the western flank.

In July, 1915, a special contingent of twenty-eight British officers and men, led by Lieutenant Commander G. Spicer-Simpson, arrived at Cape Town with a fleet intended for Lake Tanganyika: two forty-foot motor launches, named *Mimi* and *Toutou,* each carrying a three-pounder gun. Loading men and vessels aboard a train, Spicer-Simpson traveled as far as the railroad went, north of Elizabethville, in the Belgian Congo. Ahead lay 150 miles of forest and a mountain range that towered to six thousand feet. Using tractors, oxen, block and tackle, and temporary bridges, the crew hauled, tugged, pushed, lifted, and lowered their equipment over the mountains, hacking a path through the forest ahead of them as they went. At last they arrived at the Lualaba River, and the launches finally had water under their keels. It was a mixed blessing, however, for the river was barely navigable in places. With great difficulty the little fleet traveled 400 miles to Kabalo. Again the boats were taken out of the water and put aboard a train for the short trip to their destination, Albertville, on the western shore of Lake Tanganyika. The weary crews launched their boats and prepared them for action.

While a Christmas service was being held at Albertville on December 25, 1915, the German steamer *Kingani* was sighted on the lake. Quickly the *Mimi* and the *Toutou* gave chase and attacked. Much smaller but more maneuverable, they forced the *Kingani* to surrender and added her to their fleet as HMS *Fifi.* A storm claimed the *Toutou* not long after this, but in February, 1916, the *Mimi* and the *Fifi* took on the *Hedwig von Wissmann,* almost three times the *Fifi's* size. A running battle followed, the ships racing along for three hours, covering thirty miles of lake before the German vessel was sunk. Zimmer, with two of his largest ships destroyed, accepted defeat. He scuttled his other vessels and retired from the area, leaving the lake to the British Royal Navy.

21

Verdun

From the North Sea to the mountains of Switzerland in 1916 hundreds of thousands of weary, grimy men were living in holes in the ground, laying siege to other men in similar holes a few hundred yards away. The bloody battles of 1914 and 1915 had put them there, and it seemed they would never get out. Many thousands of promising young men had been put permanently to rest in the ground after those battles, and many thousands more would follow before at last the deadly siege was broken. The battles had yielded little to offset the dreadful losses, yet despite the tremendous cost of the first year and a half and the promise that the price would continue to be exorbitant, neither side dared think of surrender. Leaders on both sides were searching desperately for a way to break the stalemate as 1916 began, for almost all agreed that the war must be won or lost on the Western Front. As the first requisite, they were making great efforts to build up strength in France in men and equipment, and planning how they would be used.

Great Britain in January, 1916, was facing a manpower problem. The million men who had rushed to enlist in a great surge of patriotism in the first weeks of war had been fed into the machine, and four hundred thousand of them were dead or wounded. Now the supply of eager young men was running low, and if Britain's armies were to play their part in France it was apparent that a tradition hallowed by centuries would have to be abandoned. So it was that on January 12, 1916, the House of Commons passed the first draft act Britain had ever had. Before long a new crop of trained conscripts was on its way to France.

The Western Allies had suffered greatly in their operations from the lack of a unified command and joint strategic planning such as became the rule in World War II. General Joffre was dependent on the cooperation of the British. Usually they gave it, but their own ideas sometimes suffered in the process, and sometimes they were better than Joffre's.

In December, 1915, General Joffre invited representatives of Britain, Russia, and Italy to a conference at his headquarters at Chantilly. He was eager to undertake a major offensive on the Western Front as early in 1916 as possible, and anxious to have something going in other theaters so that the Germans would be tied down, and thus unable to use their interior lines to rush forces back to counter his attack. So it was agreed that all four Allies would launch offensives as close to the same date as possible. Joffre himself had his eye on the Somme River area, despite the fact that strategically it was of little importance. Apparently his reason for selecting this area was the fact that both French and British forces were there and could undertake a joint operation. On December 29 he told Haig that what he wanted was a combined offensive on a sixty-mile front on both sides of the river. Haig preferred an attack in Flanders, but after presenting his case, he quickly abandoned his preference and set to planning for Joffre's, even convincing himself it had real merit.

On the other side Von Falkenhayn too was planning. He was convinced that Britain was Germany's prime enemy; but Britain was inaccessible, and so he must bring her down by so weakening her ally, France, that the French would have to make peace. Britain, he believed, would be unable to carry on alone. So Von Falkenhayn planned to stage an offensive which would cause excessive French casualties and bring the French people to demand a negotiated peace. He succeeded in creating a battle that came to be known as the Hell of Verdun.

VERDUN

Verdun, on the Meuse River, was in a loop in the battle lines north of the St. Mihiel salient. Since Roman times Verdun had been fortified, and its fortifications had been changed many times before the great Vauban himself, in the seventeenth century, constructed the strongest fort he could. Thereafter the fortress was modified and modernized numerous times. Despite its supposed strength, it was forced to surrender after a brief siege in the Franco-Prussian War of 1870. The territorial losses of France in the Treaty of Frankfort after that war placed Verdun near the new frontier. Intensive French efforts further improved the fortifications, with a series of small outlying forts, roughly in a circle, connected by tunnels and trenches. As a result of this work, when World War I began some twenty forts and forty smaller posts, all heavily reinforced with concrete, ringed the town. However, after similar forts at Liège and Namur fell speedily in the first days of the war, French leaders drew the conclusion that the great fortification complexes of the nineteenth century, including Verdun, were useless against modern artillery.

In August, 1915, the commander at Verdun was ordered to remove artillery pieces, ammunition, and personnel from the fortifications. From these were created forty-three batteries of heavy guns that went to Champagne to support Joffre's great offensive. The garrisons in the forts at Verdun were reduced, and the works were allowed to decay. Like the rest of the front, this sector sprouted trenches and dugout command posts, some tunneled deep beneath the almost deserted forts.

The French anticipated no action at Verdun, and the quiet that prevailed for months had given the men in the garrison a false sense of security. Their commander, General Herr, however, was well aware of the vulnerability of his post. In vain he begged for men, matériel, and guns when signs pointed to a German offensive, perhaps even in the Verdun area, in late January. However, as a result of Herr's expressions of alarm, Joffre finally turned his attention to Verdun and sent Herr two new divisions. They arrived in the area before the Germans attacked, but only because bad weather delayed the offensive. The artillery was not replaced.

Von Falkenhayn's choice of Verdun as his target was made partly for strategic, partly for sentimental reasons. The fortress was, he believed, of such deep traditional importance to the French that they would never surrender it but would continue to send more and more troops to hold it. The primary key to victory in the war, he thought, was to kill as many Frenchmen as possible, and at Verdun he believed he could best accomplish this purpose. Of course, it would also be desirable to gain control of the fortress, for it was within artillery range of the German-controlled coal fields at Briey. The German area around Verdun had a good railway supply network behind it, and it happened to be in the sector commanded by Crown Prince Wilhelm. Von Falkenhayn could hardly overlook the desirability of managing a victory for him.

The French front-line trenches at Verdun formed a semicircle outside the line of forts, facing roughly northeast, and cut by the wide Meuse River. Von Falkenhayn's plan was to attack on the right bank, the east side of the river, on a five- to seven-mile front between the river and the Woëvre plateau. Although Prince Wilhelm and his staff argued for an attack on a broader front, on both sides of the Meuse, Von Falkenhayn was in supreme command, and he held out for the narrow front.

In preparation for the attack, in which artillery was to play the key role, during January, 1916, the Germans assembled 542 heavy and 306 light artillery pieces, and 152 large mine throwers, with almost three million shells to feed them. Von Falkenhayn also moved up six more infantry divisions. Very little of this was known to the French. Although apparently they expected an attack somewhere, it was not until late in January that they began to suspect that Verdun might be the target. They had no idea how strong the attack might be.

The German front east of the Meuse was held by three German corps: the VII Reserve, the XVIII, and the III Corps. The V Reserve Corps had recently been relieved from the front but would be available later. Farther east, in the Woëvre sector, were two divisions of the XV Corps and the 5th Landwehr Division. The French had the XXX Corps under General Chrétien in the area to be attacked, the II Corps in the Woëvre, and the VII Corps, under General Bazelaire, on the left bank of the river. Two divisions, the 37th and 48th, were in reserve south of Verdun. In addition the XX Corps was on its way from Charme to Bar-le-Duc, thirty miles south of Verdun, but in the area chosen by Von Falkenhayn for the attack there were six German divisions to two French. One of the railway lines, running south from the French front to the rear, had been cut by the Germans when they occupied the St. Mihiel salient in 1914. The other line, to the west, ran close behind the front and was cut by German artillery fire on the first day of the battle. This left only a single narrow-gauge railway line and an unpaved road for supply and communications with the base at Bar-le-Duc.

The German artillery opened fire in the cold early morning of February 21, 1916, and poured shells—explosive, gas, shrapnel, and tear gas—on the French front all day at the rate of one hundred thousand rounds an hour. The metallic rain wrought terrible destruction, completely demolishing large areas of the French trenches, and creating great craters in the snow-covered earth. The German soldiers, who had waited for a week for the word to advance, had been told that nothing would survive the murderous bombardment. They could see for themselves the trees torn to shreds and the apparent desolation of the whole landscape. Yet when the artillery had lengthened its range and the infantrymen finally moved out at five o'clock in the afternoon, many with their guns on their shoulders, in the midst of the destruction they encountered French soldiers effectively manning machine guns. There are no figures on losses for the first day. The French lost more than the Germans, but German casualties were still heavy. When the fighting died down with darkness, the Germans were in control of the French front-line trenches in the assault zone.

The steady pounding by German artillery continued day after day, the range moving up as the infantry advanced, forced to fight desperately for the ground they gained despite the great areas of destruction created by the heavy guns. On February 24, General de Langle de Cary received Joffre's approval to withdraw his troops and artillery from the Woëvre plain. That day, too, Joffre made the decision, recommended by his Chief of Staff, General de Castelnau, to move the Second Army to Verdun and to put its commander, General Henri Philippe Pétain, in command of the defense.

February 25 was a disastrous day at Verdun. Of the ring of forts that comprised the fortification system, Fort Douaumont was the most important. The Germans were in awe of it. It was to them a symbol of the stupendous task they had undertaken in attacking Verdun. They did not know that the French August order had resulted in removal of all but one 175-mm. gun and two 75's and reduction of Douaumont's garrison from its normal complement of five hundred infantry and forty artillerymen to fifty-seven old territorial gunners and one artilleryman, with no officer among them. The reinforcements sent to Verdun shortly before the German attack had not been intended for the forts, and orders had been to extend the trenches, with no thought at all for Douaumont.

When the men of the 24th Brandenburg Regiment approached Fort Douaumont on February 25, the German artillery was still bombarding it. The soldiers advanced cautiously, expecting at any moment that the big guns of the fort, strangely silent, would open fire upon them. In amazement they found not even machine guns shooting at them. They scaled the parapet with no opposition (to find later that the main entrance was open and the drawbridge down) and took possession of the fort, its inadequate garrison surrendering without resistance. The importance of Fort Douaumont's loss to the French was great—one French general estimated it as equivalent to one hundred thousand men—and the gain to the Germans was no less significant. Word of its capture raised German spirits from the front lines back to Berlin and beyond. The symbol was in their hands! It was only part of the objective, however.

Pétain, tall, calm, highly capable, having conferred with Joffre at Chantilly, hurried to Souilly, where he established his headquarters and took up his new duties. Whether he said it or not, the word promptly went out—"They shall not pass!" His were not the first orders to hold; the French troops had been told this constantly since the assault began. But Pétain drew the defense together, built it up and organized it, and gave its men confidence, so that Verdun did not fall.

To supply the front, Pétain turned his attention at once to the single road from Bar-le-Duc. It had been widened the previous summer and was already carrying a constant stream of traffic to and from Verdun. Pétain issued strict rules: no trucks allowed to pass; trucks that broke down must be immediately dragged off the road; repair crews would work constantly to repair the road, quarrying stone from the roadsides to fill in holes caused by German long-range artillery fire, and keep the road constantly passable. All day and all night trucks traveled in both directions on this forty-five-mile stretch of road, maintaining a rate of about one vehicle every fourteen seconds. Men, matériel, ambulances, mail, guns, everything destined for the front passed wounded men being carried to the rear and men relieved by new units, in a never-ending stream. So vital was the road to the defense that one French writer gave it a name that has stuck, the name of the principal street of ancient Rome—the Sacred Way, La Voie Sacrée.

At about the time of Pétain's arrival there was a lull in the fighting. This was partly caused by the heavy expenditure of artillery ammunition by the Germans, whose supplies were nearing exhaustion. It was also influenced by one of Pétain's first directives. The French artillery on the west bank of the Meuse had been directing its fire against the front-line positions opposite it to the north, where the Germans were not attacking. But so much of the east bank was now in German hands that Pétain ordered the French guns to be turned to fire across the river at the east bank, on the flank of the advancing attackers. This maneuver at last convinced Von Falkenhayn to attack on the west bank as well, as the Crown Prince had advocated from the beginning.

On March 6 a new German attack began, hitting with particular strength on the west bank of the Meuse. Despite another long and heavy artillery bombardment, the German infantrymen still had to fight determined French defenders as they pushed across the line and worked their way slowly about two and a half miles on a four-mile front. Dominating the new battle area was a hill aptly named Le Mort Homme (The Dead Man). Again and again the Germans tried to take it, only to be driven back by the stubborn French defenders. It was not until the end of May that the Germans finally took the hill.

The French by this time had built up their strength so as to be about equal in numbers to the Germans and as well supplied with guns and ammunition, and they were repeatedly counterattacking in strength. Both sides had lost almost equal numbers of men in the long and bloody struggle. In April General Pétain had moved up to replace De Langle de Cary, and General Robert Georges Nivelle took command of the French Second Army. General Charles Mangin, who worked closely with him, was in command of the 5th Division. These two then undertook strong counteroffensives.

During the next several months there was almost incessant bitter fighting, with small gains on either side. On June 2 the Germans finally captured Fort Vaux, south of Douaumont, but its fall was a very different story. On Pétain's order Vaux had been strongly garrisoned and supplied with guns and ammunition. A determined German attack surrounded the fort, but the defenders, without food or water, held out for four days before finally yielding in their hopeless cause. On June 21 the Germans attacking Fleury, southwest of Vaux, first used the deadly phosgene gas, with great effect. But they still were held by the French short of their goal, Fort Souville.

Von Falkenhayn was relieved as Chief of the German General Staff on August 29, partly because of the failure at Verdun, partly as a result of the rivalry of the successful Von Hindenburg, who took his place, with Ludendorff as his deputy. Von Hindenburg gave orders that no new offensive be undertaken at Verdun.

On October 24 Nivelle launched a counteroffensive, which succeeded in retaking Forts Vaux and Douaumont. In mid-December another French attack regained more land. Then the long, bloody battle died out. Its cost has never been known exactly, for the published figures are inexact and conflicting. Killed, wounded, missing, the French could count their losses close to half a million, the Germans probably over four hundred thousand. Was it worth it? The front line had changed but little. The dead could not be replaced, the wounded and those lucky enough to come through unscathed lived with it for the rest of their lives.

22

The Somme

As the French staggered under the weight of the German assaults at Verdun in the spring of 1916, the importance of an offensive elsewhere took on more urgency. The operation in the Somme sector that had been decided upon at Chantilly in December, 1915, was originally planned as a joint attack in which French forces would play the dominant role. When more and more French divisions were removed from the area and rushed to Verdun, however, plans were modified to make the offensive primarily British. Joffre, Pétain, Foch, and other French leaders kept urging Haig to attack, but despite the importance of relieving the pressure at Verdun, Haig insisted on delaying until he had men and equipment ready to go. At last the attack date was set for June 29.

Haig planned to attack on a wide front and break through the German defenses. Then the British would push northeast while the French pushed southeast, opening a wide gap through which British and French cavalry would rush, to divide the Germans and so defeat them en masse. There were numerous fallacies in Haig's plan, not least of them the necessity of pushing it through before the Germans could bring up reinforcements. In order to move fast it was essential that the initial artillery bombardment so completely destroy the front-line German defenses, and if possible those behind them, that the infantry could advance rapidly and in full strength. Joffre apparently had less ambitious ideas than Haig's, his objective being roughly the same as Von Falkenhayn's at Verdun: attrition.

The soldiers who were to participate in the Somme action were predominantly men of Kitchener's New Army, volunteers who had been trained quickly and were eager to do their bit in the

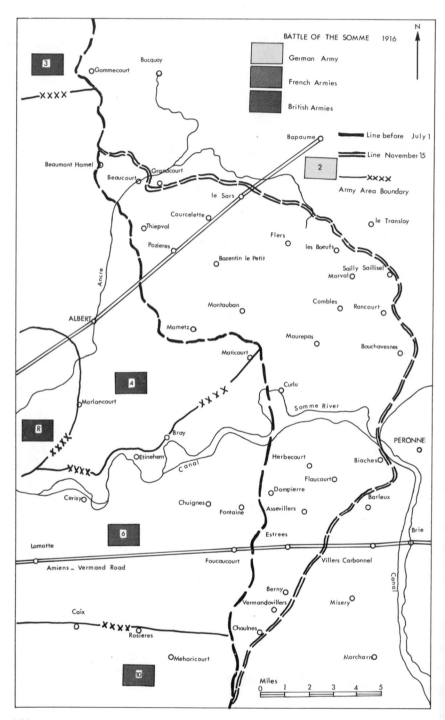

BATTLE OF THE SOMME   1916

German Army

French Armies

British Armies

Line before   July 1

Line November 15

XXXX   Army Area Boundary

N

3

2

Bucquoy

Gommecourt

Bapaume

Beaumont Hamel

Grandcourt

Beaucourt

le Sars

le Transloy

Courcelette

Thiepval

Flers

les Boeufs

Pozieres

Sailly Saillisel

Bazentin le Petit

Morval

Combles

Rancourt

Montauban

Maurepas

Bouchavesnes

ALBERT

Mametz

Maricourt

Ancre

4

Curlu

Somme River

Morlancourt

PERONNE

R

Bray

Herbecourt

Biaches

Etinehem

Canal

Flaucourt

Barleux

Cerisy

Dompierre

Chuignes

Assevillers

Brie

Fontaine

6

Estrees

Villers Carbonnel

Lamotte

Foucaucourt

Amiens _ Vermand Road

Canal

Berny

Caix

Misery

Vermandovillers

XXXX

Rosieres

Chaulnes

Meharicourt

Morcharn

10

Miles

0   1   2   3   4   5

168

fight, the best young men England could provide. General Sir Henry Rawlinson's Fourth Army, north of the Somme, was to carry the major part of the attack, while two divisions of General Sir Edmund Allenby's Third Army made a smaller attack near Gommecourt farther to the north. Lieutenant General Sir Hubert Gough's three cavalry divisions would charge through the gap made by the infantry.

Neither Rawlinson nor Allenby liked the Somme plan very much. Nor did General Foch, who commanded the northern sector of the French front, including the Sixth Army of General Marie Emile Fayolle, just south of the river. Haig was in command, though, and when their views were not accepted, they naturally followed his.

As plans for the offensive were nearing completion, word came that Lord Kitchener, Secretary of State for War, had been lost at sea. Kitchener had left Scapa Flow on the cruiser *Hampshire* on June 5, en route to Archangel and a conference with the Russian Grand Duke Nicholas. The ship had scarcely cleared the estuary when she hit a mine and sank, taking all but twelve of her crew, including the eminent passenger, with her. Serious though the shock of this event was, the loss of Kitchener to the war program was not great, for he had proved to be only moderately effective in the Cabinet post. His place was ultimately taken by David Lloyd George.

Plans for the impending battle of the Somme included a role for the Royal Flying Corps. Major General H. M. Trenchard, the Air Commander, had 185 aircraft at his disposal, which were to fly reconnaissance, photography, artillery spotting, and bombing missions. The Germans had about 130 planes, and sent observation flights almost daily over the British lines. Aerial fights were not uncommon, including nine on the first day of battle.

Opposite the British the Germans held a strongly fortified position, in fact possibly the strongest of the German front. Facing Rawlinson was the German Second Army, commanded by General Fritz von Below. He had six divisions on the front, and five in reserve. North of him was the Sixth Army under Crown Prince Rupprecht of Bavaria. The Germans had built their fortifications on a ridge with several spurs that overlooked the British lines. They were so designed that from almost any direction attackers would come under heavy crossfire. Beneath the fortifications were dugouts thirty to forty feet deep. Deep trenches, several rows of them, all equipped for fairly comfortable living, were built in two lines two or three miles apart. Behind them a third line was under construction. Each line was barricaded with twenty to thirty feet of heavy barbed wire. So well was the defense planned that a few lookouts could be left in the trenches and the rest of the soldiers could remain in relative comfort in the dugouts until called to come up. Carrying their machine guns with them, they could man the line in a matter of a few minutes.

The British were unaware of the details of the German fortifications but had planned their artillery preparations with the object of destroying as much as possible. For five days before the attack there would be a continuous night and day bombardment of the German trenches, reaching a crescendo each day in eighty minutes of concentrated firing, the first two days primarily to cut the barbed wire, the other three to destroy the trenches and other fortifications. On the day of the attack the intensive firing period would be cut to sixty-five minutes, on the assumption that this would enable the infantry to take the defenders by surprise.

At six o'clock on the morning of June 24, 1916, the British artillery commenced firing, and it continued on the following days according to schedule. The weather turned very bad, and the attack was delayed until July 1. During these three extra days, the artillery continued to pound the German defenses, firing 1,508,652 shells by the time the troops moved out. Many sections of the German front-line trenches were destroyed, but few of the deeper dugouts were touched at all. And of more immediate importance, despite the massive bombardment much of the barbed wire remained uncut.

At 7:30 on July 1, a hot summer day on the Somme, the bombardment suddenly stopped. All along the Allied front, men climbed up and over the parapets of the trenches, pushed through their own barbed wire barricade, and stepped into no-man's-land, to be greeted almost at once by machine-gun fire, in some areas by artillery shells as well. The Germans, realizing the significance of the sudden silence, had swarmed from their dugouts. Many found the trenches blasted out of existence, but the shell holes that had taken their places served equally well as protection for the men and their machine guns.

Wave after wave of British soldiers clambered over the parapets and started for the German lines. As men fell, wounded or dead under the German fire, others pushed on. A few reached the German front lines; most did not. By nightfall those who had survived the slaughter crawled back to the trenches they had left so hopefully a few hours before. Only in a few places was the story a little different. The XV Corps had advanced about three quarters of a mile and taken the village of Mametz, or what was left of it. And beside the XV Corps, on the right flank of the British forces, the XIII Corps had advanced over a mile, the farthest of any British troops that day. The corps commander, General Walter Congreve, had used a new artillery technique, a rolling barrage. When his guns ceased firing at the German front line, the gunners raised their sights and laid down a curtain of fire in front of the advancing infantry. As the line advanced, the range was lengthened periodically. Consequently the Germans were never able to establish a defense line.

At Foch's recommendation the French south of the Somme had delayed their attack until 9:30, rightly assuming that the Germans would have decided they were not coming and so be unprepared. The French had more artillery than the British, and it was more effective. Their sector was almost straight, not bulging here and there like that of the British, and the Germans opposing them lacked the commanding observation positions they had north of the Somme. The attempt at surprise worked, and the French soldiers overran most of the German line and pushed ahead half a mile beyond. Their part of the attack was relatively successful and the cost in casualties not excessively heavy. The British assault, on the other hand, was a dreadful, costly failure. Almost sixty thousand British soldiers were dead, wounded, or missing by the end of the day. Well over nineteen thousand were dead.

Strategically the operation should have ended there, for there was no longer—if there ever had been—a possibility of breaking through the German line before they could get reinforcements to the area. There remained only the objective Joffre had sought from the first, attrition of the German forces, and the diversion of effort from Verdun. It is probable that Haig did not fully realize the extent of the first day's losses. In any case, he never considered abandoning the effort but told Rawlinson to continue the attack the next day.

The Germans were also determined to continue and to hold the land they occupied. Moreover they had orders from Von Falkenhayn: "Not a foot of ground must be voluntarily abandoned. Only over our dead bodies will the enemy advance."

The attacks continued, interrupted at times by counterattacks, and the casualties on both sides mounted. On July 7 it began to rain hard, and the trenches as well as the churned-up, pockmarked terrain between became bottomless, gluey mud. Gradually the British gained ground, until by the end of the second week most of the German first line was in British control. In the early hours of July 14, Rawlinson tried a night attack, and with it he used a rolling barrage. Five miles of the German second line were taken. Another attack, farther north, on July 23 was less successful, but two Anzac divisions of General Sir Herbert Gough's newly established Fifth Army did succeed in taking the remains of the town of Pozières.

The battle dragged on with the same dreary pattern. Gains were scarcely noticeable and losses were enormous, as the attrition continued week after week. Only one event really interrupted the awful, monotonous carnage. For many months the British had been working on an answer to the stalemate in France, a machine combining firepower and protection, that could cross no-man's-land unharmed and ride across the enemy's trenches as if they were level ground. The Somme offered an opportunity to try it. This marriage of armor to a tractor-driven vehicle had been spurned by the British Army when it was suggested to them in 1914. When the British War Office ignored a proposal that such a vehicle be developed, Winston Churchill provided funds from the Admiralty for its development, wholly on his own responsibility. Demonstrations of the new invention (called "tank" during its development, as a sort of code to conceal its true identity) in February, 1916, were greeted with great enthusiasm, and the Army promptly ordered a hundred of them.

Under urging from Joffre, Haig developed plans for a new offensive on the Somme in September, 1916. Despite the fact that those who were responsible for developing the tanks were insistent that they not be revealed to the enemy until a large number of them were available, Haig decided that this was the perfect place to try them out. He ordered all that had been produced to be sent to France so that he might use them in his September offensive.

The British attacked on a ten-mile front from Combles northwest to the Ancre valley on September 15, 1916, twelve divisions facing six and a half divisions of Germans. Once again three days of heavy bombardment alerted the Germans to the approaching attack, but they were unprepared for the appearance of the new armored tanks. Forty-nine of them had reached France, but only thirty-six arrived at the fighting front. Few of these accomplished anything, for no one knew just how to use them. As the strange machines rumbled across the rough ground, they struck awe into the hearts of the Germans who were near them. Primarily because of their psychological impact they did make some unmeasurable contribution toward the gains of the day, which were the greatest of any day of the long campaign. Allied advances went as deep as a mile and a half and more in the center, where Flers was taken. One tank entered the town.

Haig has been much criticized for disclosing the existence of the tank in this relatively ineffective fashion rather than waiting until larger numbers were available. It is interesting to note that six months later there still were only forty-eight tanks available for the Battle of Arras. How much longer the tank could have been kept a secret is problematical. On this occasion Haig was acting in accordance with his intention of making this the big breakthrough he sought, and for that reason perhaps he was justified in using the tanks. In any event, as in the case of all radically new weapons, no one knew what the potential of the tank was, and there is no assurance that it would have accomplished any more in a later first appearance than it did at the Somme.

Haig attacked again in strength later in September and took more of the devastated territory. The weather grew worse and worse, mud deepened, and then snow and bitter cold added to the misery of the men in the trenches. General Gough attacked with seven divisions on November 13 on both sides of the Ancre River, and gained yet more ground. But a blizzard on November 18 and rain the following day put an end to the fighting and finally terminated the Battle of the Somme.

The battle had lasted a little over four and a half months, and nowhere had the Allied line advanced more than eight miles. About three million men had participated in the operation on both sides. No one knows exactly how many of these were casualties, for there are no complete official casualty figures. Best estimates seem to be 475,000 British, 195,000 French, and for the Germans about 500,000. Britain had lost the best of her young manhood, for these were largely the high-spirited, eager volunteers of the New Army who fought at the Somme. Those who were there and survived to fight another World War—among them Wavell, Churchill, and Alexander—were determined not to let such wholesale, pointless bloodshed happen again.

But what of the attrition so evident in the figures? There is ample evidence that the bloodletting at the Somme combined with the carnage at Verdun greatly weakened German morale, and the losses of men and officers were sadly felt by the German Army. Both actions contributed to the Kaiser's decision to replace Von Falkenhayn as Chief of Staff at the end of August.

23

Jutland

The German naval command chafed under the restrictions that had been placed on submarine warfare in August, 1915. Early in 1916 support for the Navy's desire to use U-boats more effectively came from Von Falkenhayn, who wanted help in the stalemate on the Western Front, either by a direct confrontation of the two fleets or by increased U-boat activity. On January 18 Vice Admiral Reinhard Scheer replaced Admiral Hugo von Pohl as commander of the High Seas Fleet. A more aggressive man than Von Pohl, Scheer was eager to use his ships and ready to argue for his views. Pressure from Scheer and Von Falkenhayn finally secured the Kaiser's approval in March to sink merchant ships within the war zone. Outside the war zone armed merchant ships would be sunk, but neither armed nor unarmed passenger vessels were to be attacked by a submerged submarine.

At once Allied ship sinkings rose. Then the *UB–29* put a torpedo in the passenger steamer *Sussex* as she was making her regular crossing between Dieppe and Folkestone. The vessel was not sunk, but several passengers, including Americans and Spaniards, were killed. Protests came promptly from the United States and Spain. As a result the Kaiser placed new restrictions on U-boats. Announced in May as the "Sussex Pledge," the new rules provided that unless a ship tried to escape she would not be attacked by a U-boat until her papers had been examined and her crew and passengers had been removed. To Admiral Scheer this was preposterous. He withdrew his U-boats from the sea and limited their activities to operating with the fleet.

Although all or parts of the British and German fleets ventured into the North Sea several times in the first months of 1916, only a few minor elements met each other until the last day of May.

The British were planning to make a foray into the Skaggerak in an attempt to attract the High Seas Fleet, when an intercepted German message on May 30 revealed that the Germans were

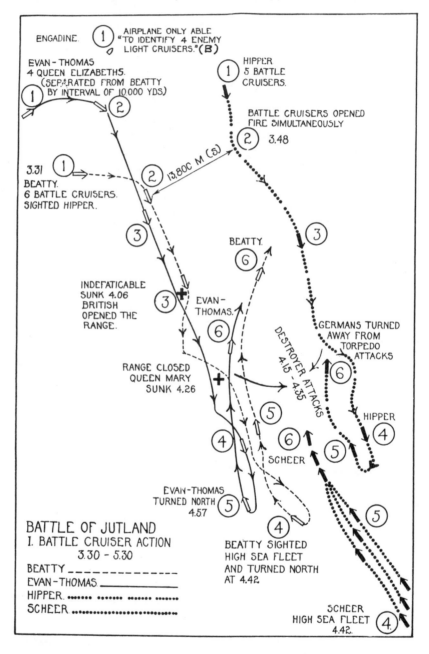

ENGADINE. ① AIRPLANE ONLY ABLE "TO IDENTIFY 4 ENEMY LIGHT CRUISERS."(B)

EVAN – THOMAS
4 QUEEN ELIZABETHS.
(SEPARATED FROM BEATTY
BY INTERVAL OF 10,000 YDS.)

HIPPER
① 5 BATTLE
CRUISERS.

BATTLE CRUISERS OPENED FIRE SIMULTANEOUSLY
② 3.48

3.31 ①
BEATTY.
6 BATTLE CRUISERS.
SIGHTED HIPPER.

② 13,800 M (5)

BEATTY.
⑥

③

INDEFATICABLE
SUNK 4.06
BRITISH
OPENED THE
RANGE.

③ ✠ EVAN – THOMAS.

⑥

GERMANS TURNED
AWAY FROM
TORPEDO
ATTACKS

RANGE CLOSED
QUEEN MARY
SUNK 4.26

✠

DESTROYER ATTACKS 4.15 – 4.35

⑥

⑤

④

⑥

⑤

HIPPER
④

SCHEER

EVAN–THOMAS
TURNED NORTH ⑤
4.57

BATTLE OF JUTLAND
I. BATTLE CRUISER ACTION
3.30 – 5.30
BEATTY _ _ _ _ _ _ _ _ _ _ _ _
EVAN–THOMAS _____
HIPPER. •••••• •••••• •••••• ••••••
SCHEER ••••••••••••••••••••••••••

④

BEATTY SIGHTED
HIGH SEA FLEET
AND TURNED NORTH
AT 4.42

⑤

SCHEER
HIGH SEA FLEET ④
4.42.

about to set out. Admiral Scheer's plan was to send a force to attack Sunderland, on the coast of England, and he had already sent submarines to stand by off the British naval bases to watch

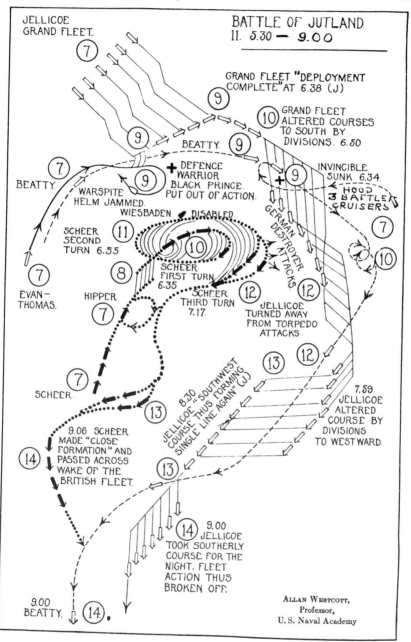

BATTLE OF JUTLAND
II. 5.30 — 9.00

for warships putting to sea. Bad weather caused Scheer to change his plans and try something closer to home, an exercise to try to lure the British into the Skaggerak. The message the British intercepted included orders for the High Seas Fleet to assemble in Jade Bay, prepared to put to sea.

The Admiralty, not knowing from the intercepted message just what the Germans planned to do, ordered Admiral Jellicoe to get the Grand Fleet under way, prepared for whatever might develop. By 11 P.M. on May 30 the whole British fleet was at sea. Admiral Jellicoe in the *Iron Duke* with ninety-nine ships, including twenty-four dreadnoughts, three battle cruisers, and a screen of light and armored cruisers and destroyers, was proceeding from Scapa Flow and Invergordon. Vice Admiral Beatty had steamed out of Rosyth with fifty-two more ships, including four fast, new battleships and six battle cruisers. Both British fleets headed roughly east, with the intention of rendezvousing about ninety miles west of the entrance to the Skaggerak if nothing had been sighted by 2 P.M. the following day.

The High Seas Fleet did not get under way until three and a half hours after the Grand Fleet was at sea. Leading as it headed north from Jade Bay was Admiral Franz von Hipper with forty ships, including five battle cruisers, five light cruisers, and thirty destroyers. Admiral Scheer followed, about fifty miles behind, in the battleship *Friedrich der Grosse,* his main body of the fleet including sixteen modern battleships, six older ones, six light cruisers, and thirty-one destroyers—a total of fifty-nine vessels.

Both British and Germans observed radio silence as they ploughed along through the water. Hence neither knew that the other was at sea. Listening radios in London picked up only the acknowledgment of messages for Admiral Scheer by a ship safely anchored in Jade Bay.

Beatty's orders were to turn north for the rendezvous with Jellicoe shortly after 2 P.M. if nothing had been sighted. Just as he was about to change course, the light cruiser *Galatea,* easternmost of his screening force, sighted smoke to the east. With the *Phaeton* she hurried off to investigate.

A short time before, the German cruiser *Elbing* had sighted a Danish freighter and sent two destroyers to see what she was. Coming upon the German destroyers, the *Galatea* identified them from a distance as German cruisers and opened fire, thereby starting the action. At once Beatty changed course and with two squadrons of battle cruisers headed southeast toward the area of Horns Reef, hoping to cut between the German ships and their base. Behind him, Rear Admiral H. Evan-Thomas with the four battleships did not receive the visual signal to alter course for several minutes and so was some distance behind when he finally turned.

The German light cruisers had by this time rushed over to join the fight, and they followed the British light cruisers, which had turned back to the northwest, hoping to lead the enemy back toward the main body of the Grand Fleet. Von Hipper, with the battle cruisers, was coming along behind them on a course so nearly parallel to Beatty's in the opposite direction that the two forces might have missed each other entirely had not Beatty decided to turn northeast. Admiral von Hipper, aboard the *Lützow*, sighted the British battle cruisers coming up at about 3:20, a few minutes before Beatty was aware of his approach. Von Hipper changed course at once to southeast, to try to lead the British toward Scheer, who was still some distance away. At about 3:30 Beatty, sighting the Germans, also changed course, to the east and then southeast, so that the two fleets were soon on almost parallel courses, both heading toward the approaching Scheer.

The Germans, coming within about seventeen thousand yards of the British ships, opened fire and were immediately answered. In the fight that followed it was the British who suffered more. At about 4 P.M. a direct hit on the *Lion's* amidship turret knocked it out and killed all but one of the gun crew. Fire would have spread to the ammunition magazines alongside the turret had not the commander of the gun crew ordered the turret doors closed, although it meant certain death for himself. Five minutes after the *Lion's* disastrous hit, the *Indefatigable* was sunk by the *Von der Tann*.

Evan-Thomas and the battleships at about this time came within range of the German battle cruisers. The fifteen-inch shells of the British guns drove Von Hipper to increase his speed to get out of range of the battleships and closer to Beatty's battle cruiser force. Shorty thereafter the *Derfflinger* scored five hits on the *Queen Mary*, causing her to turn over and sink. Except for the *Seydlitz*, which lost a turret, the German battle cruisers suffered little from British fire.

Seeing British ships disappearing beneath the water, Admiral Beatty, on the bridge of his own seriously damaged *Lion*, gave no thought to turning away. "Chatfield," he said to his flag captain, "there seems to be something wrong with our bloody ships today!" and he ordered him to turn toward the German battle cruisers. Beatty sent his destroyers into the fight, hoping that their torpedoes could find a German cruiser target. As the destroyers headed in Von Hipper's direction, however, he turned his cruisers away, sending his own destroyers to meet Beatty's. British destroyers scored better than the larger ships, badly damaging two German destroyers that eventually were sunk.

Shortly after 4:30 Commodore W. D. Goodenough, in command of the 2nd Light Cruiser Squadron, sighted Scheer's battleships coming up from the southeast. When Beatty also saw them, about fifteen minutes later, he turned and headed toward the approaching Jellicoe, still about fifty miles away, hoping that Scheer would see him and follow. Von Hipper meanwhile had turned and fallen in ahead of the German battleships, somewhat to the rear of Beatty but close enough so that from time to time shots were exchanged between the two battle cruiser squadrons until Beatty speeded up to hasten to join Jellicoe.

Evan-Thomas, behind Beatty, was soon under fire from the ships of both Von Hipper and Scheer, until he too put on more speed and drew away. Goodenough, true to his job as scout for the fleet, darted up to within thirteen thousand yards of the German battleships in order to count them and determine their identity, course, and speed. Maneuvering skillfully, he dodged their shells and sped away. Another destroyer attack at about this time was led by Commander Barry Bingham in the *Nestor*. A hit forward on the *Seydlitz* caused her to list, but thanks to watertight bulkheads she did not sink. However, two of the British destroyers, including the *Nestor*, were lost.

About twenty-five miles in front of the battleships of the British Grand Fleet as it approached was the 3rd Battle Cruiser Squadron, commanded by Rear Admiral H. L. A. Hood, in the *Invincible*. The light cruiser *Chester* was about five miles to the west at 5:36 P.M. when she met the German Scouting Group II, which was ahead of the High Seas Fleet. The Germans attacked and immediately knocked out the *Chester's* fire-control communications system. Otherwise the cruiser was not significantly damaged, and she escaped as Hood's battle cruisers came up. Their fire stopped the *Wiesbaden* where she was and badly damaged the *Pillau* and the *Frankfurt,* at the cost of one British destroyer.

Just before Beatty came in sight of Jellicoe's ships, he turned and opened fire again on Von Hipper, damaging the *Lützow* and most of the other German battle cruisers, and causing Von Hipper to order a turn toward Scheer. Within range of both German units came the British cruiser *Defence,* hastening to try to finish off the *Wiesbaden.* In view of practically everyone in the British fleet the *Defence* was blown to bits by German gunfire.

Beatty crossed in front of the British battle fleet and took up position with Hood ahead of it. Evan-Thomas turned north to fall in behind Jellicoe's ships. In executing this order the *Warspite's* rudder jammed, which caused her to turn at full speed in a large circle, a great target for the German ships, who took advantage of it and damaged her severely.

Jellicoe then formed his battleships in line ahead, steaming in single file to perform the classic naval maneuver known as crossing the T. At the head of the Grand Fleet, Hood first came in range of Von Hipper's battle cruisers. In the ensuing battle the *Lützow* was put out of action and the *Invincible,* with Admiral Hood aboard, was sunk. Von Hipper left the *Lützow* and boarded a destroyer. For three hours he tried in vain to get to another battle cruiser and put his flag aboard.

By this time the whole area was covered with smoke and haze, and visibility was very poor. At 6:30 Jellicoe's ships finally sighted the approaching Germans and opened fire. Scheer could see nothing but the flashing of guns on the horizon and the big shells flying at his ships from ahead and to the left, while to the right the battle cruisers were shooting it out. In order to get out of his dangerous situation in a hurry he ordered his ships to execute a complicated maneuver, a *Gefechtskehrtwendung,* in which the ships at the rear turned about first and those ahead followed in order, while destroyers laid a smoke screen. The maneuver was accomplished with no difficulty. Jellicoe could not see what was happening and knew only that his target was no longer visible.

Afraid to venture into an area that might expose his ships to torpedo attacks he kept on going, then turned to a more southerly course. Scheer, thinking he could pass behind the British fleet and head for home, after a short time on the new westerly course quickly turned his battleships back toward the east.

Shortly after 7 P.M. the German dreadnoughts and battle cruisers were again steaming directly toward Jellicoe's line and under attack from most of the British capital ships. Again Scheer could see little but the flash of guns and the rain of shells, but this sufficed to convince him he should again get out of the way as rapidly as possible. For the third time in about forty minutes he reversed his course, ordering his four remaining battle cruisers and his destroyers to proceed to the attack to cover the withdrawal of the German battleships. Under command of Captain Hartog of the *Derfflinger*—Von Hipper had not yet caught up—the battle cruisers sped past the entire Grand Fleet, at a range of little more than seven thousand yards, drawing the fire of the British battleships. The *Derfflinger's* guns were soon all knocked out, but the rest of the German ships fired back as they continued their "death ride." In rushed the German destroyers, loosing their torpedoes at the mighty British ships. But Jellicoe had seen them coming and ordered a turn away to avoid the deadly fish. Unfortunately for Jellicoe's place in history, this maneuver cost him his chance to catch the German battle fleet. When he turned back fourteen minutes later Scheer's big ships were out of sight. Since that time there has been endless discussion among naval critics as to whether Jellicoe should have turned toward the Germans instead of away in order to avoid the torpedoes.

Completely out of contact, Scheer decided the British had gone off to the east, and he headed south for the safety of Jade Bay. Jellicoe, however, by this time was going southwest in order to get between the High Seas Fleet and its anchorage. As darkness fell, Beatty's battle cruisers again spotted the German battle cruisers and old battleships and exchanged fire, causing some damage. The Germans broke it off by turning west to join the rest of the High Seas Fleet. Jellicoe then realized that he had accomplished his purpose of getting between the Germans and their base, and he determined to continue on a southerly course in order to be in a good position to resume the fight when day broke.

He drew his ships closer together, with destroyers and light cruisers in the rear area and battle cruisers ahead.

Scheer by 9:30 was about nine miles west of Jellicoe and eight miles behind Beatty. Determined not to risk another engagement and anxious to get his ships safely home, he ordered the fleet to head directly for Horns Reef, firing on anything they encountered. Word of this order was radioed from the Admiralty to Jellicoe an hour and a half after it was given. He took no action, however. The German course took them right across the Grand Fleet, about six miles behind the dreadnoughts, through the midst of the destroyers and cruisers. On came the German ships at about midnight, their great searchlights lighting the surprised ships ahead of them to illuminate targets for their guns. The British returned the fire, but although some of the British battleships, some distance ahead, saw the lights and flashes of gunfire, no one reported the action to Admiral Jellicoe. A British torpedo struck the old battleship *Pommern* and sent her to the bottom, the only battleship lost in the action. The British cruiser *Black Prince* also sank, blown up by German gunfire.

Jellicoe turned north at about 2:30 A.M., apparently planning to draw his fleet together and head east for Horns Reef, although his intentions are not clear. Before long, however, he received word that the German fleet had already passed Horns Reef. He could not hope to catch it. After searching the area for survivors, the Grand Fleet finally headed for home, shortly before the High Seas Fleet dropped anchor in Jade Bay.

This was the only major naval engagement of World War I and, having been recorded in great detail, particularly on the British side, it has been studied exhaustively and debated repeatedly. In some sense it may be considered a German victory, since the Germans lost only 3,039 men and eleven ships to the British 6,784 men and fourteen ships.* But the battle convinced Admiral Scheer that he could not hope to win a decisive victory against the Grand Fleet. It also led him to advocate increased U-boat warfare as the only decisive use of German naval power. The British lost the chance to gain entrance to the Baltic, but they retained

---

* Germans: one old battleship, one battle cruiser, four light cruisers, five destroyers, totaling 62,000 tons. British: three battle cruisers, three armored cruisers, eight destroyers, totaling 112,000 tons.

control of the North Sea. They also realized that their ships had been vulnerable because they were insufficiently armored, and took measures to remedy this situation.

POST-JUTLAND NAVAL ACTION

Admiral Scheer did not anchor his ships permanently after the Battle of Jutland. When the damage had been repaired he decided to go through with the project he had originally planned for May 31, a raid on Sunderland. With submarines along for protection, Von Hipper would take two battle cruisers and three battleships in to bombard the town, while Scheer stood behind him with the main body of fifteen battleships, and zeppelins scouted ahead and north toward the bases of the Grand Fleet.

Again, on August 18, 1916, the Admiralty learned that the High Seas Fleet was going out, and ordered the Grand Fleet to get under way, prepared for whatever developed. In the southern regions of the North Sea, Commodore Reginald Tyrwhitt would take his Scouting Force to watch for the German ships.

The British submarine *E–23* was patrolling at 3 A.M. on August 19, when she spotted the High Seas Fleet, steaming west in the North Sea. Commander R. R. Turner fired two torpedoes as the ships passed within range. Both missed their targets. A third, however, hit the last ship in line, the battleship *Westfalen*. She stayed afloat and, escorted by destroyers, went slowly back to Wilhelmshaven. About an hour later the German submarine *U–52* more than evened the score by sinking the cruiser *Nottingham,* part of the Grand Fleet's escort, with two torpedoes.

Around noon Admiral Scheer received a report from one of his zeppelins of the sighting of Tyrwhitt's ships, southeast of the High Seas Fleet and heading north. To Scheer this force seemed worth attacking, and he changed his course and headed back to the east to try to cut them off. Tyrwhitt, however, having seen no Germans, himself had turned around and headed back south to his patrol area. Thus, when Scheer arrived at the area where he expected contact, there were no British ships to be found.

Meanwhile, the battle cruisers of the British Grand Fleet were only about thirty miles from Von Hipper's when the Germans reversed course. Unaware of that maneuver, however, the Fleet continued on its course and missed the Germans entirely. Scheer ordered his fleet to continue east, heading for home. At about 5 P.M. some of Tyrwhitt's ships spotted the Germans, but although they followed along for two and a half hours they found no opportunity to attack, and Scheer ignored them.

One more British ship fell victim to a submarine as the Grand Fleet, having seen no Germans, was returning to its bases. Two torpedoes from the *U–66* hit the cruiser *Falmouth,* cutting her speed to two knots. Eight destroyers moved in to escort her on the long trip home. The next day at noon they were still with her when the *U–63* came up undetected and put two more torpedoes in her. The *Falmouth* remained afloat for eight hours before disappearing beneath the waves of the North Sea.

The High Seas Fleet never again went so far from home. Only once, on October 18, 1916, did the whole fleet come out at all. At about 6 A.M. on October 19 the British submarine *E–38* sighted it. Maneuvering carefully, her commander finally attacked and hit the cruiser *München,* last ship in the line. This was the only contact, for there had been no advance notice of the German sortie.

It was over a year before another British submarine had an opportunity to attack a German warship. In November, 1917, the *J–1* sighted four German battleships which had come out to assist two U-boats grounded off Jutland. The British skipper, Commander Lawrence, moved in to four thousand yards and skillfully fired four torpedoes, hitting both the *Kronprinz* and the *Grosser Kurfürst.* When the two damaged ships returned to port, Scheer was rebuked by the Kaiser for having risked his battleships, and he never did it again.

GERMAN DESTROYER ACTIVITY

Scheer might have to keep his battleships at anchor, but there was no such restriction on destroyers, and he was determined to increase their usefulness. In October, 1916, two flotillas of destroyers were transferred to Zeebrugge, the U-boat base in Belgium. Aware of this move, the British expected trouble and had not long to wait.

In the evening of October 25 the destroyers set sail for Dover Strait, the vulnerable space between Britain and France, where nets had been installed in the hope of trapping German submarines. A little after 10 P.M. the German destroyers appeared, sank four of the drifters that guarded the net, and damaged a fifth, then sank a British destroyer that hastened to the rescue. One German destroyer flotilla went through and sank the only ship in sight, an empty transport. Turning about, the ships sank four more drifters and headed back to Zeebrugge.

Meanwhile six British destroyers from Dover and five from Dunkirk had been sent to the rescue, not knowing what they would find or what to do when they did. In the confusion that followed, three of them were damaged by the Germans, who readily identified them and fired accurately as they rushed by, before the British had a chance to recognize the Germans.

German destroyers successfully raided Ramsgate and Margate on November 23, with no interference from the British. British destroyers looked a little better a few nights later when they attacked some more Germans on the way to Zeebrugge. They damaged one, which hit a second, but the British themselves lost the *Simoom* to a German torpedo.

MORE GERMAN RAIDERS

In contrast to the German High Seas Fleet, whose movements were greatly restricted by its size and vulnerability, were the surface raiders that managed to slip out of German ports and into the Atlantic without being detected. Carefully disguised, and sailed by picked crews, they supplied the Germans with vivid reports of derring-do that brought flashes of cheer into the prolonged drabness of a war whose effects were felt even in the villages farthest removed from the fighting fronts.

In January, 1916, a German merchant ship, the *Moewe,* disguised as a Swedish vessel, managed to elude British patrols and lay a minefield north of Scotland. The old battleship *King Edward VII,* steaming along unaware of the danger, hit one of the mines and went to the bottom. The *Moewe,* long gone from the area, stayed at sea for the next two months, preying on shipping in the South Atlantic, and finally returned unscathed to Germany at the beginning of March. A second raider, the *Greif,* was detected and sunk by British patrols, but not until she had sunk an armed merchant cruiser, the *Alcantara.*

So successful was the *Moewe* that she put to sea again on November 22, 1916. Eight days later she sank the *Voltaire,* a British refrigerator ship. Her presence in the Atlantic might have gone longer undetected had she not stopped a Belgian relief ship and let her go, having taken the precaution to destroy her radio. As soon as the ship reached port her skipper reported her experience, and the British were alerted to search for the *Moewe.*

Five more British ships had been captured by the *Moewe* by December 12. Removing the crews from three, the German captain, Commander Count zu Dohna-Schlodien, sank them. He put a prize crew on the *Yarrowdale,* which was loaded with munitions, and sent her with four hundred prisoners back to Germany. Another crew took the *St. Theodore,* with a load of coal, to the South Atlantic for a later rendezvous with the *Moewe.* Zu Dohna subsequently transformed her into a raider, the *Geier,* and in that role she sank two ships. When her coal supply was exhausted the *Moewe* sent her to the bottom. The *Moewe* herself stayed out until March 22, when she again sailed serenely into port in Germany, having sunk or captured twenty-seven ships.

Meanwhile the *Yarrowdale* had been rechristened *Leopard* and sent to sea disguised as a Norwegian ship named the *Rena.* She was proceeding north of the Shetland Islands on March 16 when a British boarding steamer, the *Dundee,* accompanied by the cruiser *Achilles,* hailed her and sent a boarding party to look at her papers, keeping her four-inch guns trained on the German ship. Suddenly the *Rena* fired two torpedoes at the *Dundee* and tried to flee. But the fire of the *Dundee* and the *Achilles* was too much. Down she went, and the boarding party with her.

In the last week of November, 1916, another raider, the *Wolf,* about the same size as the *Moewe,* with Captain Karl Nerger in command, took a course through the icy waters far to the north of Scotland and headed for the distant waters of the Indian Ocean, laden with mines and carrying a small seaplane. Two months later two freighters struck mines she had planted ten days before off the Cape of Good Hope. Off Cape Agulhas on February 17 another ship fell victim to another of her mines.

Capturing two ships, Nerger fitted out one of them, the *Turritella,* as an auxiliary minelayer, but she was blown up by her own crew after failing to escape from a British sloop. The *Wolf* continued on her way, around Australia and New Zealand, between the Solomon Islands and New Guinea, over to Singapore, and then to the Indian Ocean, capturing and sinking ships as she went. On February 19, 1918, she sailed triumphantly home, having been at sea for fourteen months, traveled sixty-four thousand miles, and sunk 150,000 tons of shipping.

Best known of the raiders was the *Seeadler,* whose colorful captain, Count Felix von Luckner, added to his fame by lecturing about his exploits after the war. The *Seeadler* was a full-rigged sailing vessel, disguised in complete detail as a Norwegian ship, even to a crew with a high percentage of men who spoke Norwegian. Besides her sails she was equipped with a powerful engine. Passing undetected through the British patrol late in December, 1916, Von Luckner sailed to the South Atlantic, where he captured a number of ships, mostly sailing vessels. The prisoners whom he took aboard the *Seeadler* found her equipped with everything to make them comfortable and her captain the most genial of hosts. He had collected 260 unwilling guests by March 21, when he captured a French sailing ship, the *Cambronne,* transferred all the prisoners to her, and sent her to Rio de Janeiro, while he set sail for Cape Horn.

Five weeks later, with three American schooners added to his victims, Von Luckner sailed his ship to the uninhabited island of Mopelia in the South Pacific. His crew was tired and many were ill with the disease of the sailing man, scurvy. They were still recuperating there on August 2, when a heavy sea drove the *Seeadler* upon a reef. She was broken to bits. Von Luckner, with three officers and two men, set off in one of the ship's boats to look for help, but they were captured in the Fijis and sent to jail in New Zealand for the rest of the war. Those who had stayed on Mopelia seized a French schooner that came by and sailed to Easter Island, only to be taken prisoner by Chileans and interned in Chile, a dull fate for a gallant crew.

24

The Brusilov Offensive

LAKE NAROCH OFFENSIVE

By early 1916 much of the manpower Russia had lost in the disastrous fighting the previous year had been replaced with fresh troops. Equipment, artillery, and ammunition remained in short supply, however, for Russian industry could not produce fast enough to keep up with the army's demands. At Chantilly in December, 1915, the Russian representative had agreed that his country would mount an offensive in coordination with the British, French, and Italians the following June. Plans for it were being made in February, when the German attack at Verdun caused Joffre to beg the Czar to do something to take the pressure off the French. Although the Russians were not ready to undertake an offensive, the Czar agreed to try.

The Russian front at this time was held by three groups of armies: the northern, commanded by General Aleksei Nikolaevich Kuropatkin; the western or central, commanded by General Aleksei Ewerth, and the southwestern, commanded by General Nikolai Ivanov. It was decided to use eighteen divisions from the northern and central groups in an attack on a ninety-mile front straddling Lake Naroch. Unfortunately this was an area where the German Tenth Army had built a particularly strong defense system.

On March 18, 1916, in the usual miserable cold of the Russian winter, the attack began. Artillery preparation had done little more than alert the Germans to what was coming. As the Russian soldiers advanced over the frozen ground or sloshed through the foot of water that covered the frozen lakes and rivers, German gunners poured their fire upon them. It was much like the

Somme, with the added misery of winter. The operation contin- ued until March 26 before it was abandoned. Progress had been no more than a few hundred yards at the most, and Russian casu- alties amounted to 110,000, of whom 10,000 were prisoners. Ger- man losses, about 20,000, had no visible effect on the Western Front.

On April 14 the Russian Stavka met, with the Czar presiding, to discuss plans for the June offensive. General Alekseev pre- sented a plan for the northern and central groups to attack north of the Pripet River, while the southwestern group remained on the defensive. Kuropatkin and Ewerth, having so recently suf- fered a new disaster, were reluctant to strike again at the strong German positions facing their armies. But Brusilov, who had re- placed Ivanov in command of the southwestern group, approved the plan, urging that his group should attack with the others in order to broaden the front and prevent the Germans from shift- ing reserves freely behind the lines. His arguments were persua- sive, and it was agreed that although he could expect neither reinforcements nor artillery, his command should attack when the others did on June 15. He would advance into Galicia; the other two would strike for the Vilna area.

In May there came another request for help from Joffre. The Germans were still hitting hard at Verdun, and now Italy was reeling back under an Austrian attack in the Trentino. Again the Czar was eager to help. When Alekseev asked the group com- manders if they could step up their schedules, the able Brusilov reported that he could be ready by June 1, if Ewerth could attack beside him. But Ewerth could not. So it was agreed that Brusilov would attack on June 4, and Ewerth would follow on the four- teenth.

The artillery strength of Austrian forces in Galicia had been cut back in order to build up for a planned offensive in Italy. They were left with 1,301 guns, opposed to 1,770 in Brusilov's group. Brusilov had a little over a half-million soldiers, about the same as the opposing Austrians. From south to north the Austrians had five armies—the Seventh, Austro-German Southern, Second, First, and Fourth—plus two independent corps. Brusilov had the Ninth, Seventh, Eleventh, and Eighth Armies.

Brusilov's plans depended heavily on achieving surprise, and all his preparations were made in the greatest secrecy. The attack was to be made along a front of three hundred miles, and his forces were distributed accordingly, with strongest concentrations at both ends. Thus there was no obvious assembling of forces to attract attention. Nor was there a long, revealing artillery preparation in the customary fashion, and the assault troops were not moved into the front line until the night before the attack.

The Russian guns finally opened up on the morning of June 4. Six hours later the first wave of troops moved out. The heaviest attacks came in about ten places where Brusilov hoped for breakthroughs. Along the rest of the line the Austrians were kept busy with diversionary attacks so that they could not shift reinforcements to other areas. The Russian attack was so unsuspected that on most of the front the first line of Austrian trenches was overrun during the first three days. The Russian Eighth Army, on the right flank, captured Lutsk and penetrated about twenty miles, as the Austrian Fourth Army melted before the eager Russian soldiers. On the left the Russian Ninth Army did equally well, capturing Chernovtsy and pushing on into eastern Galicia and Bukovina. So thoroughly were the Austrians demoralized that by June 6 about forty thousand prisoners were in Russian hands, and more were surrendering at the rate of over ten thousand a day.

While Brusilov's men were moving rapidly ahead and the defense was crumbling before them, word came from Alekseev that Ewerth's attack on Brusilov's right was being postponed. Then it was canceled altogether and a smaller attack, at Baranovichi, eighty miles north of Pinsk where it would do Brusilov no good, was substituted. Ewerth was afraid to attack the well-prepared Germans in front of him. Brusilov was furious. The two army corps he was given as reinforcements were no substitute for an offensive that would keep the Germans from rushing troops to the aid of the hard-pressed Austrians. The attack at Baranovichi was made on June 13, with only three divisions. They were repulsed, and a second attempt on July 3 did no better.

By mid-June Brusilov's left wing had advanced thirty miles and his right was twenty-five miles beyond Lutsk, but the operation was slowing down, for ammunition was low, transport inadequate, and reserves insufficient. On June 16, with the Hungarian General Terszyanski replacing Archduke Joseph in command of the Austrian Fourth Army, and three German divisions under

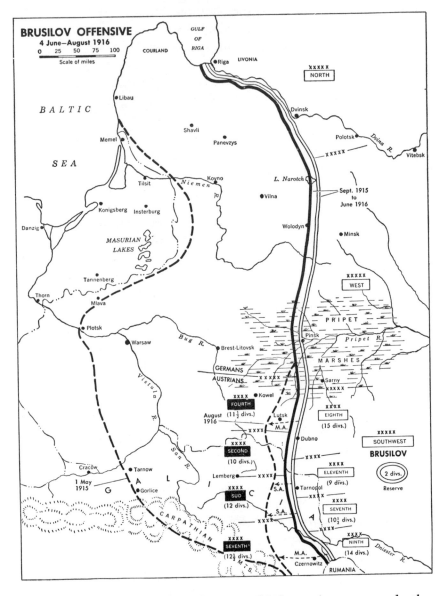

General Georg von der Marwitz added to the command, the
Austrians counterattacked on the northern end of the line. Some
territory was regained, as much as eight or nine miles in places,
but there was no breakthrough, and the offensives on both sides
soon halted.

The lull in Galicia and the absence of activity on the other parts of the Russian front gave the Germans an opportunity to send reserves to shore up the Austrian forces. Fifteen German divisions, including some from the Western Front, plus troops and artillery from the Italian front, and all aircraft units that could be spared, were sent to the embattled area.

The sorry performance of the Austro-Hungarian armies finally resulted in a unified command for the Eastern Front, something the Germans had tried to secure from the beginning. Although Conrad refused to yield, Emperor Franz Joseph, under pressure from the Kaiser, at last agreed. Command of the front from the Baltic to just south of Tarnopol was given to Von Hindenburg on July 30, 1916. Archduke Carl, with a group of armies, retained command independently of the rest to the Rumanian border; but with German General Hans von Seeckt assigned to his staff, Carl also came close to being under Von Hindenburg's control.

On the Russian side of the front Brusilov too had received reinforcements, despite the inadequacies of Russian transport and supply. Minor action had continued, and on July 28 Brusilov launched a new offensive. Some gains were made, but the cost was heavy. The Russians attacked again in August and in September, gaining all of Bukovina and climbing the lower slopes of the Carpathians. But losses mounted, and with no support elsewhere, having used up his reserves and run short of ammunition, Brusilov could go no farther.

What had Brusilov accomplished? While the offensive had been tactically successful, strategically there was little gain, for the Russian Stavka had given Brusilov little support. Alekseev, not understanding Brusilov's idea of a surprise attack all along the front, had tried to get him to change his plan and had made no preparations to move forces from the north to exploit his success. With the militarily inexperienced Czar in overall command of the Russian armies, Alekseev was actually the commander. Yet he lacked the rank to force Ewerth and Kuropatkin to carry out their part of the offensive. Brusilov's troops had caused the enemy about a million casualties, almost half of them prisoners, but Russian losses came to almost the same figure, and probably contributed to the subsequent collapse of the Russian Army.

On the other side, however, Brusilov's offensive had all but ruined the Austro-Hungarian armies and shattered Austrian pride by forcing them under German control. It had caused the halting of the Austrian offensive in Italy and had reduced the pressure at Verdun by requiring the transfer of units from the Western Front. It also resulted in Rumania's finally entering the war on the side of the Allies.

25

Rumania's Short War

Like Bulgaria, Rumania had remained neutral and encouraged both sides to make offers for her support. In her case the Allies could offer more, for the territory she coveted belonged to Austria-Hungary and Bulgaria, both Central Powers. As Brusilov's offensive moved rapidly forward, Rumania finally talked in earnest with the Allies, and on August 17, 1916, signed a secret treaty. Von Falkenhayn, realizing what Rumania was doing, rushed preparations to meet an offensive he expected the Rumanians would make in Transylvania. Rumania declared war on the Central Powers on August 28, ten days earlier than Von Falkenhayn had anticipated.

The Allies were hopeful that Rumania would join them in an effort to cut German communications with Turkey, but as Von Falkenhayn surmised, her eye was on Transylvania. A part of Hungary at the time, it had been promised her as part of the victors' spoils, but her government was determined to occupy it as soon as possible. Consequently the Rumanian military leaders planned to attack there with three armies, leaving only one, the Third, to defend the Bulgarian border.

Von Falkenhayn, meanwhile, had made plans for a twofold attack on Rumania, from Transylvania and from Bulgaria, to converge upon Bucharest. Having been relieved as Chief of the General Staff on August 29, 1916, he hastened to take command of the German Ninth Army, which had been reconstituted with three German and two Austrian divisions and was stationed in Austria-Hungary. With the Austrian First Army on his left he assembled his forces in western Transylvania.

The First, Second, and Fourth Rumanian Armies had started for Transylvania immediately after the declaration of war and

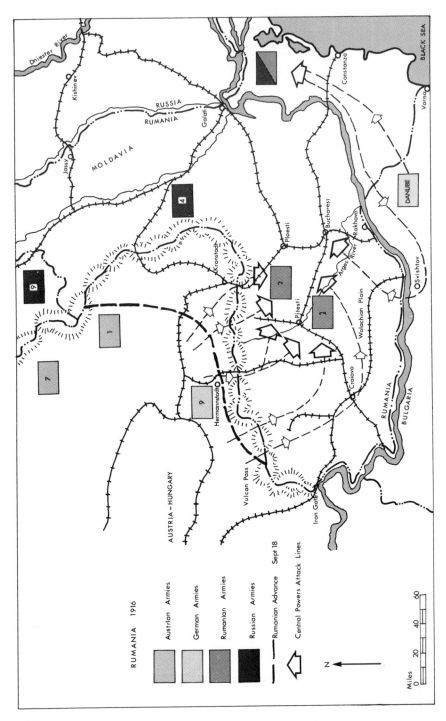

RUMANIA 1916

Austrian Armies

German Armies

Rumanian Armies

Russian Armies

Rumanian Advance Sept 18

Central Powers Attack Lines

Miles
0   20   40   60

N

AUSTRIA – HUNGARY

Dniester River

Kishinev

RUSSIA
RUMANIA

Galati

Jassy

MOLDAVIA

4

9

1

7

Kronstadt

Ploesti

9

Hermannstadt

Vulcan Pass

Iron Gate

2

Bucharest

Pitesti

Craiova

Walachian Plain

Arges River

Rakhovo

Svishtov

RUMANIA

BULGARIA

Constanza

DANUBE

Varna

BLACK SEA

196

were across the border before Von Falkenhayn arrived in Austria-Hungary. At first they met with little opposition as they advanced slowly through the Transylvanian Alps, their units divided among several passes on a two-hundred-mile front. They were on the plain beyond the mountain when Von Falkenhayn's army turned them back on September 30 at Hermannstadt. The Austro-Germans attacked again on October 8 at Kronstadt, driving the Rumanians back into the mountain passes. There they stayed, stubbornly defending the passes while Von Falkenhayn tried to cross first one, then another. Finally, after being reinforced by five German divisions, he concentrated overwhelming force at the Vulcan Pass and pushed through. By late November his troops were pursuing the retreating Rumanians in the Walachian Plain.

Meanwhile the three Rumanian armies had scarcely started into Transylvania when Field Marshal von Mackensen, with a mixed force of Germans, Bulgarians, and Turks, crossed from Bulgaria into southern Rumania on September 1 and pushed ahead toward the Black Sea port of Constantsa and the railroad line leading from it. The Rumanian Third Army hastened to the area, joined by a division of Serbian volunteers and three divisions moved down from Transylvania. Three more were sent from Russia. Von Mackensen was halted long enough to add two Turkish divisions to his army. Then he tried again. A shortage of ammunition and equipment on the Rumanian-Russian side helped him, and on October 23 the port and the railroad were in his hands. Once his position was secure he divided his force, leaving part to defend the area, and with the rest turned west to Svishtov, to join Von Falkenhayn.

The two German commanders met west of Bucharest on November 27. At the Arges River the combined forces attacked the Rumanian Army on December 1. The battle raged for three days before the Rumanians withdrew and, abandoning Bucharest, retreated to the north and east. Von Falkenhayn's troops entered the city on December 6.

Then the invaders fell prey to the forces of nature. Rain, incessant, torrential, turned streams to rivers, and rivers, with very few bridges left standing, became impassable. Cold weather and shortages of food added to the problems. As 1916 ended, the Ru-

manians halted on the far side of the Siret River. The province of
Moldavia was all that remained to them of their country. They set
up a temporary capital at Jassy, where it remained for the rest of
the war. Their support of the Allied cause had been brief, ineffective, and, for them, disastrous.

26

Austrians in Italy, 1916

FIFTH BATTLE OF THE ISONZO

Like the Russians, the Italians received a plea from Joffre in February, 1916, for some sort of diversionary attack to reduce the pressure at Verdun. General Count Luigi Cadorna, the Italian commander, responded with the Fifth Battle of the Isonzo, fought from March 9 to 17. Although the men were tired and their supplies were short, Cadorna prepared plans in haste and made his attacks both north and south of Gorizia. Nasty weather, including fog, rain, and snow, made progress impossible, and after a futile week Cadorna called a halt.

THE TRENTINO

During the long winter Austrian Field Marshal Conrad von Hötzendorf had decided that the time was right to launch an offensive operation from the Trentino down into the Italian plain. If successful, he could cut the Alpine and Isonzo fronts from the rest of Italy. Von Falkenhayn opposed the idea and refused to help, but he had no control over Conrad, who proceeded with plans and the buildup of forces for the attack.

Conrad assembled two armies in the valley of the Adige, the Eleventh, commanded by General Viktor Freiherr von Dankl, and the Third, under General Kövess von Kövessháza. Together they comprised 350,000 men on a front of thirty miles. They had 2,400 guns, some of them taken from the armies in Galicia.

After Cadorna's intelligence sources informed him about the Austrian buildup, he began to move troops from the Isonzo area to reinforce the First Army and to build up a new Fifth Army in the area of Treviso and Vicenza. He also ordered the commander of the First Army, General Roberto Brusati, to strengthen his defenses. But Brusati did little about it. Cadorna replaced him with General Guglielmo Pecori-Giraldi on May 8, but when the Austrians attacked, a week later, the army was still unprepared.

The usual preliminary artillery attack was effective, and when the Austrian infantry advanced they easily pushed the First Army defenders back. Although Italian resistance stiffened, in the first five days the attackers had gained five miles. By the end of May they had captured Arsiero and Asiago in fierce, often hand-to-hand fighting.

On June 2 Cadorna stiffened the Italian defense by throwing in the Fifth Army. By this time the Austrians were feeling the results of long, inadequate supply lines, insufficient reserves, and difficult terrain. By June 10, about twelve miles from the point of origin, they had slowed almost to a halt. On the sixteenth the Italians counterattacked. Conrad's forces had been depleted in the preceding week by the demands of the Galician front. Men and guns had been taken from Italy and rushed to bolster the Austrian armies staggering under the weight of the Brusilov offensive. Now outnumbered in Italy, the Austrians were ordered back to strong defensive positions, in a line only a short distance forward of their original front. The threat to Italy was over. It had been a costly fight for the Italians, whose casualties amounted to about 147,000, compared with the Austrians' 81,000. But for Austria-Hungary not only had it gained nothing, it had contributed to Brusilov's success by using men and artillery which might otherwise have been in Galicia to strengthen the Austrian defense.

SIXTH BATTLE OF THE ISONZO

For the Trentino operation Conrad had also transferred troops from the Isonzo area, as had Cadorna. But Cadorna had the advantage of interior lines and adequate railroads. When the Trentino offensive ended he quickly moved troops back to the Isonzo, and by August 6 he was ready to attack there once again. This time he was well supplied with artillery, and he opened the attack with an extremely heavy bombardment. Behind it the attack proceeded swiftly. Italian soldiers swarmed over the heights north and south of the town of Gorizia. On August 9 Gorizia itself fell. To the south the Italians advanced on the Doberdo Plateau, pushing the Austrians from the defenses east of Monfalcone.

Monte San Michele, the key to the Carso Plateau, was now in Italian hands, and by August 17 Italian troops controlled the western end of that inhospitable area, thirty miles of which separated them from Trieste, Cadorna's objective. The Carso, or Karst, which lay ahead, is a dry, barren area, with shallow soil and large areas of bare limestone which made it necessary to blast or drill out gun emplacements and other defenses. The rigors of the terrain are matched by the climate, which tends to be hot by day and icy cold at night. Crossing the Carso would not be easy.

THREE MORE BATTLES OF THE ISONZO

Cadorna planned a series of operations, setting limited objectives and short periods of time, to be separated by periods of rest and recuperation, in order to conserve his resources. Each operation is considered a separate Battle of the Isonzo: the Seventh fought from September 14 to 17, the Eighth from October 10 to 12, and the Ninth from November 1 to 4. The Austrians moved thirty-five divisions into the area to meet the attacks and held the Italians to slight gains, exacting a heavy toll of casualties.

Torrential rains and bitterly cold weather forced a halt to operations in the Isonzo area at the end of November. Ice and snow made mere existence difficult and coordinated military action impossible. Both sides took advantage of the break in activity to build up their defenses and strengthen their forces both in the Isonzo area and in the Trentino. Since August Italy had been at war with Germany as well as Austria, and the Italians expected they would soon be facing German troops. They intended to be prepared for an attack early in 1917.

27

Salonika

After the Bulgarians drove the Allied Salonika Force back into Greece in December, 1915, the Armée d'Orient, or the Armées Alliées en Orient—it was called by both names—dug in on a seventy-mile front running from the Vardar Marshes to the Strymonic Gulf, twenty-five miles from the nearest Bulgarian posts. There four French and five British divisions, united in a loose sort of command under French General Maurice Sarrail, waited, plagued by malaria and paratyphoid and uncertain in their relations with the politically confused Greeks. While they waited they constantly worked at fortifications, constructed roads and railroads toward the Serbian border, built up supplies, and gradually increased in strength to about 250,000 men. By the spring of 1916 Salonika was one of the best-defended cities in Europe.

As part of the attempt to pull German forces away from the area of Verdun, Joffre ordered Sarrail at the end of January, 1916, to prepare for an operation that would convince the Bulgarians and the Germans that he might be about to launch an offensive from Salonika. Von Falkenhayn at the same time, as part of his preparations for the Verdun operation, sent some German troops to Bulgaria and urged his allies to try an offensive against Salonika to draw French and British troops away from the Western Front. General von Gallwitz started preparing for an attack, but the limitations of supply lines and weather gradually put an end to preparations, and Von Falkenhayn himself ordered them stopped in March. Clearly such an operation would need help from the Western Front, and he could not spare it.

In April the French left the fortified area around Salonika and moved closer to the frontier. Two British brigades went over to the region south of Lake Doiran. There British cavalry skirmished with some German cavalry units on April 10. Joffre by this time was trying to persuade the British to support a major offensive in Macedonia. It might, he argued, bring Rumania and Greece into the war and force the Central Powers to move reinforcements from other areas. The British, however, were opposed to the idea. They doubted that either of those things would happen, but fundamentally they were opposed to becoming involved to any large extent in the Balkans. It was finally agreed at least that the British force in Macedonia would not be reduced, and the British appointed a new commander for their forces there, Lieutenant General George F. Milne, a man they thought could stand up against the dictatorial ideas of General Sarrail.

In May Bulgarian troops crossed the Greek border in the Struma valley and, with the approval of the Greek government, occupied Fort Rupel. They set up a new defense line ten miles within the Greek border, convincing Sarrail that an offensive must be mounted by summer to drive them out. In retaliation the French took over control of the city of Salonika, blockaded Greek ports, demanded that the Greek Army be demobilized, and insisted on a change of government, because they considered the existing one pro-German. With Allied warships off the coast, the Greeks gave in.

Russian successes in Galicia and Rumania's increased interest in entering the war on the Allied side aroused British support for an offensive from Salonika in the summer of 1916. Even before Rumania made it conditional on her declaration of war that such an operation be undertaken, Sarrail was making preparations. Six reconstituted Serbian divisions and a Russian brigade joined his force in July. In August some Italian and Albanian units arrived, bringing the total strength to 350,000. They were stretched out along a front of 170 miles westward from the coast to Florina. Before preparations to attack could be completed, however, the Bulgarians took the initiative.

Two German divisions, one transferred from the Western Front, had been provided to strengthen the Bulgarian force. Commanded by General Arnold von Winckler, these divisions were in the center of the front. The right was held by the Bulgarian First

Army under General Kliment Boyadjief. It would make the main attack, while the Bulgarian Second Army, based on Fort Rupel, was poised to attack into eastern Macedonia.

Attacking down through the Monastir Gap on August 17, the Bulgarians caught the Serbians, who had expected to be attacking in a few days themselves, off guard and pushed them back from Florina. Another attack farther east drove the French back across the Struma River near Seres, while still farther east the Bulgarians advanced to the coast with little opposition, and a Greek corps in the forts at Kavalla surrendered to them. But British troops destroyed bridges across the Struma and prevented the Bulgarians from crossing. And the Serbians, despite repeated attacks, stiffened and held firm.

Sarrail revised his plans, and on September 12 the Serbs spearheaded an Allied counterattack in the west. The terrain was mountainous, and Bulgarian outposts controlled the highest, best defense points. Gradually the Serbs scaled the heights and the Bulgarians withdrew to the Crna River. The offensive was renewed on November 10 in bitter cold, made worse by gale-driven snow. Again the Bulgarians moved back, and on November 19 Monastir fell to the French and Serbian cavalry.

There the advance halted. The Bulgarians, despite German reinforcements, were on the verge of collapse, but the Allies had pushed to their limit. They too were on the point of exhaustion, and they were running short of supplies. Their casualties since action began in August had reached about fifty thousand. The Bulgarians counted ten thousand more than that. Since neither side would divert forces from the Western Front to support this theater, the front remained quiet until May, 1917. Sarrail's attempt to launch an offensive before that was frustrated by the Serbs, who refused to cooperate. After two ineffective weeks he called it off.

28

The Less-Known War against Turkey—1915-1916

There was never any doubt that the primary enemy for the Allies in World War I was Germany. Nor after Gallipoli was there any doubt that the Western Front would be the decisive one, that until victory was won or lost there the war would continue. Yet in several other areas, of which the Eastern Front was the most important, there was significant fighting. For both Germany and the Allies these lesser fronts were diversions that they could not afford to ignore, and although the outcome was not influenced by them, each made some contribution to the total war. Among them was Mesopotamia.

MESOPOTAMIA

After the British seized Al Qurna in December, 1914, there was no military action in Mesopotamia for several months. Having decided to pursue the program they had begun, the British delayed attacking until they had built up a corps of two divisions under the command of General Sir John Nixon. The Turks too had been strengthening their forces in the area, in a semicircle facing the British positions. On April 12 about fifteen thousand of them attacked at Shaiba, southeast of Basra, only to be driven off. Behind them they left automobiles, river boats, and equipment, all of which the British put to good use.

The roads of Mesopotamia were rivers, and the strategy to be followed there was influenced by these waterways. On the last day of May, 1915, a reinforced brigade led by Major General

Charles V. F. Townshend started up the river from Al Qurna to attack the Turkish camp on high land to the north. The attack was successful. Pursued by the British, the Turks fled upriver to Amara. There Townshend, with a party of thirty sailors and soldiers, accepted the garrison's surrender on June 3.

The main body of Turks had withdrawn to Kut-el-Amara, where the Tigris is connected to the Euphrates by a branch called the Shatt-el-Hai. The western end of this connection is at Nasariya, only one hundred miles from the British base at Basra. In July Major General George F. Gorringe led an expedition by land from Al Qurna to Nasariya, where he was joined by gunboats that had come up the Euphrates from Basra. The Turks were driven out on July 25 and went via the Shatt-el-Hai to join the garrison at Kut-el-Amara.

In anticipation of a British attack, the Turks blocked the Tigris with booms and stationed about ten thousand men under Nur-ud-Din Pasha on both sides of the river, seven miles east of Kut. General Townshend, with eleven thousand troops, came up the river on September 27, 1915, and with a small force attacked the Turkish garrison on the south side of the river.

Knowing that the main Turkish force was on the other side, the next morning Townshend opened an attack on the center of the Turks' front and sent the bulk of his troops around their left wing in an attempt to encircle them. However, the Turks avoided envelopment and fled up the river to Ctesiphon, twenty miles southeast of Baghdad, Townshend following as far as Aziziya, more than half way to Ctesiphon.

The lure of Baghdad was strong, and Nixon was eager to take the ancient city. He could not attempt it, however, without permission from his superiors, the Viceroy of India, Lord Charles Hardinge, and the Secretary of State for India, Austen Chamberlain. In response to Nixon's request, Chamberlain said he might "march on Baghdad if he is satisfied that the force he has available is sufficient for the operation." Nixon thought it was, and with the added strength of two divisions which had been promised to him earlier he was confident he could also hold it.

Townshend at Aziziya was three hundred miles from his base at Basra. He had fifteen thousand men but an inadequate supply of boats, and his men were weary and half sick from the heat. Although he was well aware that delay would make his job harder by giving the Turks time to build up, Townshend waited at Aziziya for about six weeks, during which he received some of the supplies he needed but none of the reinforcements for which he hoped. On November 11, 1915, he at last moved out.

At first the British attack met with success, but as Townshend's hopes grew, Nur-ud-Din, at Ctesiphon, received thirty thousand new troops. With overwhelming strength he pushed the British back, all the way to Kut, where Townshend and his men took refuge. Sending a cavalry brigade and all the sick and wounded back to Ali Gharbi and to Basra, with nine thousand men Townshend prepared to stand siege. He had not long to wait. By December 7 Kut was surrounded by Turks.

For almost five months Townshend held out against continual bombardment, hoping for relief. Three different expeditions were sent by the British in futile attempts to break through to Kut-el-Amara. But the Turks drove them all back. Only a few supplies were dropped from airplanes to the garrison, a pitifully small amount for the thousands of sick and hungry men. Finally Townshend gave up. On April 29, 1916, he surrendered, the first British commander to yield a major force to an enemy since the Battle of Yorktown.

THE CAUCASUS

For centuries the people of once-proud Armenia had been subject to Russia, Turkey, or Persia, for their lands had long been divided among the three nations. In the summer of 1914 both Russia and Turkey promised the Armenian people living in their countries independence in return for loyal support for the war and, in the Turkish case, for inciting the Russian Armenians to revolt. As a result, about two hundred thousand Armenians served in the Russian Army during the war. When the Turkish Armenians refused to try to influence their fellow countrymen to rebel, however, the Turkish leaders seized on the opportunity to destroy them. A deliberate program was launched to wipe out or deport the entire race. Women and children were sold into slavery, and an estimated five hundred thousand men, women, and children were killed or starved to death in 1915. As Talaat Bey calmly told the American ambassador, Mr. Henry Morgenthau, "I am taking the necessary steps to make it impossible for the Armenians ever to utter the word autonomy during the next fifty years."

While this genocide was going on, the Russians and Turks were fighting in the same area of the Caucasus. Several battles were fought in 1915, with no significant strategic results. But in January, 1916, the Russians, under General Nilokai Yudenich, broke through the Turk defense line at Koprikeui and drove the Turks back sixty miles to Erzerum. Miserably cold and snowy weather forced the Russian attack to halt, but it was started again in strength on February 11, 1916. After five days the defenders of Erzerum surrendered, yielding 235 officers, 12,750 men, and 312 guns. Yudenich did not stop but pushed on through Mush and Akhlay to Bitlis, which he took on March 2.

The surrender of Kut released some Turkish units from Mesopotamia to strengthen the force in the Caucasus area. Thus reinforced, the Turks regained some territory, but they lost it and more as soon as the Russians started attacking again in July. Russian troops had been landed at Atina on the Black Sea in March and secured control of the coast as far as Trebizond, which they took on April 18. The renewed offensive in July netted them Baiburt, between Erzerum and Trebizond, and Erzinjan, a hundred miles west. All of Turkish Armenia was in Russian hands. Although the Turks retook Mush and Bitlis in August, they could not hold the cities, which were back in Russian control within seventeen days. For the remainder of 1916 the Caucasus was very quiet.

29

"Laon in Twenty-Four Hours"

NIVELLE TAKES COMMAND

By the end of 1916 French soldiers were exhausted, civilians discouraged, and Cabinet members in an anguish of frustration over the heavy losses and small gains of two years of war. Joffre's repeated vain attempts at a breakthrough on the Western Front had caused the French government and people to forget his brilliant performance at the Marne in 1914 and to consider him a profligate squanderer of French lives. It was time for a change. On December 12 Premier Aristide Briand called upon General Robert Georges Nivelle, commander in the last, successful weeks at Verdun, to replace Joffre as commander in chief of the French armies. Self-confident, articulate, charming, Nivelle was very different from calm, methodical, silent Joffre, and the change brought with it a new hope for success.

Nivelle's plan for success was an offensive in the same area that had appealed to Joffre, the Noyon salient. Nor was the concept much different. British would make a heavy diversionary attack from the north, quickly followed by a massive French assault from the south; the two would then combine to flatten the salient, destroying or driving out the Germans who had held it. Nivelle's innovations were in the size and speed of the attack and in the use of a rolling artillery barrage, such as he had used with striking success at Fort Douaumont. He set specific time goals, including a decisive breakthrough in the first twenty-four or at most forty-eight hours. "Laon in twenty-four hours!" was his pledge to the government, and these words became a rallying cry to his officers and men.

It was essential to Nivelle's philosophy that this cry and the concepts behind it be hammered into the consciousness of all his officers, down to company commanders. A memorandum issued on December 16 and widely distributed emphasized the idea that the coming attack was an all-out offensive aimed at destroying the principal German forces. It also included important tactical details, such as the fact that no earthwork protection was to be provided for the French artillery because Nivelle had observed that German counterbattery response to preparatory bombardments was usually weak.

General Haig was at first favorably impressed by Nivelle's energy and practical experience, but approval changed to troubled doubt when Nivelle won the support of Lloyd George, who, without informing Haig, placed him under Nivelle's command. Eventually it was agreed that Nivelle would be in command for the great spring offensive only and that Haig could appeal any orders he considered perilous to his forces. Then Haig went loyally to work preparing the British part of the operation, a preliminary assault in the area of Arras, north of the main attack. French troops, despite the losses and exhaustion they had suffered at Verdun, were to make the main effort, striking the Noyon salient from the south, along the Aisne River. To France, therefore, would go the glory of the decisive breakthrough, which would drive the Germans at last from her soil.

U-BOATS BRING A NEW ALLY

As 1916 passed, Germany increasingly felt the pinch resulting from Britain's blockade. Supplies of food and vital raw materials were short. Little was getting through from abroad, but while the U-boats were closely restricted the Allies continued to receive shipments from overseas. There was no end to the war and the shortages in sight, for the battles in the west had not achieved the victory for which Germany longed.

Limited though they were by the Sussex Pledge, U-boats in November, 1916, sank more than a quarter of a million tons of shipping. It is not surprising that many in Germany believed that if only the U-boats could sink on sight they could account for twice as much and in a short time could cut so deeply into the vital British supply lines that Britain would be forced to sue for peace. Chancellor von Bethmann-Hollweg, however, had had enough protests from the United States over American lives lost to U-boats. German military men assured him that if the United States did go to war next time it happened, she was so unprepared that Britain could not hold out long enough for her to send effective help to France. Nevertheless, Von Bethmann-Hollweg did not care to risk their being wrong. Under pressure from General Ludendorff and after long arguments in the German government, however, the Chancellor finally conceded that unrestricted submarine warfare might result in a German victory. With his approval, orders were issued by the Kaiser, and on January 31 the American ambassador to Germany was informed that as of the following morning all shipping in the waters around Great Britain, France, Italy, and in the Eastern Mediterranean would "be stopped with every available weapon and without further notice."

It seemed at first that the gamble would pay off. From an average of 37 British ships lost per month from August to December, 1916, the sinkings jumped to 105 in February, 1917, 127 in April, until 1 out of 4 ships that sailed did not come back. Nothing that was tried to prevent sinkings seemed to work, and the British Admiralty grew as pessimistic as the German Naval Staff was optimistic.

Von Bethmann-Hollweg was right, however. On February 3, 1917, President Woodrow Wilson severed diplomatic relations with Germany. As he was reporting the action to a joint session of Congress, the American freighter *Housatonic* was being sunk off the Scilly Islands. Her crew in their lifeboats were towed by the submarine *U–53* until her skipper found a British trawler to take them safely ashore.

More ships were sunk in the weeks that followed. The United States declared a condition of armed neutrality, and put guns on her merchant ships. In February a new element was added when the British intercepted a note from the German Foreign Minister, Arthur Zimmerman, to the German minister in Mexico and handed a copy to the U.S. ambassador in London, Walter Hines Page. In it Zimmerman proposed that if the United States declared war, Mexico should ally herself with Germany "to reconquer the lost territory in New Mexico, Texas, and Arizona." Publication of the note in the United States press on March 1, 1917, added fuel to a fire of anti-German sentiment that was already hot. Another month went by and several more U.S. vessels were sunk before President Wilson, on April 2, went to the Congress and asked for a declaration of war. "The world must be made safe for democracy!" he said. Four days later the United States was in the war.

LUDENDORFF'S WITHDRAWAL

General Ludendorff had no offensive plans for 1917. He was confident that an Allied offensive would be launched and repulsed on the Western Front at high cost to the Allies. He also anticipated effective economic results from the unlimited U-boat attacks. The combination, he hoped, would accomplish what none of the bloody campaigns of the preceding years had done and bring the Allies to beg for peace.

Haig had kept up repeated limited attacks during most of the winter. They hurt the Germans, although British gains were small. Reports of plans for a great Allied spring offensive persuaded Von Hindenburg and Ludendorff to make a crucial decision, to give up considerable conquered territory but at the same time greatly strengthen the Germans' defensive position, by withdrawing from the Noyon salient to a line that in places was twenty-five miles farther east. The carefully prepared Siegfried Stellung, called the Hindenburg Line by the Allies, was twenty miles shorter than the old line and could be held by thirteen fewer divisions. It was laid out in the most complicated German system, heavily fortified and liberally supplied with guns. Front-line trenches were designed to delay and then yield, to draw attackers on to less penetrable fortifications behind.

In front of the Hindenburg Line the Germans created a great barren wasteland, liberally sown with booby traps, as they withdrew from their old trenches. Methodically they held off the Allies as they pulled back and destroyed every creation of man or nature that could possibly be of use. Villages were burned, every road and railroad blasted, every apple orchard chopped down, and even a great château leveled. Most of the German troops carried out the orders with sorrow, for many of them had been living for two years in the houses they burned, and had come to know the women and children whom they herded into the few remaining villages and left as a ration burden on the French. Ludendorff later claimed that he had ordered that wells not be poisoned, observing a traditional taboo of civilized warfare, but Allied accounts assert that wells were fouled or otherwise made unusable.

The first notice the British had that the Germans were withdrawing came when German artillery fire started falling on what had been German front-line trenches on February 24. The withdrawal continued until April 5. At first the Allies were pleased at this development, but time would prove the wisdom for the Germans of Ludendorff's action.

NIVELLE STRANDED

The German withdrawal gave Nivelle most of the territory he had hoped to seize, as the Noyon salient melted away. Three of the five French armies slated for the attack were cut off from their objectives by the devastated area. As Winston Churchill wryly remarked in his account of these events, "However absorbed a Commander may be in the elaboration of his own thoughts, it is necessary sometimes to take the enemy into consideration." Nivelle pushed ahead with his plans, nevertheless, asserting that nothing important had changed. He pointed out that both the main British attack in the north and the main French attack in the south would strike beyond the flanks of the Hindenburg Line in any case. This was true, barely, but Ludendorff's shortened lines allowed him to shift reserves and strengthen these threatened areas, which were already protected by formidable natural obstacles—Vimy Ridge in the north and the Craonne Plateau in the south.

While the Germans were pulling back and leaving Nivelle geographically stranded, changes in the French government were eroding his political support. The Briand government fell in mid-March over an issue unrelated to Nivelle, and a new government headed by Alexandre Ribot was formed. The new Minister of War was Paul Painlevé, a brilliant mathematician and reasonably able statesman, who had opposed Nivelle's appointment from the first and had resigned from Briand's government in protest against it. Only a few days before the British attack was to begin he strongly urged Nivelle to reconsider the advisability of changing or abandoning his plans. But Nivelle was unshakable. The German withdrawal had freed more French divisions than German, he said, for French lines as well as German had been shortened. Confident of success, he saw no cause for worry. Besides, if he did not gain decisive victory in forty-eight hours, he would call off the attack. There would be "no more Sommes." Painlevé could have canceled the approaching offensive only by relieving Nivelle of command. Psychologically and practically this was almost impossible, for all preparations were made, troops were moving into their pre-attack positions, and the British had already started preparatory artillery bombardment.

Nivelle's confidence was not shared by his own army group commanders. Pétain doubted that he had the resources to carry out the ambitious plan. Franchet d'Esperey refused to take responsibility for approving it. General Alfred Micheler, whom Nivelle chose to lead the main attack when Pétain balked, himself became pessimistic. Only Nivelle and General Charles Mangin and Nivelle's chief of staff, Colonel d'Alençon, remained enthusiastic. D'Alençon knew that he was dying of tuberculosis and was determined to see Nivelle win the war immediately.

THE BRITISH AT ARRAS

The British bombardment began on April 1, along a fourteen-mile front, from Croisilles in the south to just north of Vimy Ridge. It was the most massive bombardment ever carried out, expending eighty-eight thousand tons of shell in contrast with the fifty-two thousand tons that had prepared the way for the Somme offensive in 1916. The initial assault, already postponed from April 4 to April 8, was delayed one more day at Nivelle's request, to Easter Monday. In the huge underground chalk cellars and caves of Arras the British and Canadian troops waited. "Confident and seasoned," Haig had described their appearance when he inspected them before the battle.

With snow and sleet in their faces but morale high, on a cold April morning the troops moved forward behind a rolling barrage. There were twelve divisions on the British front. On the right was General Sir Edmund Allenby's Third Army, with the

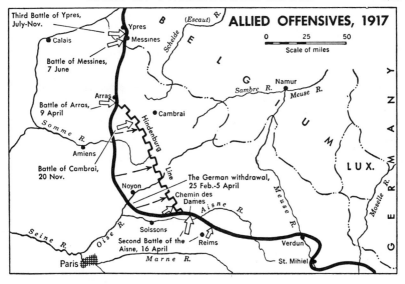

VII, VI, and XVII Corps right to left. On the left was the First Army of General Sir Henry Sinclair Horne, with the Canadian Corps and the XXIV and I. Allenby's sector ran from eight miles south to about three miles north of Arras. Only the right wing of Horne's army was involved, but the Canadian Corps on his right was facing Vimy Ridge, the most formidable obstacle and prized objective of the entire offensive. The extraordinary flatness of the Flemish countryside gave this low but dominating ridge critical importance, and the Canadians hoped to take it the first day. They fought the few muddy miles to the ridge's crest, battling determined German resistance, and were rewarded by a view across miles of the Douai plain—and miles of German positions. The northern end of the ridge still remained in German hands, however.

Between Vimy Ridge and the Scarpe River, in Allenby's sector, the XVII Corps of Lieutenant General Sir Charles Fergusson made progress that was dramatic for the trench-deadlock period of World War I. His men broke through the first, second, and third German lines, advancing three and a half miles, and taking the town of Fampoux. It was the longest one-day advance since 1914. As the bad news flowed into German High Command headquarters back in Kreuznach, Ludendorff grew anxious to the point of panic. The stolid strength of Field Marshal von Hindenburg, Ludendorff's nominal superior, then came into its own as he calmed his brilliant chief of staff with a hand on his shoulder and the words, "We have lived through worse times than this together."

Vimy Ridge and Fampoux marked the important Allied gains of the first day. The right wing of Allenby's army attacked objectives that had been altered by the earlier German devastation program and made slow progress. On April 10 the Canadians secured the rest of Vimy Ridge, but all along the front the going was slower. While British artillery and supplies were being slowly dragged up behind the attackers, over the newly captured shell-cratered land, the front-line soldiers were reaching areas where barbed wire had not been cut by the barrage and enemy machine gunners still held out. They should also have been meeting German reserves, but contrary to his orders, General Baron Ludwig von Falkenhausen, who commanded in that sector, had held his six divisions of reserves—he had six in the line—too far back.

Deprived of aerial reconnaissance by the bad weather, the British commanders did not know that the German reserves were moving up. While Allenby was ordering pursuit of the enemy at full speed, a whole new army was on its way to meet him.

Gains on the third day were slight and costly. General Sir Hubert Gough's Fifth Army, ordered into action on Allenby's right, crept forward to Bullecourt, where it was halted. Near the newly captured village of Monchy-le-Preux Allenby tried to send in cavalry, always close at hand for the anticipated breakthrough. The attempt failed, with heavy loss of men and horses.

The British were now almost at a standstill. The original attack troops were exhausted and could do little more until relieved and rested. They had achieved a smashing first-day success and absorbed some German reserves, diversion enough for the French, it seemed.

On the French front the attack was finally launched on April 16. Haig waited impatiently for news, and when none came he shrewdly interpreted it as "a bad sign." By April 18 it was clear that Nivelle was in trouble, and Haig decided he must renew the British attack to support his allies. The new effort, begun on April 23, gained little, for the Germans had created a new defense line in a short time and under fire. Despite misgivings, Haig tried again on May 3. The Canadians took the town of Fresnoy, but held it only a few days. Farther south Bullecourt, by then in ruins, finally fell. But these small gains were not worth the price.

The battle dragged on through May without much change. When it finally ended, the British had lost about 150,000 men and the Germans 100,000. But the British had gained Vimy Ridge, an important anchor for the Allied line. It would prove its worth the following spring.

THE CHEMIN DES DAMES

The left end of the new defenses of the Hindenburg Line was at the Aisne River, just west of its junction with the Vesle. From there the German line ran eastward, cutting a small bridgehead south of the Aisne, around three miles wide and a few hundred yards deep, then north for several miles, giving the French a bridgehead north of the river on the rugged Craonne Plateau, or Heights of the Aisne, before curving southeastward again across the Aisne toward Reims. The old Noyon salient had thus been re-placed with a smaller one, which became known as the Laon Cor-ner, after the city which sat behind the German lines, about mid-way along the base of the new bulging triangle.

The Craonne Plateau, traversed by steep ridges and deep ra-vines, all generally parallel to the river and to the front, was one of the most naturally defensible regions of the entire Western Front. The chalky rock lent itself readily to construction of trenches and tunnels, and the Germans had laced the area with them. Dominating the plateau, and extending generally east and west for several miles between the Aisne and Aillete Rivers, was the Chemin des Dames Ridge, taking its name from an ancient road which followed the crest from Fort Malmaison to Craonne. Most of the ridge was in German hands, but some parts of its eastern section were within the French bridgehead north of the Aisne.

A key element in Nivelle's plan was a massive assault to seize this highly fortified Craonne Plateau. The Germans could not eas-ily plug the gap thus created, he reasoned. He would promptly widen it by pouring in reserves, who would completely rupture the German lines as they swept forward, first toward Laon and then northeastward toward the Meuse near Sedan.

On a front less than fifty miles wide, roughly between Soissons and Reims, were massed the four armies of General Alfred Micheler's Reserve Army Group. General Mangin's Sixth Army and General Olivier Mazel's Fifth Army were in the line. Behind them was General Denis A. Duchêne's Tenth Army, and then General M. E. Fayolle's First Army, forming, as one American observer remarked, "a column of armies." In all, these four armies comprised 1,200,000 men, with seven thousand artillery pieces. Opposing them were the German Seventh Army of General Max von Boehn, and the First Army of General Fritz von Below (brother of Otto von Below). German strength in men and guns in the area was less than half that of the massed French armies.

The Germans, however, were aided not only by the strength of the natural formations, which they had improved with fortifications, but also by considerable knowledge of the French plans. They had observed the massing of the French forces, and they naturally connected this buildup with earlier reports of Nivelle's widely publicized boasts of plans for a sweeping victory. Then, on April 6 Boehn's troops captured a copy of the plan of the French Fifth Army to make the main effort against the Chemin des Dames Ridge east of Craonne. Thus informed, the Germans added still more cleverly concealed machine-gun nests—many lined with concrete—to the hundreds already emplaced. Then, despite a massive and prolonged pre-assault bombardment by the French, on April 15 German artillery which had survived the barrage struck columns of French tanks moving toward their jump-off positions, destroying many of the armored vehicles. At about the same time German planes, which had been massed in the region, swept the skies of French reconnaissance planes and artillery observation balloons.

Nonetheless, by the time the French soldiers climbed out of their trenches, at 6 A.M. on April 16, French artillery had put most of the German guns out of action. Behind a rolling barrage, in a cold rain mixed with sleet, the infantry advanced. Close behind the moving wall of exploding shells the French troops pushed on to the first line of German trenches, meeting with little resistance, partly because of the effectiveness of the artillery preparation and partly because there had been few defenders there anyway, in accordance with the German doctrine of flexible defense in depth.

Then, as the infantry approached the second line of trenches, they began to encounter the deadly fire of machine guns and rifles. German soldiers had crawled from their holes and dugouts as soon as the barrage rolled over them. Soon the entire French line was bogged down, while the barrage continued ahead, doing little damage to the dug-in Germans. German counterattacks stopped the advance completely in several places.

Thanks to the promises and inspiring words of General Nivelle, French morale was high. Reforming, the troops again surged forward, into more machine-gun fire and carefully planned counterattacks. Mazel's troops, who were making the main effort, were unable to get beyond the first line of German trenches. Mangin's men, to their left, made slightly better progress, some even reaching the German third line before being stopped.

Nivelle, forgetting his promises about ordering a halt if he did not gain immediate success, ordered the attacks to continue. Day after dismal day the French drove doggedly ahead, paying heavily for every foot they gained. Around Fort Malmaison they drove the Germans back two and a half miles and captured a large number of heavy guns. By May 5 they had cleared all of the Chemin des Dames Ridge, but the Germans still held higher positions on beyond, and the French soldiers had lost hope of ever achieving a breakthrough. They went no farther, and the battle slowed and finally stopped. How many men were casualties in this futile battle has been a cause for dispute ever since it ended. A reasonable figure seems to be about 120,000 for the French and considerably fewer for the Germans. Losses were less severe than in some of the earlier battles, but this was supposed to be a quick and easy victory.

Probably nothing reveals the character of Nivelle better than his own reaction to the failure of his offensive. Accusing some of his commanders of failing to carry out his orders properly, he relieved his most loyal and effective subordinate, Mangin, of command of the Sixth Army, with the clear implication that if he had tried harder Laon would have been taken. On May 15 Nivelle was himself relieved, to be replaced by Pétain. General Foch came out

of semi-retirement to replace Pétain as Chief of the General
Staff. Nivelle was gone, but he left a legacy of bitterness and
hatred that could not be so easily banished.

MUTINY AND PÉTAIN

On May 19, 1917, a group of soldiers at a replacement depot in
central France refused to obey orders to entrain for the front; instead they rioted, destroying much of the installation. Similar
disorders quickly spread throughout the French Army. Before
the end of the month approximately half the units of the army
were out of action, troops either refusing to fight or refusing to
replace the dissidents at the front.

The immediate cause of the mutiny was the sense of frustrated
despair and war-weariness that swept through the ranks as Nivelle's proud boasts came to naught. But there were deeper causes
for complaint than this tragic failure. In many ways the Army of
the French Republic was the most autocratic and insensitive military organization among the major powers of Europe. Neither
Russian nor German officers demanded more of their men, or
gave less attention to the soldiers' needs and interests. Discipline
was draconian, and offenses were severely punished. French military food was poorly prepared; home leaves were irregular and
haphazard, and all leaves had been canceled since February.

France had efficiently marshaled her industry and technology
in support of the war effort. But little of these skills was applied
to the needs of the troops. Railroads could promptly deliver masses
of ammunition to the front at the time and place needed; but
soldiers trying to get home on leave were left to the mercies of an
inefficient railroad system, and often used up most of their precious leave time in railroad stations or in marshaling yards.
Worst of all was medical care. Hospitals were inadequate and
short of technicians and medical supplies. Wounded soldiers had
to wait for hours for treatment, often lying in filthy cattle cars
that had been converted to temporary use for medical evacuation.
If they did not die of neglect, they contracted equally fatal teta-
nus or gangrene. One of the principal thoughts in the minds of
the mutineers, as they refused to go into battle, was a memory of
groaning wounded men waiting for treatment.

Fortunate for France at this hour was the nature of the man

who had just been named commander in chief. Henri Philippe Pétain had many shortcomings, but at this moment in history his nation needed and profited from his strengths and virtues. Bachelor Pétain had never been distracted from single-minded devotion to his duties by social demands or any sort of frivolity. As a line soldier his efforts had been consistently focused on getting the most from his soldiers by thoughtful, paternalistic attention, a policy which had always won him loyal and enthusiastic response from his men. He had consistently opposed the concept of *offensive à l'outrance,* "offensive to the uttermost," the concept that had dominated prewar thought in France and condemned thousands of French soldiers to death in the first battles of 1914. Pétain's opposition to this concept had condemned him to military obscurity before the war and during its early months.

Pétain mistrusted the current theories of warfare, which seemed to him (only half correctly) to rely more on emotion and intuition than reason. His own conclusion was that firepower rather than willpower would be the determinant of twentieth-century warfare. Perhaps most important was his feeling of humanitarianism, which caused him to care for his soldiers. Men commanded by Pétain used their weapons better, fought harder, and suffered fewer casualties than those in comparable units of the French Army. Accordingly, since war began, promotions had rapidly come his way.

Now faced with an army torn by dissension, Pétain refused to call the situation mutiny; it was "collective indiscipline." Quickly ascertaining which units could be relied upon, he deployed them into defensive positions along the entire front. At the same time he clamped a complete blackout of news on the army and, with government approval, on all means of public communication in France. Then he moved rapidly to deal with the thousands of examples of indiscipline. Deftly combining firmness with understanding, he arrested the ringleaders and had them quickly tried. Thousands were sentenced to death, but most of them went to prison or to new units where they were kept under strict surveillance. A few publicized executions, combined with the sudden disappearance of the most outspoken mutineers, led most of the troops to believe that the death sentence was being imposed on all the condemned, whereas in reality only fifty-five were shot.

While punishments were being carried out, with equal promptness and efficiency Pétain began to correct the abuses that had so long existed in the French Army. He visited every division, spoke inspiringly and encouragingly to the men, listened to their complaints, and corrected all the legitimate grievances he could.

Slowly the French Army began to recover its morale. By summer it was once more a fighting instrument, responsive to its commander and capable of holding the front. Pétain knew, of course, that it was not yet a fully reliable instrument; but during the remainder of the year he systematically set about to restore the spirit and the fighting qualities that had so suddenly evaporated after the ill-fated Nivelle offensive. By the end of the year he ordered a few carefully limited attacks, in areas where success was likely. The troops responded as he hoped; some small ground gains were made; most importantly, the French Army began to regain its self-confidence and its fighting capability.

Because of the effectiveness of the French censorship, the Germans had no inkling of what was going on in France for several weeks. Had they realized the situation, they could have marched right through the French Army. By the time rumors began to filter to them through neutral Switzerland the crisis had passed. German probes along the front were repulsed by the reliable units that Pétain had put in the line. The Germans could make no major effort because all of their reserves had been attracted to the northern part of the front by a series of British offensives.

30

Flanders' Muddy, Bloody Fields

Toward the end of 1916 Field Marshal Haig had begun to make plans for an offensive in Flanders, for he believed that the broad plains offered the greatest chance of a major success. Aside from his natural belief in the superiority of the British troops over the French, Haig thought it would be easier to overcome German defenses in the flat region of Flanders than in the hills farther inland. An offensive there would force the Germans to deploy more troops to defend the open terrain, and cause a consequent increase in problems of supply and reinforcement farther from the German frontier. If a breakthrough could be made in Flanders, Haig argued, the entire German position in Belgium and northern France would be threatened, forcing an extensive withdrawal, perhaps back as far as the border of Germany.

Haig's plans were discarded and his manpower diverted to the attack at Arras when the British government endorsed the Nivelle offensive. In late April, 1917, when it had become apparent that the French operation had failed, Haig returned to plans for an offensive in Flanders before the Germans could replace their losses and redeploy reserves that had been sent to the Aisne. This time he had the support of Prime Minister Lloyd George, who, although he distrusted Haig, realized that his plans for Flanders offered the only hope for a substantial success on the Western Front in 1917. Although the British as yet had no idea that the French Army was on the verge of mutiny, it was clear that it was suffering so severely that something would have to be done to prevent the Germans from taking advantage of French weakness. Furthermore, the situation on the Eastern Front was also becoming desperate, and the hard-pressed Russians needed action in the west to divert as many Germans as possible. Finally, the British

223

were feeling the effects of the German submarine campaign, and it had become a matter of vital importance to the government to capture the major German U-boat bases at Ostend and Zeebrugge on the Belgian North Sea coast.

Haig was almost ready to launch his Flanders offensive when he was secretly informed of the outbreak of the French mutiny. Pétain promptly appealed to him for major efforts to divert German reserves from the French front. Although the magnitude of the French disaster was not yet clear to Haig, he sensed that a determined German effort against the French Army could knock France out of the war. It was this assessment, more than any other single factor, which caused Haig to press forward with plans for a series of offensives to keep the Germans fully occupied until the end of the year. Until the offensives could begin, he ordered a renewal of the Arras assaults in an effort to attract German attention away from the French.

MESSINES AND PLUMER

Because of the urgency of the submarine threat to Britain, Haig had decided that his first major objective should be the Belgian North Sea ports. His plan was to strike northeast from Ypres toward Bruges, forcing the Germans to abandon Ostend and Zeebrugge or be cut off and pinned against the coast and the southwestern portion of neutral Netherlands. But before he could use Ypres as the base for such an offensive, Haig realized that he would have to eliminate a German salient south of Ypres, enclosing Messines Ridge. The low ridge dominated the devasted city of Ypres and its approaches, and the salient provided a base from which the Germans could threaten the communications lines behind a British attack to the northeast.

Both Ypres and Messines lay within the sector of the British Second Army, commanded by short, homely General Sir Herbert Plumer. Plumer's unprepossessing appearance had always created doubts in the minds of his superiors, but he always performed his duties well, and since no one could find a reason not to promote him, by 1915 he had become one of the most senior British generals. Reluctantly the War Office had recognized his seniority by appointing him to command of the Second Army. For two years he had performed well. But Haig, apparently still influenced by appearances, had avoided giving Plumer a major mission. Early in 1917, however, when Haig had begun his preliminary planning for the Flanders offensive, he could find no reason to put another general in charge of the operation to reduce the Messines salient. So the job was given to Plumer.

Plumer was making detailed plans while the major battles were being fought at Arras and the Aisne. In mid-May, when Haig ordered him to go ahead with the operation, Plumer was almost ready. In the intervening months he had had his engineers drive twenty shafts deep under the German lines, some under the crest of the ridge itself. While his engineers were packing these mines with TNT, Plumer ordered his artillery to begin a massive preparation. For seventeen days the British guns sprayed explosives along the German lines south of Ypres.

Just before dawn on June 7, 1917, one million pounds of TNT were detonated under the German Messines lines. Thousands of yards of German trenches were obliterated, and the crest of the ridge disappeared. The vibration from the mass explosion could be felt in London. The earth was still trembling when Plumer's troops rose from their trenches and swept past the smoking craters and into the second line of German trenches. In the first few minutes, almost seven thousand dazed Germans were captured. By evening the entire ridge was in British hands. The lines had moved eastward about two miles, completely eliminating the Messines salient. In the next few days there were a few more carefully limited assaults, to solidify the newly won positions.

In this brief battle the British suffered about seventeen thousand casualties, the Germans over twenty-five thousand. It was the first time in the war that the British had inflicted more casualties on the Germans in a major engagement than they had lost themselves. But particularly noteworthy, even though the objectives had been limited, it was the first battle on the Western Front which had gone exactly according to plan. Haig's respect for Plumer rose considerably.

THIRD YPRES

Despite Plumer's striking success, however, Haig continued with plans to use General Hubert Gough in command of the major offensive to liberate the Belgian ports. Gough's Fifth

Army, shifted from farther south, had begun to take over the narrow Ypres sector north of Messines while Plumer's operation was under way. Unfortunately Gough lacked Plumer's planning ability, organizing skill, and qualities of leadership. Haig's decision to give him the command was probably his worst of the war.

The date for launching the new offensive was delayed by the redeployment of the Fifth Army and by the largely symbolic shifting of General François Antoine's small French First Army to a narrow sector between Gough and the Belgians. Then indecision in London, where Lloyd George was having second thoughts, caused still more delay. The Prime Minister was hesitant to give final approval to another major offensive on the Western Front, where casualtites would certainly be great and results were unpredictable. However, under pressure from the Chief of the Imperial General Staff, General Sir William Robertson, and from Admiral Jellicoe, who had become First Sea Lord and was anxious to reduce the submarine threat, Lloyd George approved the offensive.

The Third Battle of Ypres began on July 31, after a two-week bombardment culminated by three days of intensive shelling. The German Fourth Army, ably commanded by General Friedrich Sixt von Armin, had received ample warning of the impending British attack and was well prepared. After easily yielding the first line of trenches to the British assault in accordance with the doctrine of flexible defense in depth, the Germans launched planned counterattacks which slowed, although they did not halt, the British advance.

Then came the autumn rains, almost a month early, making this Flanders' wettest August in thirty years. Over the centuries the Flemish farmers had developed an intricate system of drainage canals which reduced the ever-present danger of floods in the flat clay fields. Now the churning effect of hundreds of thousands of high-explosive shells had almost completely obliterated the network of canals. Water from the heavy rains stayed on the surface of the clay soil, draining off only into such depressions as trenches and shell craters. As a result, in August of 1917 the pleasant fields of Flanders became an almost impassable sea of mud.

It may be doubted if, delayed and well-advertised as it was, the British Flanders offensive could ever have been successful. With the interference of mud even more implacable than that of the Germans, success became impossible. Haig was tempted to halt the offensive. Yet he was unprepared to mount a major attack elsewhere, and he knew it was essential to maintain constant pressure on the Germans to keep them from shifting their reserves against the French.

So the dreadful attack continued, day after day, and week after week. With the help of British air superiority, some ground was gained, and the German reserves were pinned down. Otherwise the only accomplishment was to swell the tragically mounting British casualty lists.

Haig, realizing that Gough lacked the ability to direct a major operation under these dreadful conditions, shifted the Second Army front northward and gave Plumer responsibility for the Ypres sector. Gough's Fifth Army assumed a secondary role. In typical methodical fashion Plumer planned and executed three limited attacks. After each success there was a pause to shift artillery, supplies, and reinforcements forward in preparation for the next limited offensive. By October, with much smaller losses than Gough's operations had inflicted, the British front had been advanced two or three miles and part of Passchendaele Ridge was in British hands. Believing that the French had recovered sufficiently to permit the British to relax their pressure, and certain that the Belgian ports could not be reached before winter closed in, Plumer and Gough recommended that the offensive be halted.

THE HORROR OF PASSCHENDAELE

Haig next made the second most serious mistake of his career. He decided to continue the Ypres offensive. If he could drive the Germans completely off Passchendaele Ridge and out of the village beyond it, he thought, the British would hold a more easily defensible line during the winter and be prepared for an earlier renewal of the offensive in the spring. Apparently Haig had also gained so much confidence in Plumer by this time that he didn't believe the task would be too difficult.

The rains that had abated somewhat in September and early October became intensive again. Bitter chill was added to the discomforts and problems of combat in a treeless, slippery morass. Adding a further element of terror was the first use by the Germans of mustard gas, which settled in a deadly film on the damp ground and in the ponds and puddles to be found everywhere in the crater-filled countryside. British and Germans agree that conditions were the worst of any in the war. To the horrors on the ground the Germans then introduced another. With partial air superiority, for the first time they provided their troops with close air support, strafing the British soldiers with machine-gun fire.

Despite all the discomforts and hazards, the British, with dogged gallantry and devotion, clawed their way forward a few hundred yards. On November 6 the Canadian Corps finally seized the remaining portion of Passchendaele Ridge and the adjacent village. By the middle of November the battle was over.

The cost had been high. British casualties since July 31 exceeded 300,000; German losses were about 260,000. But even more serious from the British standpoint was the effect on the relationship between the British government and the Army's high command. Lloyd George, appalled by the casualties and the small gains they had bought, felt that they corroborated his earlier doubts about the offensive. He was confirmed in his distrust of Haig and Robertson and his estimate of his own strategic judgment, ignoring the fact that some kind of offensive had been essential to prevent a complete defeat of France and that his own delayed approval had given the Germans time to prepare and had squandered the good weather of July and September.

CAMBRAI

Haig had expected the Ypres-Passchendaele battle to be over in October, and had planned to follow it up with an immediate blow farther south, near Cambrai. He thought that the Germans would not be expecting another assault so late in the year, and there might be a good chance for a breakthrough. He also saw an opportunity to experiment with the two hundred tanks that were available to him.

The delays and unexpected losses at Passchendaele, however, made the prospects for a successful assault more doubtful. Adding to the difficulties was the impact of the Italian disaster at Caporetto. To bolster sagging Italian morale, five British divisions, under General Plumer, were rushed to Italy. (Six French divisions had also gone.) But even though these circumstances reduced the offensive force available to General J. H. G. Byng's Third Army to a total of six divisions, Haig still felt that the situation offered great possibilities for surprise. He knew that the Germans were aware of the depleted British situation on the Western Front, and thought they would be even less suspicious of an impending attack than they might otherwise have been.

Haig's estimates of the potentialities both of surprise and of the tanks proved to be well founded. General Georg von der Marwitz's Second German Army was totally unprepared for the sudden, violent, brief artillery preparation which fell on its trenches at dawn on November 20, just southwest of Cambrai. They were even less prepared for the appearance of some two hundred British tanks out of the smoke, dust, and gas fumes. Behind the tanks came the assaulting waves of the six British divisions.

Briefly the German defense collapsed completely. On a six-mile front the British tanks and infantry advanced for more than five miles. By this time they had outrun their supporting artillery, and the left rear of the advancing troops was threatened by the Germans defending the village of Flesquières. They were well supported by artillery, which knocked out many tanks and held up the British infantry. On balance, however, up to this point this had been the most successful attack mounted by either side since September of 1914.

Now, however, the lack of sufficient manpower was to prove a critical handicap to the British. Haig had no more reserves to throw into the gap to exploit the success. On the German side, Crown Prince Rupprecht of Bavaria, commanding the German Northern Army Group, rushed reinforcements to Von der Marwitz. Although the British were finally able to capture Flesquières, and to push on a little farther toward Cambrai, by November 29 they were still about two miles from the devastated city.

The next day the Germans launched a major counterattack. The British were able to hold most of their gains, but the salient they held was narrow and quite deep, permitting the Germans to bring effective fire to bear on the British from three directions. On December 3 Haig ordered a withdrawal, back almost to the line from which the attack had started. There the lines stabilized on December 7. Each side had lost about forty-five thousand casualties in the battle.

Haig had failed to make the breakthrough he had hoped for. However, he and his army profited greatly from the lessons learned at Cambrai. It had finally been clearly demonstrated that the benefits of surprise were greater than those of a prolonged artillery preparation. And the value of the tanks which Churchill had foreseen in 1914 had been proved, even though more of them fell victim to mechanical failures than to enemy guns. Both of these lessons had an important influence on battlefield tactics from then on.

31

Crisis in Italy

TENTH BATTLE OF THE ISONZO

General Cadorna's spring offensive in 1917, originally intended to support the Allied offensives in France, was delayed until the late spring finally melted the snow and movement became easier. It was May 12 when the Italians once more attacked in the Isonzo area.

Cadorna's plans this time were for a double offensive, one against the Bainsizza north and east of Gorizia, the other (delayed in order to convince the enemy that the first was the main one) on the Carso. Its objective was the Austrian strongpoint at Monte Hermada.

The attack opened with a tremendous artillery bombardment along the entire Isonzo front, which demolished the Austrians' first line of trenches. Behind it the infantry advanced with little opposition, securing positions that held in the face of Austrian counterattacks. On the southern end of the front on May 23 the Third Army, commanded by the Duke of Aosta, fired a ten-hour artillery barrage and then moved out through the shattered Austrian lines. Overhead military and naval planes supported the advance. From the sea British monitors fired on the flank of the Austrian defenders.

At first the Italians moved ahead, for the Austrians had been taken by surprise. By May 26 units of the Third Army were at the foot of Monte Hermada, but they went no farther. Losses had been heavy, and ammunition was running low. There were no reserves to put in. When Cadorna halted the battle two days later, Hermada was still in Austrian hands.

General Borojević von Bojna had called for help when the Italians attacked. Three divisions were rushed to him from the Russian front. On June 4 his troops counterattacked, driving the Italians back from some of their newly won positions during four days of fighting.

Meanwhile Cadorna had been preparing for a limited offensive in the Trentino. Satisfied that the Austrian counteroffensive was over, he proceeded with his schedule and attacked in the mountains with twelve divisions and twenty-four Alpine battalions. The gains were minimal and losses were great. After two and a half weeks fighting ceased.

ELEVENTH BATTLE OF THE ISONZO

Once again Cadorna returned to the attack in the Isonzo area. Assembling fifty-one divisions and 5,200 artillery pieces, he struck on August 18, 1917. Again the Third Army tried to capture Monte Hermada, but the Austrians counterattacked and drove the Italians back. The Italian Second Army had better success, capturing Monte San Gabriele and most of the western half of the Bainsizza Plateau. But casualties were very heavy, and both sides were exhausted when the battle ended on September 15.

Morale among the weary Italian soldiers had reached a low after months of misery and heavy casualties with no appreciable gain. At home the civilian population had grown generally disillusioned with the war. Food and coal supplies dwindled, labor disappeared into the army, rationing was imposed, and nothing but bad news came back from the front. Defeatist propaganda peddled by German and Austrian agents was gaining ground and spreading among soldiers as well as civilians. Cadorna had hoped that his last two offensives would revive morale, but when they yielded little gain they only added to the disillusion.

CAPORETTO

Austrian morale too was low, for the Austrians had suffered as heavily as the Italians in the repeated Battles of the Isonzo. Had Cadorna been strong enough to launch one more offensive, the front might well have collapsed before him. The Austrian Emperor, Karl I (Franz Joseph had died in November, 1916), fearful of a disaster on the Italian front, asked the German High

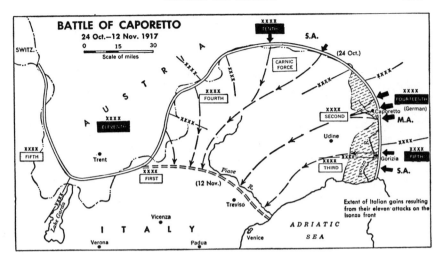

BATTLE OF CAPORETTO
24 Oct.–12 Nov. 1917

Command to relieve Austrian troops in Russia and Rumania so that he could concentrate his efforts against the Italians. The Germans, however, preferred to leave the Austrians where they were. Instead of relieving them, they agreed to send seven German divisions, with supporting artillery, air, and supply units, to the Italian front. With General Otto von Below in command, the divisions were sent at once, to be combined with eight Austrian divisions in a new Fourteenth Army. It was to be used in a great offensive on the Isonzo.

Word of the German preparations reached Cadorna, who ordered his Second and Third Armies to prepare a strong defense in depth. The commander of the Second Army, General Luigi Capello, not realizing the urgency of the situation, delayed his preparations so long that little had been done to strengthen his position, and his forces were deployed for attack rather than defense when the blow came. General Cadorna himself had misinterpreted the intelligence he received. He did not expect the main attack to come in the Second Army area and so had stationed his reserves so far south that they could not be rushed to Capello's assistance.

The German attack started with a brief but heavy artillery bombardment in the early morning hours of October 24, primarily in the area between Plezzo and Tolmino. The barrage of explosive shells and poison gas caused panic among the poorly prepared troops of the Second Army. Rain and fog added to the horror when the bombardment stopped and the men of the Fourteenth Army started moving across the front. They were well-disciplined soldiers, specially trained in a new system of tactics recently developed by the German General Staff and first tried on the Russian front by General Oskar von Hutier. Basic to the system was the preparatory bombardment. A second important element was the rolling barrage which supported the advancing infantry. Light artillery and mortars were used also for close support. Then instead of throwing the entire weight of the attack against the Italian strongpoints, the German commanders sent smaller forces through weaker zones on either side. Other units followed along to capture the strongpoints that had been cut off.

Unable to hold the German attackers, the Italian Second Army withdrew toward the Tagliamento, leaving equipment and supplies behind. Beside the Second Army the Italian Third Army also pulled back. It had been under lighter attack from the Austrian Fifth Army, but Cadorna ordered it back lest it be pushed down to the Adriatic Sea. Pursued by the Austrians, the Third Army crossed the Tagliamento on November 1.

All along the Italian front the Austrians and Germans pushed ahead. In the Trentino the Italian Fourth Army was also forced to pull back, leaving some of its units cut off in the Carnic Alps. Cadorna's hopes of holding on the Tagliamento were dashed when Austro-German troops crossed the river near Pinzano-Cornino, about forty miles above the river mouth, on November 3. Unable to hold the lower river, Cadorna ordered a withdrawal to the Piave River. On November 10 the Austrians attacked from the Trentino and took Asiago. But by now they were outreaching their supply lines and could go no farther. From Monte Pasubio to the Piave and along the river to the coast the Italians dug in as the Austrian-German offensive came to a halt.

The disaster of Caporetto, or Twelfth Battle of the Isonzo, as this battle is called, had cost the Italians 320,000 casualties. Of them about 275,000 were prisoners, the remainder killed or wounded. Several thousand badly needed guns and untold amounts of equipment and supplies had been lost. And the Austro-German forces were left in position to invade the rich valley of the Po.

The enormity of the disaster brought the dissident factions in Italy together in determination for revenge. The Italian government fell on October 30, and a new one promised better days. Production rates increased. Morale climbed. The armies behind the Piave were soon reequipped with new production artillery and munitions. From France and England came help to the stricken Italians. Before the end of October a French contingent arrived in Italy; the first British troops, led by capable General Plumer, came on November 10. By mid-December six French and five British divisions had formed a reserve behind the Italian lines.

The Battle of Caporetto also convinced the Allied leaders of the need for closer coordination. Early in November British Prime Minister Lloyd George, French Premier Painlevé, and General Foch rushed to Italy to confer at Rapallo with the new Italian Prime Minister, Vittorio Emanuele Orlando, and his Foreign Minister, Sidney Sonnino. From this conference there developed the Allied Supreme War Council. With political and military representatives from each of the Allied governments, the Council at last provided some unity to the war effort. General Cadorna was relieved of command and sent to Versailles as Italy's military representative, and General Armando Diaz took over command of the armies of Italy.

Diaz found himself with only thirty-three of the sixty-five divisions that had been available before the Battle of Caporetto. He went to work at once to organize the defenses west of the Piave, relying primarily on the Fourth and Third Armies and using the Allied troops as they arrived. Throughout November and most of December the Austro-German forces made several attempts to cross the river, but the Italian line held. Except for artillery duels and some small Italian actions that regained a few points, activity on the front stopped entirely on December 26.

32

The Russian Revolution and the Campaign of 1917

The collapse of the Brusilov offensive was a heavy blow to morale among the soldiers of the Russian Army. Short of food, clothing, equipment, and ammunition, and fighting in the worst of weather, they had little faith in the leaders who seemed to care little about them. At home, too, shortages were wearing down the already half-hearted support for the war which stretched endlessly ahead. The oppressive government of Czar Nicholas II ignored the demands from all sides for reform, and dissident groups within the country were constantly gaining support. When the Russian legislative body, the Duma, proposed formation of a coalition government and institution of a reform program in September, 1916, Nicholas refused to accept it and prorogued the Duma.

In early March, 1917, the crisis in Russia reached a head. Striking factory workers, women waiting in lines for food, and women celebrating Women's Day created large crowds in the streets of Petrograd. Demonstrations against the government and against the war soon developed as more and more people went out into the streets. The Czar ordered troops out to fire into the crowds, but many of the soldiers joined the people. Police did fire on the demonstrators, over sixty of whom were killed. The time had passed, however, when Nicholas could hold power even by force.

On March 12 a Soviet of Workers' and Soldiers' Deputies was organized in Petrograd. The Duma, refusing to disperse, formed a Provisional Government on March 14. The following day a deputation visited the Czar at Pskov to recommend and accept his

236

abdication and that of his sickly young son. The Czar's brother Michael, next in line, refused the throne, and the dynasty came to an end.

The Provisional Government, while it had no real legitimacy, was the closest thing to a legitimate government remaining. However, it represented primarily the conservative professionals. The socialist Soviet of Workers' Deputies, rapidly gaining strength in Petrograd and soon joined by other soviets in other cities, represented the working class. For a time neither faction was able to take complete charge of the government. Creation of a legitimate government depended on a national election, and the Provisional Government decided that such an election was impossible while the nation was at war.

Watching from the sidelines, the German military leaders saw a breakdown approaching in Russia. They had refrained from initiating any major action that might strengthen the patriotic sentiment in Russia and bring competing groups together. They now added another element to the situation by facilitating the passage across German territory to Russia of the Bolshevist revolutionary V. I. Ulyanov (Lenin) and about two hundred other radical Russian exiles who had been living in Switzerland. German agents also stepped up efforts to spread antiwar propaganda among Russian soldiers and factory workers.

Despite major domestic problems crying for solutions, the Provisional Government, and particularly the Foreign Minister, P. N. Milyukov, was convinced that the war must continue. He reassured the worried Allies that Russia would continue to fight. The Petrograd Soviet agreed to support the war but declared that there should be no war indemnities or annexations of territory. Since Milyukov had said that Russian aims included annexation of Constantinople, the Straits, and the Ukrainian provinces of Austria-Hungary, compromise was necessary. This resulted in a declaration that Russia aimed for "the establishment of durable peace on the basis of national self-determination." When Milyukov again assured the Allies on May 1 that Russia would fulfill her wartime agreements, the Soviet decided he must go, and organized mass demonstrations against him and against the continuation of the war.

The Provisional Government fell on May 15, and a new coalition was formed, including a number of socialists. One of them, Alexander Kerensky, became Minister of War.

While these developments were going on at home the army also had been involved in the growing socialist movement. In mid-March the Petrograd Soviet had ordered the creation of committees in all army units to exercise political authority over the soldiers, while the officers were limited to strictly military matters. In some units the committees increased the men's will to fight and raised their morale, but in many they initiated a complete breakdown of organization and discipline. Fanned by political agitators, many of them Bolshevists sent out by the Petrograd Soviet, antiwar feeling and resistance to military authority spread throughout the army.

THE KERENSKY OFFENSIVE

Kerensky, although aware of the dissension among the troops, still thought they could carry out a successful offensive in Galicia and hoped that it might serve to raise the morale and improve the discipline of the army. General Alekseev was replaced as commander in chief by General Brusilov in early June, and Brusilov began to prepare for an offensive to capture Lvov. Using personal knowledge of the area and the enemy fortifications there, he planned the attack in detail, assembling two hundred thousand men, carefully selected for their reliability. They were organized in three armies, the Eleventh, Seventh, and Eighth.

Russian artillery began firing on June 29. Two days later the Russian Seventh Army moved out, south of Lvov, and easily overran the first line of Austrians, who had not considered the Russians capable of attacking. On July 2 the Eleventh Army attacked at the juncture of the Austrian and German forces, and six days later the Eighth Army, on the south flank of the Seventh, also attacked. The Eighth met with great success, breaking through the Austrian line and seizing the hamlets of Halich and Kalush just south of Lvov. These were destined to be the last Russian victories of the war, however, for the surprised Austrians and Germans quickly regained their composure.

Although some German units had been removed from the Eastern Front during the preceding months, there still were plenty of reserves available to move to the critical area. Soon the Russians were under counterattack. With their ranks thinned by heavy losses in their own offensives, they wilted under the Austro-German pressure. A disorganized retreat soon became a rout, as the Russians fled before the pursuing enemy. By July 23 Russia's southwestern armies were no longer a viable fighting force. With negligible opposition the Germans and Austrians reclaimed all the territory Brusilov had won in 1916.

RIGA

When Russia's Coalition Government still showed no desire to make peace, the German leaders decided to launch another offensive. For the objective they selected the strongly fortified salient around Riga, at the mouth of the Dvina River, a little more than three hundred miles from Petrograd. The plan was for General Oskar von Hutier to attack from the south with the Eighth German Army. While the main force crossed the Dvina in the vicinity of Uxhall, to envelop Riga from the east, a smaller force would attack from south and west of the city.

Von Hutier made his plans carefully and trained his troops thoroughly to carry them out. He, like other military leaders on both sides, had come to believe strongly in the advantage of surprise, and his tactical planning, based on new combat-group concepts developed by the German Army General Staff, was designed to achieve it. A brief but heavy artillery barrage opened the offensive on September 1. Behind a rolling barrage the assault troops, who had moved into position the night before, advanced with little resistance. The Russian Twelfth Army abandoned its defenses and withdrew to the north.

The Riga operation was a direct threat to Petrograd itself. To add to the pressure on the Russian capital the Germans occupied two islands off the Gulf of Riga, Oesel and Dago, with sufficient forces to impress the Russian government with the possibility of an attack on the capital. The Germans had no intention of proceeding toward Petrograd, however. Although no one knew quite what was happening in the Russian government, it was apparent that there was no single-minded determination to fight. The Russian Army was falling apart, and to some extent the Germans were aware of it. Many of the Russian troops were deserting and heading for home, for rumors were rife that the vast estates of the nobility were to be divided among the people. The people, in fact, were already taking that problem into their own hands. Many of the estates near the front were plundered and their owners murdered by returning soldiers.

The reins of power in Russia were being pulled and twisted as several factions fought to gain control. Kerensky had become head of the Provisional Government on July 20, but he could not control all the elements struggling for power. At length, on November 6, 1917, Lenin, leading the Bolsheviks, successfully overthrew the Coalition Government. At once invitations went to all belligerents to negotiate peace, with no indemnities or annexations. The invitations were not accepted, and on December 15 Lenin and Trotsky signed an armistice with Germany.

The Bolsheviks anticipated a revolution in Germany similar to their own and accordingly made every attempt to foment it. When peace negotiations began at Brest Litovsk on December 23, Trotsky found the Germans insistent on detaching Poland, Latvia, and Lithuania from Russia and encouraging the Ukraine in its demand for separation. Trotsky accordingly declared a condition of "no war, no peace" and went home.

To prod the Russians, the Germans set their armies in motion again, moving out on February 18, 1918, along the whole Eastern Front. There was no army to stop them, and the Bolsheviks chose to accept German terms rather than risk destruction. Returning to Brest Litovsk they signed the peace on March 3. By its terms Finland and the Ukraine were recognized as independent. Estonia, Latvia, Lithuania, Poland, and part of Byelorussia went to Germany, at least for the duration of the war, and part of Transcaucasia went to Turkey. Since the Ukraine was to pay for independence by supplying grain to the Central Powers, one of the most important effects of the British blockade was countered. The coal-mining and metallurgical industries in Transcaucasia would counter others.

THE OTHER RUSSIAN FRONT

In the south, meanwhile, General N. N. Baratov occupied Hamadan in Persia early in 1917 and then pushed along toward

Baghdad. By March 17 he was within 150 miles of it, at Kerind. That same day Russian forces in the mountains occupied Van.

From Kerind a squadron of Cossacks, 115 of them, rode south in a dramatic dash and appeared in the British camp at Ali Gharbi on May 18, but they were the only Russians that got that far. The Turks in the area were strong enough to drive the Russians back all the way to Hamadan.

When the Czar and his government fell before the revolutionaries, the Russian units in the Caucasus melted away. But the Turks by then did not have strength enough to exploit the favorable situation offered them in the area, and the fighting simply came to an end.

33

Advance in Mesopotamia

After the surrender of General Townshend at Kut-el-Amara in April, 1916, the British went on the defensive in Mesopotamia. General Sir Percy Lake, who had relieved Nixon as commander in January, developed base facilities, built up a fleet of river transports, and reorganized his forces with reinforcements which were sent by the British, primarily from India. Meanwhile the Turks, to meet the Russian threat against Baghdad through Persia, reduced their strength in front of the British.

In August General Sir Frederick S. Maude, a very capable officer and immensely popular with his men, took command in Mesopotamia, relieving General Lake. With about forty-eight thousand men in his command, Maude formed two army corps, under Lieutenant General A. S. Cobbe and Lieutenant General W. R. Marshall, and assigned their first objective—to force General Nur-ud-Din's XVIII Corps, two hundred thousand men, out of Kut. Maude's plan was to drive the Turks from the south bank of the Tigris River, opposite Kut, and then to use his superior strength and mobility to effect a crossing of the river either to the east or west, and to envelop the Turk defenses at Kut. While Marshall's corps on the west advanced along the railroad, through Es Sinn, toward Kut, Cobbe's corps would drive north toward the river between Kut and Sanna-i-Yat.

The attack was launched on December 13 but had to stop on the twenty-sixth because of heavy rains. When it resumed on January 6, 1917, progress was slow, but by February 16 both British corps held the south bank of the Tigris along a twenty-five-mile front east and west of Kut, and Cobbe's right flank was securely entrenched north of the river at Sanna-i-Yat. On February 17 Cobbe began a major attack at Sanna-i-Yat, threatening to enve-

TURKEY IN THE WAR

Miles
0   100   200   300

243

lop Kut from the northeast. Nur-ud-Din rushed his reserves .to bolster his left, as Maude had expected. During the night of February 22–23 Marshall's corps made a surprise crossing of the river just west of the Turkish fortifications and seized a ridge only five miles from Kut. Both British corps then began a double envelopment. Nur-ud-Din, realizing the hopelessness of his situation, moved out of Kut on February 24 and withdrew toward Ctesiphon.

For almost a year the defenses at Ctesiphon had been unused. The condition of the fortifications was so poor that the commander of the Turkish Sixth Army, Halil Pasha, did not even try to make a stand at Ctesiphon. He had no reserves, since he had sent them all to Persia to meet the Russian threat. With the eleven thousand remaining men of the XVIII Corps he decided that he would try to hold Baghdad.

The advancing British stopped briefly at Aziziya to establish a base, including an airfield from which they soon had fourteen planes flying observation. Then with Cobbe proceeding on the west bank and Marshall on the east, on March 4 the British advance toward Baghdad was resumed. On March 7 Marshall's corps reached the Diyala River where it joins the Tigris. For three days the British were held up by stubborn Turkish resistance. Breaking through on March 10, they were forced to fight again as the Turks attempted a desperate stand on the outskirts of Baghdad. This time a dust storm came to the aid of the defenders, who extricated themselves from battle under its cover. Cobbe, who had been advancing west of the Tigris, had met less resistance, and his troops were already crossing the river into the city when Marshall's weary men marched in on March 11, 1917.

It was a great day for the British. The disgrace of the surrender of Kut was avenged, and all reveled in the conquest of the great and famous Baghdad. To the Turks and the Germans its loss far outweighed the victory at Kut.

Maude continued his advance after the capture of Baghdad, sending three columns west and north, one up the Euphrates, one up the Tigris, and one up the Diyala. The central force, following the road to Mosul, took Samarra on April 23 and held against a Turkish counterattack the following week. The column advancing up the Euphrates was soon halted below Ramadi, where the

Turks who had withdrawn from the south had established a new base.

The extreme heat of summer brought all operations to a halt. Despite temperatures that hovered near 120 degrees in the shade, Maude made active preparations for a fall campaign. He decided to make his main effort up the Euphrates, and so shifted the bulk of his forces over opposite Ramadi.

The British attacked on September 27, and the next day the Turkish commander at Ramadi surrendered. Maude then shifted his main strength to his right and advanced up the Tigris. On November 2 Tikrit was captured. The British were in control of all of Mesopotamia for a hundred miles above Baghdad.

Shortly after this General Maude contracted cholera and died in Baghdad, deeply mourned by his men as well as by Britishers everywhere. General Marshall took over the command.

34

Out of the Land of Egypt

SINAI

Most of the troops evacuated from Gallipoli in late 1915 were sent to Egypt, which since December, 1914, had had the status of a British protectorate. The troops were not there solely for defense of the Suez Canal, however, for plans were being made for an offensive against the Turks in the Sinai Peninsula and Palestine. A British army under General Sir Archibald Murray began to assemble between the Nile delta and the Canal. Since neither railroad transportation nor water was available in the desert area of Sinai, British engineers were put to work constructing a rail line and a pipeline to support the operation. Protected by a division of British troops, by the spring of 1916 the head of the rail line had reached Romani. Work on the pipeline was progressing at a somewhat slower rate.

The Turks, farther along the coast at El Arish, were determined to halt the British advance, but the British easily repulsed several raids in early 1916. In late July the Turks mounted a major effort against the British railhead. A Turkish column commanded by German General Friedrich Kress von Kressenstein, and supported by German and Austrian artillery units and an Arab camel corps, moved down the coast toward Romani. On August 3 they attacked in force. Fighting continued until the next afternoon, when the British infantry charged from their entrenchments with bayonets fixed. While the Turks were attempting to deal with the unexpected counterattack, they were struck in the flank by British cavalry. The Turks broke and fled, abandoning many heavy guns. They had suffered more than five thousand casualties, about five times as many as the British.

Slowly the rails and pipeline were extended, a covering force constantly preceding the work, and the main army following behind. By December British troops had reached El Arish and found it abandoned. The Turks had withdrawn to Gaza and Beersheba, where they were preparing fortifications. Below the border of Palestine only two Turk outposts remained, Magdhaba and Rafah. Magdhaba fell two days before Christmas. By January 9, 1917, after a sharp two-day fight at Magruntum, Rafah was in British hands. The British were ready to move into Palestine.

REPULSE AT GAZA AND BEERSHEBA

The first British objective was Gaza, whose many wells could supply water for the ten thousand horses of Major General Sir Philip Chetwode's Desert Corps, spearhead of the British attack. Thick hedges of cactus formed a natural defense about the city, and the Turk defenders had not considered it necessary to improve much on what nature provided. They had, however, prepared an extensive line of fortifications between Gaza and Beersheba, blocking the only possible avenues of approach to Palestine from Egypt.

Major General Sir Charles Macpherson Dobell, commander of the British forces assigned to the attack on Gaza, launched the assault in thick fog on March 26, 1917. British cavalry of the Desert Corps rode east and north to surround the city, while infantry attacked from the south. Both groups were making progress through the unfinished Turkish defenses, and the infantry had entered the town, when a false report reached Chetwode that the infantry attack had failed. Accordingly, he ordered his cavalry to withdraw. The infantry also pulled back in uncertainty. Too late the British commander found that they had been misled by faulty communications. They tried to return the following day but failed, for Kress von Kressenstein had mounted an enveloping counterattack against the vital line of communications behind the British right flank. To avoid being cut off, Dobell again withdrew, having lost four thousand men to the Turks' two thousand during the two-day battle.

On April 17 Dobell made a second attempt to take Gaza. By this time the Turks had greatly strengthened their defenses. Dobell's plan was to attack from the southwest with three divisions on a two-mile front, supported by naval gunfire from offshore. The approach he had selected slopes gradually upward toward the city. As the British troops moved slowly up the hill they found the Turks waiting for them. The battle continued for three days, but in the end the British were again driven off, suffering 6,500 casualties while the Turks lost 2,400.

After this second failure, General Murray was replaced by General Sir Edmund Allenby, transferred from command of the Third Army in France. Allenby, an enormous man with an enormous temper, found morale low among these men who had recently failed twice at Gaza. He promptly removed his headquarters from Cairo to the front at Rafah, just across the border into Palestine, a move that made him popular with the troops. They soon grew to know and respect this dynamic man who kept popping up unexpectedly in their midst. By his calm confidence and firm assertion of authority he restored the fighting spirit of his army, as he prepared to continue the offensive.

Allenby demanded and received reinforcements, bringing his command to a total of eighty-eight thousand men. These he divided in two corps, the XX and XXI, commanded by Chetwode and Lieutenant General Edward Bulfin, and the Desert Mounted Corps, under Australian Lieutenant General Sir H. G. Chauvel.

The Turks, realizing that they faced the likelihood of a stronger attack, also built up their forces in the Gaza-Beersheba area to about thirty-five thousand men, and strengthened their defenses. Their troops, still commanded by Kress von Kressenstein, were now designated the Eighth Turkish Army. Overall command of the defense of Palestine was given to General Erich von Falkenhayn, former Chief of the German General Staff. He began to establish a new Seventh Army near Jerusalem, bringing down from Aleppo reserves that had been assembled to recapture Baghdad.

THE BATTLE OF BEERSHEBA
(THIRD BATTLE OF GAZA)

Allenby planned to mount a single offensive to take both Gaza and Beersheba and the strong line of fortifications between the cities. Beersheba, about thirty-two miles southeast of Gaza, and replete with wells, would be attacked first, while a feint was made at the more formidable fortifications of Gaza. Once Beersheba was taken, the British would swing around and take Gaza. Elaborate plans were made, so successfully concealed that the Turks believed that all British forces were concentrated in front of Gaza.

British artillery started pounding Gaza on October 27 and continued through the thirty-first, joined by naval guns from ships off the coast on October 30. The three divisions of the XXI Corps then began a demonstration, leading the Turks to expect a repetition of the Second Battle of Gaza. Meanwhile the XX Corps with four infantry divisions, and the Imperial Camel Corps Brigade, plus a strong artillery contingent, were moved secretly toward Beersheba. The attack there on the morning of October 31 took the Turks completely by surprise. Although they fought stubbornly, by nightfall Beersheba was in British hands, all the precious wells intact. The XX Corps then turned to work its way toward Gaza, meeting up with stiff resistance from the Turk defenses in the hills. The Desert Mounted Corps struck north, toward the Turkish line of communications.

During the night of November 1-2, Allenby launched an attack on Gaza, sending the XXI Corps along the coast. With the infantry were eight tanks, the only ones outside Europe. The defense was typically stubborn, and the attackers made little progress until November 6, when the XX Corps reached the left flank of the Gaza defense line. The Desert Mounted Corps was approaching the coast farther north. The Turkish resistance collapsed, and on November 7 Gaza was at last taken by the British.

JUNCTION STATION

The Turkish Eighth Army, withdrawing from Gaza up the coast, was pursued by Allenby with three mounted divisions and two infantry divisions, while the remainder of the army rested and reorganized at Gaza. At Junction Station the Turks halted and dug in, their left flank covered by the hastily assembling Seventh Army. Von Falkenhayn himself took over command of the two army fronts, which he planned to extend from the sea to Hebron, south of Jerusalem.

Junction Station was a key point on the railroad line from Aleppo. The road branched there, one branch going east to Jeru-

salem, and the other south to Beersheba. The town was important, moreover, for it was the site of a water-pumping plant
that would be invaluable to the British forces. Allenby prepared
at once to attack the defending Turks.

Taking advantage of the fact that the Seventh and Eighth
Turkish Armies had not yet joined, Allenby swung one calvary
division to his right, southeast of Junction Station, while with his
infantry and two cavalry divisions he attacked the Turks in front
of the city. The rest of his cavalry drove north near the coast,
around the Turks' right flank.

The Battle of Junction Station began on November 13 and
lasted for two days. By this time the Eighth Army was again
threatened with encirclement and once more retreated northward. The British fell heir to the pumping station, two locomo-
tives, and sixty railroad cars. Along the coast to the west Allenby's
cavalry continued to rush along, and on November 16 occupied
Jaffa, fifty miles from Gaza.

THE ARABS REVOLT

At about the time General Murray had been establishing a base
at Romani in 1916, and shortly after the surrender of Kut, the
Grand Sharif of Mecca, Husein ibn-Ali, anxious to be rid of his
Turkish overlords, declared the Hejaz to be independent. Rallying
the other Arab tribes to his cause, with his sons Feisal and Ab-
dullah he proceeded to harass the Turks in the area. After capturing the Turkish garrison at Mecca he took Taif and Jeddah and
sent his son Feisal to take Medina. Feisal and his men cut the
railroad line north of Medina but failed to take the city, and it
stayed in the hands of the Turks throughout the war.

The British, recognizing that the Arab revolt could help their
campaign in Palestine, set up a supply base for Feisal at Rabegh,
on the Red Sea. There Feisal went, after giving up on Medina. In
January, 1917, he was joined at Rabegh by a young British lieutenant, Thomas E. Lawrence. This gifted, romantic character
knew the country and the language and had adopted Arab dress.
The full extent of his contribution to the Arabs' cause is impossible to evaluate, but there is no doubt that he was highly popular
and an inspiration to them. He also proved to be a capable leader
of irregular forces, and some competent authorities believe that

he was an authentic military genius. He was probably responsible for most of what was accomplished by Feisal and his Arab forces during the remainder of the war.

In January Feisal, hoping to divert the Turks who were threatening to attack Mecca, took his own men, by then numbering about ten thousand, up the Red Sea coast from Rabegh to attack Wejh. British ships carried his equipment and put a landing force ashore on the coast. This group reached Wejh before Feisal and his troops, who, afoot and by camel, had to cross 150 miles of desert. Upon arriving, Feisal, following Lawrence's plan, immediately joined the attack, which was already under way. The Turk defenders were driven out, leaving equipment and arms behind them.

During February the British landed other forces at Dhaba and Moweilah, until by the end of the month the Red Sea shore as far as the Gulf of Aqaba was under British-Arab control. For the remainder of the war the Arabs repeatedly attacked the railroad line and struck at Turk garrisons in the Hejaz, making it valueless to the Turks.

TO JERUSALEM

While the Turkish Eighth Army had been fleeing up the coast, the Seventh Army had organized the defense of the Judaean hills, south of Jerusalem. Supplies for the army came to the area of Jersualem by road from Nablus, almost directly north. Allenby decided to try to cut that road.

Leaving one cavalry division and one infantry division to watch the Eighth Army, which held the coastal plain north and east of Jaffa, Allenby sent part of the XX Corps—two infantry divisions and one cavalry division—east into the rugged hills of Judaea. The troops advanced in two columns over the difficult roads in bad weather, taking with them only the equipment that donkeys or camels could carry. Progress was slowed further by Turkish strongpoints in the hills, and on November 24 the columns halted altogether, confronted by well-entrenched, well-equipped Turks west of Bethlehem and Jerusalem. A few days later the Turks tried to cut this British force off from the rest of Allenby's army, on the coastal plains, but the attack was repulsed.

Sending in fresh divisions from the XX Corps to relieve the

weary men opposite Jersualem, and having established a strong supply line to the area, Allenby ordered a new attack along the entire front.

On December 8 the 60th Division, in the center of the XX Corps, struck at the chief Turkish positions west of Jerusalem, driving the Turks out. The Seventh Army began to withdraw from Jerusalem. At dawn the following morning the mayor, realizing his city was defenseless, walked out of the city gates, accompanied by his staff, prepared to surrender Jerusalem. As he approached the position of the nearest British unit, he saw a British soldier walking alone. It happened to be the unit's cook, looking for fresh eggs. The mayor surprised the cook by handing him the keys to the city. Later in the day the mayor surrendered more formally to the British corps commander, General Sir John Shea. He was forced to repeat the ceremony a third time the next day for General Allenby. All of this activity, in cold, wet weather, proved too much for the mayor, who developed pneumonia and died a few days later.

At the end of the month Von Falkenhayn tried to retake Jerusalem. Chetwode's XX Corps counterattacked, however, and the Turks were driven off.

So ended many centuries of Turkish Muslim rule over Jerusalem. Psychologically its capture was of tremendous importance to the Allies and a great blow to Turkish prestige. Strategically it was an important objective in the campaign to drive the Turks from Palestine and a good place to stop and prepare for the next operation.

35

Planning for 1918—
America's Crucial Role

ALLIED AND STRATEGIC ASSESSMENTS

As the winter of 1917–1918 approached it became increasingly obvious to both sides that 1918 would be the decisive year of the war. It was equally clear to both Allied and German leaders that the crucial determinant during that year would be the extent of American participation. The collapse of Russia, and the near-collapse of Italy, suggested to both sides that Germany would be able to concentrate the bulk of her best forces against the Western Allies in 1918.

The overwhelming German successes at Riga and Caporetto had demonstrated to the Allies that the German armies were still strong and able despite three wearing years of war. These operations had also revealed new and effective tactical measures that rendered the Germans even more effective. In contrast to these evidences of enemy strength, Allied leaders saw dangerous weaknesses in their own forces. The French Army, seriously hurt by the losses suffered in the great battles on the Western Front, had not yet recovered from the mutinies that followed the disastrous Nivelle offensive. In Britain the supply of manpower was nearly used up, and the entire nation was still shocked by the dreadful losses in the 1917 offensives in Flanders. Allied leaders knew that Germany was also suffering severely from the casualties that her troops had suffered in France and Belgium and that she was feeling the effects of over three years behind the blockade. But they saw no indication that the German armies' combat effectiveness had suffered at all. In both Paris and London there were gloomy doubts that Allied forces would be able to prevent a German breakthrough in the west in 1918 unless American manpower could be brought in to bolster the sagging French and British armies.

On the other side of the line the situation seemed no less gloomy, however. German leaders were acutely aware of how severely the strength of their army had been sapped by the combined effects of fearful manpower losses, war-weariness, and the pressures of the blockade. Even more worrisome was the growing weakness and war-weariness of Germany's allies: Austria-Hungary, Bulgaria, and Turkey. Despite the encouragement which all of the Central Powers had derived from the collapse of Russia, Von Hindenburg and Ludendorff realized full well that this was only a temporary respite. The entry of America into the war provided the Allies with potential military strength considerably exceeding that which they had lost when Russia had asked for an armistice.

On the other hand, Ludendorff, who by this time had assumed the major role in strategic planning, also realized that the weight which America could add to the Allied side of the scales was still only potential. Ludendorff believed that the tiny American Army could not be expanded and trained adequately to play a major combat role in Europe before the end of 1918. The victory in Russia, combined with the recent successes in Italy, gave Germany a preponderance of immediately available military power in Europe greater than at any time since the outbreak of the war. To Ludendorff, therefore, it was obvious that Germany had a splendid opportunity to win the war in 1918. Clearly, however, it would be the last opportunity, and it must be seized and exploited before fresh American manpower could shift the scales irretrievably to the Allied side sometime after 1918.

THE AMERICAN EFFORT

When the United States declared war, on April 6, 1917, there were in the U.S. Army 127,588 officers and men. About 80,000 more National Guardsmen had been mobilized for duty along the uneasy Mexican border. In addition, the Marine Corps had about 13,000, a large number of whom were in the West Indies. The combined strength was a little more than that of the Belgian

Army, whose six divisions were holding a scant ten miles of front in Flanders. A 1,500,000-man army such as military leaders wished to provide the Allies could not be built up over night, but no time was lost in starting.

Congress passed the Selective Service Act on May 18, 1917, to draft men into the service. Already young men were volunteering by the thousands. There seemed little problem in assembling the manpower, but equipping them to fight was another matter. Guns, ammunition, clothing, all the myriad items an army needs were in short supply. It would take time to gear up industry to produce them, and months of training before the men were ready to be sent overseas. Clearly American influence would not be felt on the war fronts soon. More optimistic planners thought of mid-1918; the pessimistic doubted that many men would get to Europe before 1919.

The Air Service Section of the Army Signal Corps was in worse shape than the ground forces. There were 35 officers who could fly, but only 5 or 6 in condition for combat and none with combat experience. Of the 55 training planes, 51 were obsolete and 4 obsolescent. Planners estimated that there would have to be 7,200 officers, 54,000 men, and at least 5,400 planes to satisfy the needs of the Allies.

The United States collectively rolled up its sleeves and went to work. Vast camps were hurriedly built to house the stream of new young soldiers. The nation's tailors produced uniforms by the tens of thousands. The entire national stockpile of weapons and equipment was put to use for training. When these proved insufficient, dummy weapons—even broomsticks for rifles—were devised by the ingenious Regular Army soldiers scattered around to the new camps as training cadres. Weapons production could not hope to supply enough for the combat-ready troops before 1919, and Britain and France agreed to supply the deficit when the Americans arrived in Europe.

Supplying weapons was one thing, but providing leaders for the greatly expanded army was quite another. To begin with, there were less than 6,000 Regular Army officers and about 3,000 in the National Guard, and it was calculated that about 75,000 would be needed for an army of 1,500,000 men. Somehow they were produced. About 16,000 were promoted from the ranks, most in the early months of the war. The most promising of the

new soldiers were rushed through hastily devised training programs in three months to become "ninety-day wonders" and take
their places as second lieutenants to train others and fill out the
rosters of the newly formed companies, battalions, regiments,
brigades, and divisions.

PERSHING TAKES COMMAND

In May, 1917, President Woodrow Wilson appointed a commander in chief of the American Expeditionary Force that was
being assembled to send to France, Major General John J. Pershing. Although little known outside the Army, Pershing had
earned a reputation for toughness and ability in small-scale military operations during the Philippine Insurrection and the recent
troubles along the frontier with Mexico. On May 28 he sailed for
Europe, with a directive from the President "to cooperate with
the forces of the other countries employed against [the Imperial
German Government]; but in so doing the underlying idea must
be kept in view that the forces of the United States are a separate and distinct component of the combined forces, the identity
of which must be preserved." Pershing was given latitude in determining how the Americans would cooperate. "But," he was
told, "until the forces of the United States are in your judgment
sufficiently strong to warrant operations as an independent command, it is understood that you will cooperate as a component of
whatever army you may be assigned by the French government."
Pershing was wholly in accord with the use of Americans as independent units, and he was forced to stand firm on many occasions
against British and French attempts to flesh out their depleted
ranks with American soldiers.

Pershing arrived in London on June 8, 1917. After conferring
for several days with General Sir William Robertson, Chief of the
Imperial General Staff, and other British leaders, he crossed the
Channel to France. A few weeks later the first American units,
parts of the 1st Division, arrived at St. Nazaire. They were a
token only, however, a pledge of American dedication. The troops
had been hastily assembled and they required about four months
of training in France before they were believed ready to be put
into quiet sectors of the line.

Pershing and the staff who had accompanied him began at once planning for American participation in combat operations on the Western Front. It was soon apparent that 1,500,000 men would not be enough. With Russia about to collapse unless a miracle could intervene, Germany seemed certain to be able to shift sizable forces from the Eastern Front to the Western by 1918. Twice the 500,000 Americans Pershing had hoped to have in France by mid-1918 must somehow be provided, and 3,000,000 instead of 1,500,000 in 1919. To Secretary of War Newton D. Baker Pershing sent an urgent plea to double the manpower plans. In December Pershing raised the figures again. After the Battle of Caporetto he agreed with the dejected British and French leaders that defeat was likely if great numbers of American troops were not available in 1918. More than 2,000,000 troops would be needed, he told Secretary Baker, and 5,000,000 in 1919.

CREATING AND TRANSPORTING AN ARMY

Pershing's increased demands were received calmly in Washington, where an efficient management team for the army was functioning smoothly. In September Major General Tasker H. Bliss had taken over as Chief of Staff for the Army. After installing Brigadier General Peyton C. March as his assistant, Bliss went to Europe to observe at first hand the war administrations of the Allies. While he was in Paris in November, President Wilson appointed him representative on the Allied Supreme War Council, established after the Caporetto disaster. March became Chief of Staff. He already had the administrative machinery functioning smoothly when Pershing's request arrived.

By this time a program for training units and transporting them to France had begun to operate with assembly-line precision. Each newly established division was to receive at least six months of training in the United States and about two more in France in order to become fully familiar with its French or British equipment. This was to be followed by at least one month of combat experience in the front-line trenches in a "quiet sector" under French or British command. This schedule was followed fairly closely by most of the forty-two American divisions that arrived in France during the war. It was speeded up slightly, however, after Pershing's December message, and some divisions were put into combat more quickly than planned because of the German attacks in the spring of 1918.

The first two American divisions to arrive in France were exceptions to the schedule. The 1st Division was hastily assembled after the declaration of war, from Regular Army units on the Mexican border. Because of the need for experienced officers and men in training and administrative tasks, about two-thirds of the division strength was made up of newly recruited volunteers. Part of the 2nd Division, the 5th Marine Regiment, arrived at St. Nazaire on June 27, 1917. But the division was not established until October, when the 5th Marines were joined with the recently arrived 6th Regiment and a machine-gun battalion to form the 4th Marine Brigade. This unit, combined with the 3rd Army Brigade, then formed the 2nd Division.

Delivering the troops and their mountains of supplies to Europe was a major problem, and it occupied a great deal of Pershing's time and thought during his first months in France. It also became the prime job of the U.S. Navy in this war in which there were almost no sea battles, none at all in which U.S. ships were engaged.

Basic to the delivery problem were two facts: the Allies had a shortage of shipping, and German U-boats were sinking it at the rate of five hundred thousand tons a month in the first six months of 1917. To overcome the first, all possible shipping was diverted from other runs to the cross-Atlantic route. German ships that had sought asylum and been interned in U.S. harbors in earlier years of the war were commandeered. Despite extensive sabotage by their German crews, the ships were repaired with incredible speed and put back in service under U.S. flags and with American names. And a huge program was begun to build cargo ships quickly from standardized parts as closely as possible on an assembly-line schedule. Under a similar program, work began on 258 new, fast destroyers for convoy and patrol duty in defense against the U-boats.

Rear Admiral William S. Sims had departed from Washington for London in the last days before the U.S. declaration of war in order to coordinate possible joint American and British naval action. When Sims arrived, the United States was already at war, and his conversations took on a more urgent tone than had been anticipated. Informed at the Admiralty of the real seriousness of the U-boat menace, which had been underestimated in the United States, Sims at once urged the institution of a convoy system to protect the ships. The idea of sending ships in groups was an old one, but it had gone out of use with the development of steam-powered vessels. Now increasingly it was gaining support among British naval officers. Some opposed it, however, because it would limit the speed of faster ships to that of the slowest in the convoy. And some thought the masters of merchant ships were such an independent lot that they never would cooperate with a convoy system. There were other arguments, but no one spoke from experience.

With Sims's persistent voice added to those of the supporters of convoys in the British Admiralty, and having the promise of U.S. destroyers as escorts, Prime Minister Lloyd George ordered the Admiralty to try out the system. The first convoys proved such a success that by the summer of 1917 convoys were traveling on a regular basis, and submarine sinkings were beginning to fall rapidly. U-boat captains soon found they could not fire their torpedoes at escorted ships without being attacked by the protecting destroyers and cruisers.

New weapons also were enlisted in the fight against the U-boat. Specially designed 110-foot submarine chasers were soon in production in large numbers and proved invaluable in coastal patrol. Aboard them, and on destroyers also, was installed a new device, an underwater hydrophone which picked up the noise of submarine engines. Newly improved antenna mines were produced by thousands, and a deep minefield was laid across the English Channel, so deep that shallow draft vessels could pass but submarines would strike the mines. In the summer of 1918 a more ambitious project was begun, the laying of a minefield all the way across the North Sea from Scotland to Norway. The field was to be 230 miles long, 15 to 25 miles wide. Over seventy thousand mines had been planted by the time the war ended, but not a single U-boat was a confirmed victim.

PRESIDENT WILSON PREPARES FOR PEACE

Back in Washington, as Pershing was preparing for active American participation in the war, President Wilson was exercising his responsibility for overall coordination, planning, and ful-fillment of the tremendous mobilization effort with the same cool detachment and decentralization which had characterized his administrations as President of Princeton University and Governor of New Jersey. With few administrative failures or breakdowns, by the end of 1917 the most sweeping and rapid economic and military mobilizations in the history of the world were moving smoothly and satisfactorily to provide a trained and fully operational American Expeditionary Force of at least two million men in France by the end of 1918.

THE FOURTEEN POINTS

President Wilson was already thinking far beyond American military participation. At a time when his counterparts in France, England, and Italy doubted whether they could survive the year, and when the German leaders were confidently planning for the offensives which they thought would bring them victory, Wilson began to consider the terms which should be the basis of a peace treaty imposed by the Allies. As a historian, well aware of the historical causes of the war in Europe, he devoted most of his thought to measures which he hoped would eliminate, or control, those causes in the future.

In an address to a joint session of the Congress on January 8, 1918, Wilson revealed to the American people—and to the world —his thoughts on the subject of a just peace, on Allied terms. He listed fourteen points, which were destined, as he had intended, to become the basis for peace negotiations, although not the basis for the permanent peace of which he dreamed:

I. Open covenants of peace, openly arrived at, after which there shall be no private international understandings of any kind, but diplomacy shall proceed always frankly and in the public view.

II. Absolute freedom of navigation upon the seas, outside territorial waters, alike in peace and in war. . . .

III. The removal, so far as possible, of all economic barriers and the establishment of an equality of trade conditions among all the nations consenting to the peace and associating themselves for its maintenance.

IV. Adequate guarantees given and taken that national armaments will be reduced to the lowest point consistent with domestic safety.

V. A free, open-minded, and absolutely impartial adjustment of all colonial claims, based upon a strict observance of the principle that in determining all such questions of sovereignty the interests of the populations concerned must have equal weight with the equitable claims of the government whose title is to be determined.

VI. The evacuation of all Russian territory, and such a settlement of all questions affecting Russia as will secure the best and freest cooperation of the other nations of the world in obtaining for her an unhampered and unembarrassed opportunity for the independent determination of her own political development and national policy. . . .

VII. Belgium . . . must be evacuated and restored, without any attempt to limit the sovereignty which she enjoys in common with all other free nations. . . .

VIII. All French territory should be freed and the invaded portions restored; and the wrong done to France by Prussia in 1871 in the matter of Alsace-Lorraine, which has unsettled the peace of the world for nearly fifty years, should be righted, in order that peace may once more be made secure in the interest of all.

IX. A readjustment of the frontiers of Italy should be effected along clearly recognizable lines of nationality.

X. The peoples of Austria-Hungary should be accorded the freest opportunity of autonomous development.

XI. Rumania, Serbia, and Montenegro should be evacuated; occupied territories restored; Serbia accorded free and secure access to the sea; and the relations of the several Balkan states to one another determined by friendly counsel along historically established lines of allegiance and nationality. . . .

XII. The Turkish portions of the present Ottoman Empire should be assured a secure sovereignty, but the other nationalities which are now under Turkish rule should be assured an undoubted security of life and an absolutely unmolested opportunity of autonomous development, and the Dardanelles should be permanently opened as a free passage to the ships and commerce of all nations under international guarantees.

XIII. An independent Polish state should be erected which should include the territories inhabited by indisputably Polish populations. . . .

XIV. A general association of nations must be formed, under specific covenants, for the purpose of affording mutual guarantees of political independence and territorial integrity to great and small states alike.

At the time the Allies made no attempt to study or discuss the Fourteen Points but gave them a sort of nodding acquiescence. Since they were the only formal statement of Allied objectives, they became a goal without ever being accepted as such.

36

The Well-Planned Offensive:
Michael

GERMAN PLANS

Prior to the collapse of Russia the German Army had been divided nearly equally between the Eastern and Western Fronts, with the strengths on each of these fronts varying between 2,000,000 and 2,500,000 men. With Russia virtually knocked out of the war in 1917, the East was drained of more than half of its strength, and the best divisions and commanders all shifted to the West. By early 1918 the strength in the East had been reduced to a bare 1,000,000 men, while that in the West was growing to more than 3,575,000, organized in 191 combat divisions. To oppose this growing German concentration of force there were about 1,200,000 British troops, in 63 divisions, and somewhat less than 2,000,000 French soldiers, in 99 divisions.

Plans for the use of the preponderant German strength in 1918 were the responsibility of Ludendorff. Although still the junior man to Von Hindenburg in the German command team, Ludendorff by this time frequently ignored his senior partner and did not hesitate to make decisions and give orders in Von Hindenburg's name, often without informing the old field marshal.

During the winter of 1917–1918 Ludendorff had the best divisions of the German Army given special training as "shock troops," familiarizing them completely with the new Hutier tactics, which had achieved such success at Riga and Caporetto. Using the same techniques—secret preparations, night concentrations, and sudden attacks without long preliminary bombardments—Ludendorff intended to launch a series of drives primarily against the British front, where he could concentrate more force than against the French. He confidently expected he could knock Britain out of the war and force the Allies to sue for peace. Complete defeat of France, he thought, would not end the war, for the British could continue to fight from a powerful beachhead in northern France, and American manpower would eventually arrive to reinforce them. If Britain were knocked out of the war, however, France could not carry on, and the United States could never bring her strength to bear in Europe.

In a search for the earliest chance of victory, Ludendorff had the German General Staff prepare several alternative sets of plans. Those given the code name "George" provided for a massive strike through Flanders. This would permit the German armies to reach the Channel coast most quickly and promised the earliest possible defeat and destruction of the British armies. However, after Ludendorff toured the front in early March, he concluded that the ground in Flanders would be too wet for a major offensive before April. Therefore he selected Operation Michael, an assault on the thinly held sector in the Somme valley between St. Quentin and Arras, where the British and French lines joined. The defenses there were weak, because the Allies thought the Germans would not attempt an offensive into the area they had themselves devastated before withdrawing in early 1917. Nor

did the Allies see any strategic advantage to be gained there by the Germans. Ludendorff, however, saw an opportunity to take advantage of the divergent interests of the French and British.

If a breakthrough could be achieved between the two Allies, Ludendorff reasoned, the French would automatically fall back to the southwest to protect Paris, while the British retired to the northwest to cover their lines of communications to the Channel ports. If the Germans could get between the two Allies, their retreating armies would widen the breach themselves. Then the Germans would swing to the north, encircling the open British right flank. In a series of assaults Haig's armies would be crushed against the Channel coast.

The ground in the Somme sector was dry enough to support operations in March, and Ludendorff ordered the initiation of Michael for March 21. Secretly, moving by night, the divisions of shock troops began to gather along the Somme front. There they joined the three armies designated to carry out the offensive, from north to south the Seventeenth, under General Otto von Below, the Second, commanded by General Georg von der Marwitz, and the Eighteenth, under General Oskar von Hutier.

ALLIED PLANS

The Allied leaders were well aware of the great preponderance of German combat strength and had heard rumors of the plans for the impending offensive. But, largely because of the great divergence of strategic opinion among the British, they were unable to agree on plans for 1918.

Prime Minister Lloyd George was convinced that there could be no solution on the Western Front. Just as the Allies had failed to achieve a breakthrough when they had held the preponderance of strength, so too would the Germans fail in 1918, he believed. He was anxious to increase Allied strength on the Turkish and Balkan fronts, instead of in France, to bring about the early surrender of Turkey, Bulgaria, and perhaps Austria-Hungary. With her allies gone, he thought, Germany would be forced to make peace.

Neither the Chief of the Imperial General Staff, General Robertson, nor the commander in chief of the BEF, Field Marshal Haig, agreed with the Prime Minister. Robertson was not opposed to continued pressure against the Turks and Bulgarians, but he agreed with Haig that the German threat on the Western Front was a most serious one. It was the one area where Britain could lose the war; and there was no assurance that victories on other fronts would hasten a German collapse.

Because of the blood-letting of the fall of 1917, Haig had three hundred thousand fewer men than he had had earlier in the year, and his armies were holding forty more miles of front, which they had taken over from the French. He had asked for six hundred thousand additional troops, to make up for losses and to give him more strength to face the expected German offensive, but by March he had received only one hundred thousand of these. Lloyd George, in fact, refused to allow more troops to be sent to Haig, fearing that he would squander them in a renewed offensive in Flanders.

The two principal Allied field commanders in France, Haig and Marshal Pétain, left with no firm direction, had to coordinate their plans as best they could. As Ludendorff anticipated, Pétain expected an attack toward Paris and Haig feared an attack in Flanders aimed at the Channel ports. They agreed to help each other wherever the blow might come, but each prepared to meet the attack he dreaded. Haig, not aware of Ludendorff's assessment of the ground in Flanders, built up the strength of his left wing, the First Army under General Henry Sinclair Horne, and center, the Third Army under General Sir Julian Byng, weakening General Sir Hubert Gough's Fifth Army on the right whose front extended beyond the Somme River. Pétain at the same time built up his reserves behind Reims and Soissons, far from the point where the Germans were planning a strike, and so played into Ludendorff's hands.

THE ASSAULT

At 4:40 A.M. on March 21, 1918, as the usual predawn fog was spreading over the countryside, the front-line troops of the British Fifth and Third Armies were subjected to a massive and intensive bombardment. Colonel Georg Bruchmüller, Von Hutier's artillery officer, had planned it carefully, and it went off as planned. Many front-line trenches were obliterated. The survivors were numbed by shock and fear as gas and smoke shells, mixed with high explosive, added to the horror. There was no dawn that morning for the soldiers of the two British armies. With limited visibility through the eyepieces of their gas masks, they could barely see three or four feet into the mixture of fog, smoke, and gas fumes.

Less than five hours after the bombardment had begun, suddenly the German fire lifted from the front-line trenches. Only seconds later a wall of grey-clad, gas-masked shock troops appeared through the gloom. The battle was quickly over in those trenches; the few who had survived the bombardment were killed or captured. The shock troops swept ahead, following closely behind their artillery's rolling barrage.

There was little variation in the opening pattern along the sixty-mile front of the two British armies. North of the Somme, however, once the first shock of the attack was over, the defenses of the Third Army began to stiffen. The fog in that sector lifted before noon and added to the advantage resulting from Byng's more thorough preparations for defense and greater density of troops. South of the Somme, where the fog persisted until mid-afternoon, there was confusion throughout the battle zone of the Fifth Army. Von Hutier's Eighteenth Army was meeting little opposition.

For the next two days Gough's Fifth Army retreated, closely followed by Von Hutier and Von der Marwitz's left wing. One division arrived to reinforce the British on March 24, but it was not enough to stop the onrushing Germans. They had advanced about thirty-seven miles by the end of the fifth day and were threatening Amiens, an important railway center which lay between the French and British armies. By this time the French too were under heavy attack. Pershing offered to provide some of the new American divisions, but Pétain preferred to use them to relieve more experienced French units from other sectors.

In the north, meanwhile, the German main effort, made by Von Below's Seventeenth Army and the right wing of Von der Marwitz's Second, was held by the determined resistance of the British Third Army. But Byng found it necessary at last to pull back his own right wing so as not to lose contact with the crumbling French Fifth Army.

Ludendorff had been counting on Von Below to make the breakthrough near Arras and was unprepared for Von Hutier's rapid advance south of the Somme. Fortunately for the Allies, he failed to realize the opportunity he had in his hands. Had he shifted the main effort from Von Below to Von Hutier, the Eighteenth Army could have exploited the breakthrough in the south and then wheeled north past Arras. Instead he ordered Von Hutier to slow down so as not to lose contact with Von der Marwitz and Von Below.

The Allies were totally unaware of Ludendorff's lost opportunity. Haig saw the breakthrough south of the Somme and the crushing defeat being suffered by the Fifth Army as a horrible disaster. Pétain saw in it a direct threat to Paris. When the two men met on March 24, Haig appealed to Pétain for the assistance he had promised to give. But the cautious French leader responded that he expected the main German attack would come in Champagne and he could not spare any of his reserves. His only concession was to put General Emile Fayolle in command of the region south of the Somme. Pétain still expected Haig to provide the reinforcements so desperately needed by General Gough.

In despair Haig sent a telegram to Alfred, Lord Milner, British War Minister, and General Sir Henry Wilson, new Chief of the Imperial General Staff, urging that a supreme commander be appointed for the Western Front. He recommended "Foch or some other French general who will fight." Haig's appeal caused both Milner and Wilson to rush to France to consult with Haig and with French military and civilian leaders.

Milner, Wilson, and Haig met with the new French Premier, Georges Clemenceau, and other French officials at Doullens, close behind the British Third Army front, on March 26. Haig urged that one man be placed in command from the North Sea to the Alps and added that he would be delighted to serve under General Foch, whom the British trusted and respected as a vigorous, gifted, fighting general. There were several recommendations as to what should be done, but finally Foch was appointed, not with the full command authority Haig had suggested, but to be "coordinator" of Allied operations on the entire Western Front. He was to "come to an understanding with" the French and British commanders, who were to furnish him with all necessary information.

Foch did not worry about semantics. He immediately tested his vague new authority by instructing Pétain to move up reserves to the region between the Oise and Somme Rivers, behind the remnants of the British Fifth Army. Pétain, realizing that the responsibility for the defense of Paris had been lifted from his shoulders, complied.

On April 3 a full meeting of the Supreme War Council was held at Beauvais, to review, clarify, and extend the emergency decisions made at Doullens. Prime Minister Lloyd George was present, as were American Generals Bliss and Pershing. The authority given to Foch at Doullens was strengthened. He was formally entrusted with the strategic direction of overall military operations on the Western Front. However—primarily at French insistence—the commanders in chief of the British, French, and American forces were to retain full control of the tactical employment of their armies. At Pershing's insistence the American Army, still not organized in France, was included, as insurance that the units arriving in France would not be used to fill gaps in the British and French Armies.

For a man with lesser strength and tact than Foch, this was still a long step short of the supreme command which had long been needed on the Western Front. For Ferdinand Foch it was enough. By a combination of skill, force of character, and personality he was able to function as a fully effective supreme commander. As General Pershing later wrote: "Once the question of supreme command was settled, the coordinated energies of the Allied armies could be directed with maximum effect toward a common end. Although dark days were still ahead, we were spared the chagrin of inefficiency through lack of teamwork. With unity of command and the still more important fact of almost unlimited American reenforcements looming on the horizon, the chances of Allied success were much improved."

THE GERMAN DRIVE FALTERS

Although it had not been evident to the worried Allied leaders when they met at Doullens on March 26, the German drive had already begun to falter, and Ludendorff had begun to accept the fact that the results of the offensive would be far less than he had hoped for. Nevertheless, the Germans continued to press slowly forward. But British and French reinforcements were filling the gaps created in the initial assault, and British aircraft were striking hard at the advancing Germans.

Vainly, between March 27 and 30, Ludendorff attempted to regain the momentum of the first days of the offensive, by shifting the main effort first directly against Arras, then back against Amiens. Both times, however, the shock troops were held almost at their starting points by the well-prepared defenses of the British Third Army. After a brief rest, one final effort was made, on April 4 and 5, to reach Amiens. The attack failed again. Ludendorff ordered a complete halt, since "the enemy resistance was beyond our powers."

Despite Ludendorff's disappointment, the German accomplishments in the two weeks between March 21 and April 5 had been considerable. Their new tactics had again proved successful, this time in the ultimate test of the trenches of the Western Front. For the first time since September, 1914, a complete breakthrough had been made, and open warfare had been renewed, even though only briefly. German troops had overrun nearly two thousand square miles of territory, and driven a salient forty miles deep into Allied territory. They had captured about eleven hundred artillery pieces and more than 70,000 prisoners, while inflicting almost 150,000 losses in killed and wounded upon the Allies, mostly the British. And, unusual in warfare and almost unknown on the Western Front, the attackers had sustained fewer casualties than the defenders.

STRATEGIC ASSESSMENT

Despite these evidences of a truly great tactical victory, there was ample reason for Ludendorff's disappointment. He knew that he had in reality suffered a major strategic defeat. He had failed to accomplish either of his two principal objectives: to destroy the British Army, and to separate the British forces from the French.

Perhaps even more serious were the manpower losses suffered by the German Army. Although they were less than those inflicted on the Allies, who had been severely weakened, the German losses had been almost entirely among the carefully trained, irreplaceable shock troops. Furthermore, rendering the German manpower situation still more critical, the gain in territory was actually a liability; more troops were required to man the lengthened lines of entrenchments, recreating the unfavorable tactical situation which Ludendorff had eliminated in early 1917 by the planned withdrawal to the Hindenburg Line. But now, for reasons of morale, Ludendorff felt that he could not abandon the ground won at such great expense, and to the accompaniment of propaganda claims of a great victory.

In retrospect the reasons for the German defeat in victory are clear. The first was insufficient mobility. Once the breakthrough was made, the German infantry was unable to move fast enough through the devastated terrain to exploit the victory before the Allies could bring up reinforcements and reestablish a defense line. Second was insufficient firepower. Slow though the advance of the infantry was, that of the supporting artillery was even slower, since the roads in the region had been almost totally obliterated. The same problem made it difficult to supply the advancing troops with reinforcements, ammunition, and equipment in sufficient quantity. Little could have been done about these problems in anticipation; nothing could be done after they had developed.

37

Backs to the Wall

THE PARIS GUN

Two days after the first German attack at the Somme the people of northwestern Paris awakened to the noise of an explosion. Paris had been bombed frequently by German planes, but usually at night to avoid interception by Allied pursuit planes and anti-aircraft fire from the city's defenses. This time, however, no planes had been sighted. Twenty minutes later a similar explosion about a mile away killed eight people and wounded thirteen. Explosions continued throughout the day, about half an hour apart, scattered throughout Paris and its suburbs. Alarm approaching panic spread through the city.

At midday fragments picked up near the sites of the explosions were identified as pieces of artillery shells. But it was easily established that there were no hidden guns between the front and the city of Paris. The closest German trenches were sixty-five miles away. Artillery ranges greater than twenty miles were unknown, and only a few naval guns could fire that far. Although it seemed to many impossible, by nightfall French artillery experts finally agreed that the Germans must have developed at least one gun that could fire sixty-five to seventy miles.

They were right. The Germans had two guns set up in the Forest of Crépy, near Laon, and a third being installed. They were enormous things, 120 feet long, and Kaiser Wilhelm himself was observing them on their first day of action.

Working frantically, the French artillerists calculated where the gun emplacements must be, in the area of Laon, and carefully studied air photographs to determine the most likely spots for them. Orders were sent to the front to move a number of heavy artillery weapons within range at once.

The firing on Paris continued on the following day, but while the gun crews were complacently eating lunch, suddenly the Forest of Crépy was swept by French artillery shells. Taken by surprise, the Germans suffered heavy casualties. The guns were not knocked out, however, and they continued bombarding Paris, but at longer intervals because the gun crews repeatedly had to seek shelter in dugouts and trenches from French artillery fire. German artillery was rushed to the area to protect the guns and soon was firing back at the French batteries.

March 29, 1918, was Good Friday, and at four-thirty that afternoon the Church of St. Gervais, in the heart of Paris, was filled with people, when suddenly it was hit by a German shell. Eighty-eight people, mostly women and children, were killed, and sixty-eight injured. When Ludendorff learned of the tragedy he ordered the long-range guns silenced during the funeral for the victims on April 2. Then they resumed firing. Impressive though they were to those directly involved, they were but a sideshow to the main action of the war.

LUDENDORFF CHANGES SCENES

Although badly disappointed with the results of the Somme offensive, Ludendorff had not abandoned hope that victory was within Germany's grasp. He knew that the British had been seriously weakened and that he still had an advantage of almost half a million men, despite the arrival of American units in increasing numbers. Ludendorff realized that although they were not yet ready for combat their arrival was narrowing the margin of time for a German offensive, since some were already relieving experienced French and British units for use as reserves.

To take advantage of the opportunity still remaining, Ludendorff decided to launch Operation George. Rapidly and efficiently he shifted his shock troops north from the Somme to Flanders. Four days after the last German assault on Amiens he was ready in Flanders.

The Allies expected that Ludendorff would attack again, and Haig thought it would be in Flanders. But neither he nor any of the other Allied leaders dreamed that an offensive there could be mounted so fast. While Ludendorff's troops were hastening north, Allied leaders confidently assumed they would have several weeks of respite.

THE LYS OFFENSIVE

In the early morning of April 9 fury erupted through fog in the Lys River valley of Flanders, just as it had nineteen days earlier in the Somme River valley of Picardy, and the initial results were similar.

The main effort was made by the German Sixth Army, commanded by General Ferdinand von Quast, attacking up the Lys River valley through Armentières and toward Hazebrouck. Farther north, driving directly toward Ypres, the German Fourth Army, under General Friedrich Sixt von Armin, made a secondary assault. However, instead of attacking along a thirty-mile front as had originally been planned for Operation George, Ludendorff was forced by reduced manpower availability to attack on a much narrower, twelve-mile front.

One reason for selecting the location of the main effort of the Sixth Army—about midway between Bethune and Armentières —was German knowledge that this section of Horne's First Army front was held by two Portuguese divisions, long overdue for relief from front-line duty. The combination of Bruchmüller's furious high-explosive bombardment, a gas attack, and smoke-thickened fog was too much for the battle-weary Portuguese. The survivors fled even before the first wave of German shock troops surged forward into the five-mile gap. The two neighboring British divisions, their flanks exposed, were also severely mauled, but by nightfall the German advance had been contained by the First Army's reserves—two divisions—along the lines of the Lawe and Lys Rivers, after an advance of nearly five miles.

Rightly expecting that most British reserves would have been attracted to the threatened First Army front, the next morning, again in fog, the German Sixth Army struck another massive blow south of Armentières, while the Fourth hit farther north on Plumer's Second Army front between Armentières and Ypres. The British were better prepared for this assault, but nevertheless they had to evacuate Armentières. The next day, April 11, German progress was slower, but by this time Haig had used up all of his reserves, and the German advance was moving dangerously close to the sea. Aware that Foch had been collecting French reserves farther south, hoping to use them for a counteroffensive, Haig sent an urgent appeal to Foch to release some of these troops to bolster the threatened British First and Second Armies. But Foch had more faith in British holding power than Haig. He refused the reserves. Bitterly disappointed, Haig on April 12 issued an Order of the Day, which concluded in these stirring words:

> There is no other course open to us but to fight it out. Every position must be held to the last man. There must be no retirement. With our backs to the wall and believing in the justice of our cause each one must fight on to the end. The safety of our homes and the freedom of mankind alike depend on the conduct of each one of us at this critical moment.

As the Germans continued to advance, taking Messines Ridge on April 16, Foch decided to commit some of his hoarded reserves. He sent three cavalry divisions and two infantry divisions to Ypres, to serve under the command of Plumer. Before they could enter the line, however, the British First and Second Armies, with vigorous support from the newly created Royal Air Force (it had replaced the Royal Flying Corps on April 1), had stopped the German drive short of Hazebrouck and Ypres.

Ludendorff, although depressed by the failure of his armies to achieve a quick victory, had not abandoned hope of taking the two cities and the Mont des Chats–Mont Kemmel Ridge between them. This is the only high ground in the area and dominates all of Flanders. To divert Allied attention from this region and to throw the British off balance, Ludendorff launched a sudden attack on Amiens on April 24. For the first time German tanks appeared on the battlefield. British tanks, by this time no longer a novelty, engaged them near the village of Villers Bretonneux, in the first tank battle in history. Like the rest of the battle, it ended in a draw. After making considerable gains in the direction of

Amiens, the Germans were thrown back by British and French counterattacks.

Although the surprise attack had failed to reach Amiens, it had accomplished its primary purpose and diverted Allied attention from the Hazebrouck area. When Ludendorff renewed the offensive with an assault on Mont Kemmel on April 25, preceded by a brief but very intensive artillery bombardment, it was successful. The French reserve divisions failed to hold. Repeated German efforts to continue and seize Mont des Chats, however, were unsuccessful.

On April 29 the German Fourth Army attacked once more farther north, again preceding the ground movement with an intensive, brief artillery bombardment. But Foch had moved French artillery and machine-gun units to the area in anticipation of an assault, and the Germans were held to only slight gains south of Ypres. Once again Ludendorff was forced to admit failure.

LUDENDORFF'S THIRD OFFENSIVE—THE AISNE

In each of Ludendorff's first two offensives the margin between success and failure had been small, and he knew it. The battered British Army had barely been able to hold the front. Since the Germans had achieved a number of local successes by attracting Allied reserves away from the main objective to a secondary area, Ludendorff decided to try the technique on a larger scale. If he could attract enough reserves away from Flanders in a diversionary attack farther south, he reasoned, another rapid assault in the north should be able to break through to the Channel ports.

The region chosen by Ludendorff for the diversion was the famous and bitterly contested Chemin des Dames Ridge, just north of the Aisne River. He ordered an attack for May 27. Preparations were pushed ahead rapidly and with great secrecy. Shock troops and other reserves were rushed to the German Seventh Army, commanded by General Max von Boehn, and the First Army, under General Bruno von Mudra. So successful were the efforts to conceal the troop movements that General Denis A. Duchêne, who commanded the French Sixth Army, lying opposite the German Seventh and the right wing of the First, refused to believe the bits of information which suggested that his sector might be the site of the next German offensive. A firm believer in the employment of infantry in masses, he also ignored instructions he had received from General Pétain to deepen his defense zone and thin out the troops concentrated in the front-line trenches.

At 1 A.M. on May 27 the most intensive artillery bombardment of the war concentrated for nearly three hours on Duchêne's seven front-line divisions. When the German shock troops moved forward, there was no resistance. By noon the attackers had crossed the Aisne River, where the surprised French had left the bridges intact, and had advanced five miles. By evening they had reached Fismes, on the Vesle River. Their advance of eleven miles was the greatest since the early days of the war.

For the third time in 1918 the Germans had achieved a complete breakthrough. Ludendorff was almost as surprised as the shocked Allies. This planned diversion had proved to be the most successful attack of the war. It called for exploitation, although it might well use up so many of the German reserves that the later attack planned as a climax in Flanders would be impossible. Yet the breakthrough presented an opportunity to reach Paris in a week, and perhaps to destroy the French Army. Ludendorff decided that he should not let the opportunity slip away.

The advance continued unabated for the next three days; on May 30 the German drive reached the Marne River between Dorman and Chateau-Thierry, an advance of more than thirty miles since the beginning of the offensive. The French capital, still under intermittent long-range fire from the "Paris Gun," was in an uproar as the German spearheads were reported less than fifty miles away and French soldiers retreated toward Paris. On Pétain's request, General Pershing released two divisions, the 2nd and 3rd, to French command, and the fresh but inexperienced American troops were at once rushed toward Chateau-Thierry, in the path of the shock troops.

THE FIRST AMERICAN BATTLES

The diversion of two divisions to help stem the German tide interrupted an orderly plan for more gradual indoctrination of the American troops which by this time were arriving in France in a steady flow. Two days before, the 1st Division, commanded by Major General Robert L. Bullard, had undertaken the first independent American action of the war. This was an assault on Cantigny, a heavily fortified village at the tip of the Somme salient that had been created by the first German drive in March. The purpose was to improve the position of the American forces by gaining higher ground. At the same time it was hoped that the appearance of Americans in battle would improve Allied morale. Although it was a relatively minor action, the American troops gained the praise of Allied observers for the workmanlike manner in which they drove out the defenders of Cantigny and threw back repeated German counterattacks. The 2nd Division was on the way to relieve the 1st, when it was diverted to Chateau-Thierry.

The first units of the 3rd Division went into action on May 31, joining French soldiers holding the line of the Marne River between Chateau-Thierry and Jaulgonne, where German troops were endeavoring to establish a bridgehead south of the river. The rest of the division was put into the line as soon as the units arrived on the following day. The Americans and French counterattacked repeatedly and threw the Germans back across the Marne. Their subsequent attempts to cross were repulsed.

When the 2nd Division arrived it was thrown in in support of two French divisions athwart the highway from Chateau-Thierry to Paris. The French withdrew as planned on June 4, and the full force of German attacks fell on the Americans, who successfully held them off.

By this time the exhausted Germans had outrun their supplies. The realization that they were opposed to fresh troops of good quality caused Ludendorff to halt the offensive temporarily. He wanted to regroup and to move up supplies and artillery. Particularly important for supply reasons was the need to widen the base of the salient which bulged deep into the Allied lines from the Aisne to the Marne. Although spreading the offensive to the flanks and shoulders of the salient would further delay the final offensive Ludendorff planned in Flanders, he felt that drawing still more Allied reserves to the south would make that offensive more successful. Furthermore, the drive to the Marne had gravely weakened French morale, and Ludendorff thought that continuing the threat to Paris might topple the Clemenceau government. If the renewed offensive did not actually reach Paris, a new attack in Flanders, in a time of political crisis and strategic indecision, would be even more likely to succeed.

One thing that Ludendorff had not anticipated, however, was Allied interference with his plans to widen the Aisne-Marne salient. He was at first annoyed, then alarmed, at a small but persistent counteroffensive directed by the U.S. 2nd Division against the tip of the salient just west of Chateau-Thierry. This attack, designed to clear the Germans from Belleau Wood, was spearheaded by the Marine Brigade of the 2nd Division on June 6. The American Marines suffered fearful casualties in the operation, but they worried the Germans greatly by their refusal to accept defeat. In the larger picture of the German operation it was a small engagement, but Ludendorff begrudged the necessity for sending reserves and increasing supplies to the tip of the salient, when he wanted them for use at the shoulders.

Doggedly the 2nd Division forged ahead through the woods, which they finally cleared by June 25. Sober German General Staff reports in early June referred to the American performance as "storm-troop quality." Realizing that nine American divisions had arrived in France in May (bringing the total to eighteen), some of the German staff officers thought that Ludendorff was losing his race with time. But he pointed out that only a handful of these divisions was yet ready for combat. He thought that, despite losses, he still possessed a superiority in combat strength. He knew that he still held the initiative. And he believed that a favorable decision could be reached before the end of July.

THE FOURTH OFFENSIVE— NOYON-MONTDIDIER

Ludendorff's plan was to eliminate the large Allied reentrant salient which lay between the salients of his first and third offensives, the one south of Amiens at Cantigny, the other around Chateau-Thierry. Von Hutier's Eighteenth Army was to drive to the southwest from the Noyon-Montdidier area, to meet a westward thrust from Soissons by Von Boehn's Seventh Army near Compiègne. These twin assaults would straighten out the line, thus reducing German manpower requirements and facilitating supply, while at the same time attracting more Allied reserves to the threatened fronts, and further increasing the growing anxiety in Paris. Again Ludendorff would use the one-two punch technique which had proved so successful in attracting local reserves during the first two offensives. Von Hutier was to start the attack on June 9; Von Boehn would launch his assault on the twelfth.

The French had anticipated the possibility of attacks in this region, and despite German secrecy, had also detected some of the preparations. General Charles Mangin, whose Tenth French Army held the most exposed portion of the line between the Oise and Ourcq Rivers, had wholeheartedly adopted Pétain's ideas for an elastic defense in depth, with only small forces in the front line. To his left, however, the French Third Army, under General Georges Humbert, had made only half-hearted accommodations to the new concept of defense in depth.

When Von Hutier launched his assault, early on June 9, his right wing enjoyed the same sort of success he had achieved in March on the Somme. Before noon his troops had advanced more than seven miles in the region west of the Oise. The German left-wing divisions, however, had been held in place, after a short initial gain, by Mangin's furious counterattacks. Despite this setback, Von Hutier continued to press forward toward Compiègne, but Pétain's waiting reserves soon stopped the drive. There was little gain on June 10, and on the eleventh Ludendorff halted the offensive. He felt confident that all of Mangin's army reserves had been committed near Noyon, and that Pétain had put in most of the general reserve near Compiègne. Thus he expected that Von Boehn's assault, scheduled for the next morning, would have little trouble.

The first great surprise encountered by the Germans in 1918 had been the fighting quality of the American divisions. The second great surprise was Mangin's defense on June 12. Despite the vigor of his actions in halting the Germans near the Oise, the fiery French general had not lost sight of the threat to his right along the Ourcq. The Germans easily penetrated Mangin's thinly held front lines, only to find themselves subjected to massive counterfire from French artillery, quickly followed by counterattacks from the waiting troops in the rear areas of the deep defensive zone. The German assault was quickly halted. Ludendorff called off the entire operation the next day.

Although the Germans had been unable to achieve a strategic decision, each of the other offensives had had startling tactical success. This one, however, as Ludendorff recognized, had been a dismal defeat.

THE FIFTH OFFENSIVE—
CHAMPAGNE-MARNE

Despite this disappointment, Ludendorff was still hopeful that elusive victory was within reach and that he could grasp it with two more rapid blows. The first of these was to be another front-straightening effort near Reims, just east of the Marne salient. Then at last would come the climactic drive in Flanders to destroy the British Army.

But time was growing short, and the odds were building up against the Germans. Fresh American divisions were arriving at French seaports at the rate of at least one a week. And nature was taking a toll of the German soldiers. From mid-June to early July the German Army was virtually immobilized by one of the worst epidemics of influenza in history. The illness was affecting the Allies also, but the poorly fed Germans were more severely hit. Despite it, by mid-July preparations for the fifth German offensive of 1918 were complete.

Von Boehn's Seventh Army was poised in the Marne salient to strike south and southeast to establish a broad bridgehead across the Marne between Chateau-Thierry and Epernay. Von Mudra's First Army and General Karl von Einem's Third were to strike south at the same time toward Châlons, to secure the upper Marne. Thus Reims would be cut off, the salient eliminated, the line shortened. With Paris threatened, all Allied reserves would flow to the area between the Marne and the Seine to protect the city. Then, in one of the lightning-fast shifts of troops for which Ludendorff was justly famous, the scene of activity would switch to Flanders for the final blow against the Channel ports.

This time the Allies learned of the imminent attack in time to take countermeasures and even carried out an artillery "spoiling" bombardment themselves, just before time for the German infantry to move into position. Nevertheless, when the attack began on July 15, for a few hours it moved ahead. Following another intense bombardment and gas attack, the German infantrymen poured across the Marne and fought their way through the first-line defenses west of Reims, penetrating as much as four miles. Only the American 3rd Division held firm at Chateau-Thierry. East of Reims the going was harder. Behind the thinly held front line was the hard-core defense of General Henri Gouraud's Fourth Army, beyond the range of the Germans' light artillery. Deprived of artillery support and meeting stubborn resistance, the advance was halted.

Once again the Paris Gun was shelling the city, creating panic as word came of the German advance west of Reims. Pétain rushed reserves to the sector, and the defense stiffened. With little progress to the east of Reims, and with the U.S. 3rd Division resisting the attacks of seven German divisions at the Paris end of the western sector, Ludendorff realized that he could gain little by continuing the battle. On July 17 he halted the offensive and turned his attention to the north, certain that the panic in Paris would have drawn the reserves from behind Haig's thinly held front in Flanders.

38

The Foch Counteroffensive

AISNE-MARNE

Napoleon, in one of his maxims, identified "the mark of genius," saying, "In war there is but one favorable moment; the great art is to seize it."

Foch proved his understanding of the art on July 17, 1918, when he gave final approval to plans for a massive counteroffensive to reduce the German salient in the Marne area. At 4:35 the following morning, less than six hours after Ludendorff had called off the fifth German offensive of 1918, four French armies, all but one including American units, jumped off in their counterattack.*

The Marne salient bulged from the line of the Vesle River a few miles west of Soissons south to the Marne near Chateau-Thierry and north again to the Vesle just west of Reims. Foch had arranged his forces with Mangin's Tenth Army, spearheaded by the American 1st and 2nd Divisions, on the left to strike from the west; in the left-center was the Sixth Army, commanded by General Jean Degoutte; to the right-center General Henri de Mitry's Ninth Army was opposite the German Marne bridgehead; on the east face of the salient was General Henri Berthelot's Fifth Army. Some of the units barely made it to their positions in the front lines in time for the attack. Only by double timing did the 1st Division take its place for the attack.

Supported by tanks, the infantry of the Tenth Army took the Germans by surprise as they moved out in the main attack on

---

* This counteroffensive, coming as it did in direct response to the German Champagne-Marne offensive, with no delay, is often combined with that and the two operations are inaccurately called the Second Battle of the Marne.

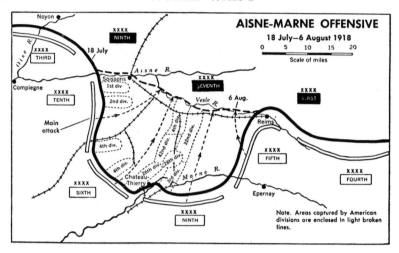

July 18. Nevertheless, they found little softening of German resistance. But the Allies had the preponderance of manpower and
artillery, and slowly they forced the Germans back. The Sixth
Army, also spearheaded by two American divisions, the 4th and
the 26th, was also gaining ground. Soon the action was joined by
the other two armies. Clearly the Allies had taken the initiative
and held it. On the evening of July 18 Ludendorff, who had received word of the attack while on his way to Flanders to direct
his long-delayed offensive there, ordered all attacks on Reims to
cease. As reports of Allied advances continued to reach him, the
next night he ordered evacuation of the Marne salient. In the orderly withdrawal that followed, priority was given to the Paris
Guns. Skillfully protected by stubborn defenses on the flanks, men
and matériel moved back to the Vesle.

As the Allies advanced into the salient, several more American
divisions became engaged in the attack. The 3rd, 28th, and 32nd
Divisions, forming the III Corps, were on the left flank of the
Ninth Army; the 42nd as well as the 4th and the 26th, forming
the I Corps, on the right of the Sixth. Each of the American divisions was twice the size of the average European division. Confident, fresh, and eager, they made up for lack of experience with
determination and soon proved themselves under fire. On July 24
Pershing at last issued an order to combine the two corps on August 10 into the First American Army.

On August 2 the Germans, having efficiently evacuated their
supplies from the salient, suddenly broke contact, except for rear-

guard patrols protecting demolitions. Contact was not reestablished until the fifth, when the Germans were encountered in carefully prepared positions, determinedly holding the line of the Vesle River. The Marne salient had been eliminated. Foch called off the offensive; he confirmed orders to Haig to start a new one within three days.

Next day, on August 6, Prime Minister Clemenceau announced the promotion of Foch to be Marshal of France. No promotion had been more richly deserved.

AMIENS

While the Aisne-Marne offensive was proceeding, Foch had directed Haig to prepare for another offensive farther north. Foch suggested Flanders, but the British commander persuaded him that greater rewards were to be gained in the Amiens sector, by freeing the railroad line and pushing back the German salient. Foch thereupon placed General Marie E. Debeny's First French Army under Haig's command. That army, side by side with General Sir Henry Rawlinson's British Fourth Army, doubled in size with the greatest secrecy, prepared to strike the nose of the German salient between Montdidier and Albert.

The Germans, not suspecting that the Allied troops had been able to recuperate so rapidly from the blows they had suffered in the spring and summer, had no expectation of another major Allied offensive, although they did anticipate some limited attacks in Flanders. Nor did their intelligence sources report the carefully concealed preparations of the Allies.

At 4:20 A.M. on August 8, without any preliminary bombardment, British, Australian, Canadian, and French troops surged from their trenches as the waiting Allied artillery began a rolling barrage. The Germans, misled by Allied deception and their own preconceptions, were completely astonished by the sudden appearance of the infantrymen and their supporting tanks. For the first time in the war entire German divisions collapsed. Reserves rushed to the front soon slowed the Allied advance, but some of the fleeing men paused long enough to taunt the arriving reserves, and to accuse them of needlessly prolonging the war.

The total Allied advance was only seven miles, less than the Germans had done on a number of occasions earlier in the year.

But Ludendorff called it "the black day of the German Army." The breakdown of discipline, even though temporary, was proof to German leaders that they were beginning to lose full control over their war-weary troops. "The war must be ended," said Ludendorff, and he reported to the Kaiser that peace must be negotiated as soon as possible, since the German Army "had ceased to be a perfect fighting instrument."

As the British Fourth and French First Armies continued a slower advance, Foch ordered the offensive to be widened. After a brief pause, from August 13 to 21, the Allied armies complied. On a seventy-mile front from Arras to Soissons the British First, Third, and Fourth Armies, and the French First, Third, and Tenth Armies struck a series of blows that sent the Germans reeling back—dogged, tenacious, and skillful, but nevertheless defeated. Ludendorff ordered withdrawal from the Somme and Lys salients. Pressed more vigorously by the British than they had expected, the Germans suffered severe losses as they fell back across the upper Somme to the Hindenburg Line.

By September 4 the Battle of Amiens was over. Haig had used up all of his reserves, and he knew that it would take a major effort to crack the strong defenses of the Hindenburg Line.

ST. MIHIEL

General Pershing, on August 30, took over control of the sector including the St. Mihiel salient, which the Germans had held since 1914. Plans were already in preparation for the first major offensive of the new American First Army, an operation to reduce the salient and straighten out the Allied line, preparatory to driving on to Metz, the important industrial and railroad center behind the front. The plan was to attack from both directions at the base of the salient, pinching it off and trapping the German units within it. A French corps was to keep them in the salient by a holding attack, while the pinching operations were done by three American corps.

Marshal Foch had approved the St. Mihiel offensive, but, on the same day that Pershing took command in the sector, Foch arrived at his headquarters to tell Pershing that he had changed his mind. He was planning to take advantage of the disorder of German divisions resulting from the recent French and British of-

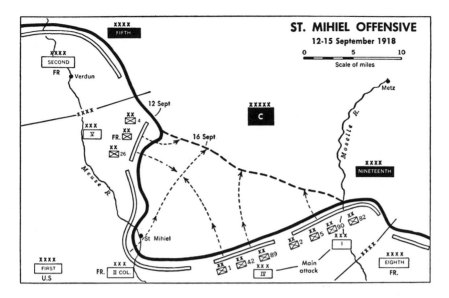

fensives. He now saw an opportunity to win the war in 1918. So he proposed that the St. Mihiel operation be limited to an attack on the southern face of the salient. He would put some of the American divisions thus freed under the French Second Army for an attack on the area between the Meuse River and the Argonne Forest. The rest would form an army to operate with the French Fourth Army on the Aisne River. Moreover he offered to have General Degoutte, who many American officers thought had unnecessarily sacrificed American troops, temporarily in charge of the new army.

Pershing saw in this another attempt to break up the Americans and delay their operation as an American army. He refused to agree. When several alternate suggestions were turned down by Foch, Pershing told the astonished French marshal: "You have no authority as Allied commander in chief to call upon me to yield up my command of the American Army and have it scattered among the Allied forces, where it will not be an American army at all." When Foch insisted, so did Pershing. "Marshal Foch," he said, "you may insist all you please, but I decline absolutely to agree to your plan. While our army will fight wherever you may decide, it will not fight except as an independent American army." After further argument Foch abruptly got up and left Pershing's headquarters.

The following day Pershing conferred with Pétain and found the French general sympathetic with his position. When Pershing and Pétain met with Foch again on September 2, the mood was calmer and an agreement was reached that included maintenance of the American Army as an independent unit. Pershing was to proceed with a limited attack on the St. Mihiel salient, starting on about September 10. By September 25 the First Army was to be prepared to participate in the attack on the Meuse-Argonne front. A sector ninety miles long, from the Moselle River to the Argonne, would be under Pershing's command. The French Fourth Army would attack west of the Argonne at the same time the Americans did.

Time was short. Although plans and preparations for the St. Mihiel operation were well in hand, complicated arrangements had to be made to move the bulk of the forces that were to participate in it to a new battlefield sixty miles away. And they must be there ready to fight two weeks after the St. Mihiel attack began.

After a four-hour bombardment and an intensive aerial attack by hundreds of Allied planes under the direction of Colonel William Mitchell, the American infantry moved out in the St. Mihiel sector in the morning of September 12. The I and IV Corps attacked across the base of the salient from the southeast, while the V Corps, which included a French division, drove from the northwest. The French II Colonial Corps made a secondary attack at the point of the salient.

Ludendorff had learned of the pending American attack and decided to withdraw from the salient. Although the attackers met strong resistance, it was actually cover for a withdrawal. When the opposing attacks met in the middle less than thirty-six hours after the attack began, most of the defenders had escaped from the trap. By September 16 the entire salient had been cleared. Pershing's staff had already begun to move forces to the Meuse-Argonne area.

"TOUT LE MONDE À LA BATAILLE"

Foch's plan for winning the war in 1918 had been modified little after his argument with Pershing. Instead of using two

French armies made up largely of American troops in the key role in the offensive, he was giving the job to the American Army, which for the operation would include some French divisions. It was not without misgiving that Foch agreed to do so. Although the American soldiers had proved themselves on the battlefield, American officers had not proved that they could operate an army.

The plan Foch had developed was based on the fact that the key to German defense of the occupied regions of France was the railroad line that ran roughly parallel to the front from Lille to Strasbourg. The German Army received all of its supplies and reinforcements over that line. Key points on the line were Aulnoye and Mézières, and it was these points that Foch aimed to capture. From Aulnoye a vital line ran back to Liège, and from Mézières a branch line ran through Rethel to the front near Reims, where smaller feeder lines carried German supplies to the vast arc of front stretching from Cambrai to Verdun. If the Lille-Strasbourg line could be seized, Foch believed, the Germans would be forced to withdraw from France. The keys to the line were at Aulnoye and Mézières.

To gain control of the railroad, Foch decided on a great two-pronged offensive. The British, though battered, had proved that they could still fight. With a reinforcing American contingent they were given the mission of breaking through the Hindenburg Line toward Aulnoye. The Americans were to spearhead a somewhat longer drive down the Meuse River and through the Argonne Forest toward Mézières. Foch realized that his war-weary countrymen could not match the vigor of the Americans and possibly not of the British, but he did not intend for them to be passive. To keep the Germans occupied all along the line and prevent them from shifting reserves to oppose the principal Allied drives, the remaining Allied forces, mostly French and British, would conduct a series of limited offensives all along the front.

This was to be an allout offensive. *"Tout le monde à la bataille! Everyone into the battle!"* said Foch. He hoped that he could seize the two key rail junctions, isolate portions of the German Army, and defeat them in detail before the end of the year. Even if the enemy managed to escape, however, he would "have to leave most of his luggage behind."

MEUSE-ARGONNE

By September 25, 1918, 220,000 men of the French Second Army had been moved out of the Meuse-Argonne sector, and 600,000 Americans, complete with tanks and guns, had moved in. A large proportion of them had made the sixty-mile trip from the St. Mihiel front. It was a movement unique in its complexity, and it involved development of a supply line that would continue to function effectively during the weeks of battle ahead.

Facing the American First Army and the French Fourth as they prepared to attack were three heavily fortified German defense lines. All natural defenses had been developed as strong points so that much of the area was dominated by machine guns and artillery, their positions often protected by reinforced concrete. The heavily wooded hills of the Argonne Forest were held by the left wing of General Karl von Einem's Third Army, part of the army group commanded by Crown Prince Wilhelm. The

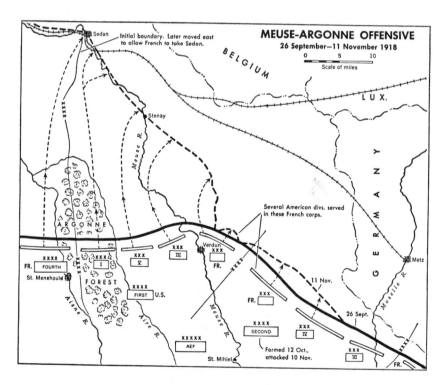

Meuse Valley, a region of steep hills through which the Meuse River flows in a deep gorge, was defended by the German Fifth Army, commanded by General Max von Gallwitz, who was also the army group commander.

Following a three-hour artillery preparation, the French Fourth Army attacked at dawn on September 26. Five minutes later the American First Army moved out. Pershing had three corps abreast: Major General Hunter Liggett's I Corps on the left, Major General George H. Cameron's V in the center, and Major General Robert L. Bullard's III on the right. The initial attack was to be toward Romagne, on a high point north of the Meuse River. The V Corps was to advance on both sides of the woods of Montfaucon and Cheppy and pass west of Montfaucon; the III Corps would protect the right flank and pass east of Montfaucon and west of the Meuse; the I Corps was to protect the left and pass through the Argonne Forest.

On the first day all the corps made good progress, although the V Corps was a little short of its objective, the III Corps through a misunderstanding failed to take advantage of an opportunity to capture Montfaucon, and the I Corps made only two miles against the difficult terrain and the German's defensive advantage in the Argonne Forest.

The Germans had been surprised by this attack so soon after the St. Mihiel operation, but by the second day reserves had arrived to stiffen their defenses. All along the front they took advantage of the terrain to pour machine-gun and artillery fire on the attackers. By October 3 American troops had overrun the first two defensive lines but were halted at the third. Their losses had been heavy, but the Germans, who had expected to be able to hold this difficult region with light forces, had been required to commit all of their local reserves and to call for more from Ludendorff, before they were able to stop the American drive.

Pershing relieved all of the divisions which had begun the initial assault with the more experienced divisions which had spearheaded the St. Mihiel offensive, and renewed the attack on October 4. But the Germans, heavily reinforced and well entrenched, refused to give way. For the next week a furious slugging match took place in the Argonne Forest, and along the heights west of the Meuse. With no room to maneuver, foot by foot and mile by mile the Americans battered their way forward in costly frontal attacks.

Prime Minister Clemenceau, bitterly disappointed by this slow progress, tried to get Marshal Foch to join him in an appeal to President Wilson to have Pershing relieved of his command. But Foch refused. He knew the difficulties of the region, and he also knew from intelligence reports and from prisoner-of-war interrogations that the inexorable American pressure was drawing German reserves from along the entire Western Front.

By the second week of October operations had been extended east of the Meuse River and it became desirable to organize the forces from there to the Woëvre in a Second American Army. With Foch's approval, Pershing took over command of the group of two armies and placed Liggett in command of the First Army and Bullard in command of the Second. Bullard's mission was essentially defensive, to keep the Germans occupied while Liggett continued the battering drive northward.

By October 20 the Germans had been driven from their last prepared fortifications in the middle of the Argonne Forest, and the American advance began to move more rapidly. The Germans had not all withdrawn, however, and still had to be reckoned with in numerous hastily built strongpoints in the rugged forest. Not until October 31 did the Americans clear the forest and reach the open ground beyond.

On the left, meanwhile, Gouraud's French Fourth Army had kept pace with the advance and reached the Aisne River. To the east, the V Corps had captured Romagne and the strategically important heights beyond, which flanked the German line on the Aisne and on the Heights of the Meuse. By this time nearly one-fourth of the entire combat strength of the German Army was concentrated in front of the American First Army.

THE DRIVE TOWARD AULNOYE

On September 27, the day after the Battle of the Meuse-Argonne began, the British First, Third, and Fourth Armies started their assault on the Hindenburg Line in the zone roughly between Cambrai and St. Quentin. The French First Army on the British right widened the line of assault as far as La Fère. The American

II Corps, composed of the 27th and 30th Divisions and commanded by Major General George W. Read, was in the center of the British Fourth Army front, attacking toward Le Cateau.

One day later, the Flanders Group of Armies launched still another offensive. Under the command of King Albert of Belgium, the Flanders Group included the British Second and French Sixth Armies and the American 37th and 91st Divisions, in addition to the Belgian Army. The British Fifth Army, between the Flanders Group and the main British attack, undertook limited actions in order to hold German reserves.

The zone facing the British effort included some of the most heavily defended areas of the entire front, and the attackers soon encountered the same sort of dogged, skillful, flexible defense that the American First Army was meeting in the rugged terrain farther south. The British Third Army, with the First on its left, managed to penetrate six miles on the first day. On the right the Fourth Army started its attack on September 29, crossing the St. Quentin Canal and penetrating the German defenses to the east. St. Quentin fell to the French First Army on October 2. Three days later the British Fourth Army broke through the Hindenburg Line. The Germans withdrew to the Selle River in good order, taking their most important supplies with them.

The Allies moved up to the Selle and renewed the attack on October 17. Although the Germans resisted stubbornly, they had no reserves to throw in, having shifted troops from the entire front to try to block the American drive toward Mézières. The British and French gained the high ground on the east of the river and pushed the Germans back. Vast expanses of deep mud, sown with mines and demolition charges, lay ahead. Through it the Allies slowly advanced, until by the end of October they had reached the next German line, from the Scheldt River south to Laon.

In Flanders the initial assault had captured the Passchendaele Ridge. Heavy rains made the roads almost impassable and so upset supply and transportation that the advance was almost completely halted for two weeks, despite the fact that most of the German forces had been removed from Flanders to face Haig's attack farther south. When the attack was resumed the armies advanced, slowly but steadily, until October 28. Then a general German withdrawal all along the line permitted them to move up to the Scheldt River.

THE FINAL OFFENSIVES

Morale in the German Army and at home had been steadily weakening as it became apparent that the Allies had seized the initiative and it was unlikely that the Germans could ever regain it. On September 29, and again on October 3, Von Hindenburg demanded that the recently appointed German Chancellor, Prince Max of Baden, immediately send an offer of peace to the Allies. "There is now no longer any possible hope of forcing peace on the enemy," he said. On October 6 Prince Max, through the Swiss government, asked President Wilson for "an armistice on land and water and in the air," on the basis of Wilson's Fourteen Points.

President Wilson refused to negotiate without assuring himself that the military dictatorship of Von Hindenburg and Ludendorff could not resume the fighting after an armistice. Consequently the original request was followed by a series of exchanges as the Germans attempted to establish an acceptable internal situation. Wilson's insistence that all occupied territory be evacuated before an armistice was granted annoyed Ludendorff, who had hoped to secure better terms, or at least delay, in order to strengthen Germany's defenses. Because he refused to admit defeat despite the obvious weakening of the front and growing internal unrest in Germany, the Kaiser was about to dismiss Ludendorff when he resigned. General Wilhelm Groener, who replaced him, took a more realistic view of the situation.

While these developments were happening the Allies had renewed their offensives all along the line on November 1. Dramatic and rapid advances were made by the American First Army, which surged north across open, rolling country toward Sedan and Mézières. The French, British, and Belgians too began to pick up speed, as German resistance weakened markedly on the whole front.

By this time the unrest that had been growing throughout Germany had broken out into open revolts in several areas. On November 3, sailors at Kiel mutinied and refused to go to sea. The spirit of revolution spread across the country and began to infect the army. With the country apparently about to collapse into chaos, the Kaiser abdicated and sought refuge in Holland on November 10. A socialist government had seized power in Berlin the day before and proclaimed a republic.

President Wilson had informed the other Allies of the exchanges with the German government, and on November 5 agreement was reached to grant an armistice. Two days later a German delegation, headed by civilian Matthias Erzeberger, crossed into the Allied lines to seek armistice terms. Negotiations continued over three days in Foch's railway-coach headquarters on a siding near Compiègne. Twice the Germans returned through the lines to report and receive instructions from the new German government. Foch, assisted by representatives of the British, French, and U.S. governments, dictated tough terms, requiring the Germans to give up so much territory and equipment that it would be virtually a surrender.

At first Von Hindenburg and Groener said the terms were unacceptable, and the German government balked at accepting them. But as the American Army rolled through Stenay toward Sedan, and the British and Belgians swept toward central Belgium, Von Hindenburg reconsidered. In the early morning of November 11 the German delegates accepted the Allied armistice terms. Word was transmitted to all of the fighting troops on both sides to cease firing at eleven o'clock that morning.

Under the armistice terms Germany was required to evacuate at once all the territory she had occupied, and Alsace-Lorraine as well. In addition to large quantities of military equipment, the German Army was to turn over to the Allies five thousand artillery pieces and twenty-five thousand machine guns and to evacuate all of Germany west of the Rhine River. The Allies were to be permitted to establish three bridgeheads east of the Rhine, at Cologne, Coblenz, and Mainz. Although this agreement was called an armistice, German acceptance of these terms was an acknowledgment of complete defeat, for further resistance or renewal of the conflict became impossible.

39

Italy and the Balkans—1918

Germany was in fact the last of the Central Powers to stop fighting. While her armies had been fighting desperately in France, in the other theaters of war her allies had finally yielded to superior forces.

During the winter and early spring of 1918, in preparation for major offensives in France, the Germans removed their seven divisions from Italy, and the Allies called six of theirs back to the Western Front. When the German offensives in the West intensified, two Italian divisions were sent to help bolster the Allied lines. Leaders on both sides began to urge their allies in Italy to attack as the battles went on. Germany called on Austria to make a major effort to eliminate Italy from the war so that Austrian divisions could be released for the Western Front. And Foch, anxious to prevent such a move, urged Diaz to attack in the Trentino before the Austrians could attack him. But Diaz preferred to build up his army and strengthen his defenses, and it was the Austrians again who made the first move.

THE AUSTRIAN ATTACK

Command of the Austro-Hungarian forces was divided between Conrad, in the Trentino, and Borojević von Bojna, on the Piave. Since neither wished to yield to the other, they planned two attacks at the same time, divided the reserves, and were forced to operate with virtually no intercommunication because of the rugged terrain that divided them.

The Austrian attack started on June 13, 1918, with a feint by Conrad at the Tonale Pass. Two days later the main offensive began on both fronts. Conrad's attack fell on a mixed force of

French, British, and Italians and initially made gains in the mountains of the Trentino. But Diaz's artillery soon commenced a strong counterbombardment. First the British, then the Italians and French, regained their equilibrium and pushed the invaders back. Borojević von Bojna's forces in the meantime gained a foothold across the Piave River in three places, and in one area penetrated three miles into the territory held by the Italian Third Army. The intensity of the battle increased as Diaz brought in aircraft and artillery. Swollen by rains, the river rose and washed away many of the Austrian ponton bridges, drastically cutting the flow of supplies to the front. Diaz rapidly moved up reinforcements, and by June 21 his troops had gained the initiative. The following night Borojević von Bojna ordered a withdrawal. The Italians crossed behind the retreating Austrians and recovered enough of the east bank to strengthen their position and secure the defenses of Venice. The Asiago area also was securely in Italian hands by July 1. Diaz refused to attempt to exploit the victory as Foch urged, however, and instead prepared his forces for a larger, coordinated offensive at a time of his own choosing.

THE ITALIAN OFFENSIVE

As the summer passed, Austrian morale dropped, in the face of shortages of supplies and food, sickness, and inadequate clothing. Reports from Austria indicated that the Austro-Hungarian government was close to collapse. Diaz was aware of this state of affairs as he planned his big offensive for the end of October. The main attack was to be made by the Italian Eighth Army under General Enrico Caviglia toward Vittorio Veneto. On the right it would be supported by the two British and two Italian divisions of the Tenth Army, commanded by British General Frederic Lambart, Lord Cavan. On the left would be the Twelfth Army, one French and three Italian divisions under French General Jean César Graziani, and the Fourth Army of Lieutenant General Gaetano Giardino. The U.S. 332nd Regiment had arrived in Italy in July and was assigned to the Tenth Army.

Diaz's plan was delayed by another flooding of the Piave River, but on October 24, one year after Caporetto, the Fourth Army started its attack, intended to deceive the enemy into thinking it

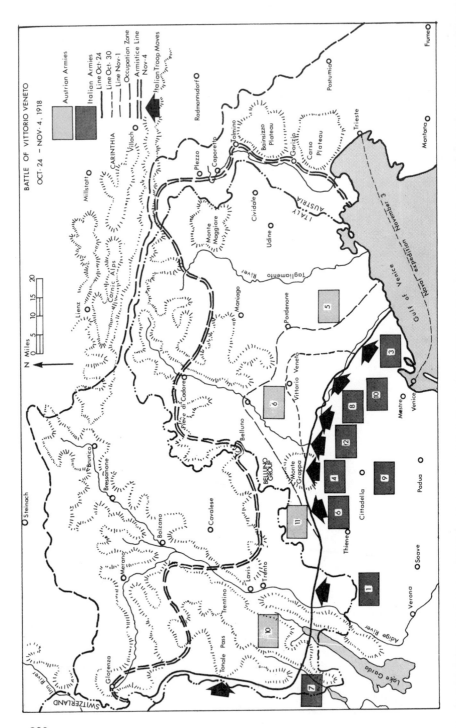

BATTLE OF VITTORIO VENETO

OCT. 24 – NOV. 4, 1918

Austrian Armies

Italian Armies

Line Oct. 24

Line Oct. 30

Line Nov. 1

Occupation Zone

Armistice Line
Nov. 4

Italian Troop Moves

N
Miles
5 10 15 20

was the main offensive. Around Monte Grappa, which the Italians had held against determined Austrian attacks almost a year before, the battle raged fiercely for three days, with little change of position, and the Austrians rushed reserves to the area as Diaz had hoped.

The main offensive, against the Austrian Fifth and Sixth Armies, began on October 26 with a heavy artillery attack. Twenty miles apart, units of the Italian Tenth and Twelfth Armies established bridgeheads across the Piave on the right flanks of the two Austrian armies on October 27. The Eighth Army pushed on through the following day. The Austrians withdrew before the attackers, having been ordered to pull back to their second line of defense. As the Italians continued their determined advance, the Austrian withdrawal became a rout. Units were cut off, and the fighting broke down into a series of isolated incidents. Whole sections of the Austrian Army, many of the soldiers Czechs, Poles, or Hungarians, surrendered. Asiago was taken on October 31. Everywhere along the Piave the Italian front was advancing, pushing the Austrians back across the Livenza River and then to the Tagliamento, the Italian Cavalry Corps rushing ahead of the infantry in pursuit of the fleeing Austrians. In the west, the Italian Sixth Army too was driving ahead. It captured the city of Trento on November 3.

The Austrians had already tried to sue for peace. A party with a flag of truce approached the Italians in the Adige valley on October 29, but since the group lacked proper credentials it was not received. A more proper party came over the next day. General Pietro Badoglio, chief of staff to General Diaz, presented terms to the Austrians on November 3. With their acceptance on the following day, an armistice put an end to hostilities between Italy and Austria. About five hundred thousand men of the Austrian Army were by then in Allied hands.

The armistice terms provided that Allied troops might cross Austria on the way to Germany and that the resources of Austria should be made available to the Allies. But Germany was about to collapse herself, and these measures never became effective.

ATTACK FROM SALONIKA

The anomalous situation in Greece, where Allied troops were stationed in a large portion of the northern section of the country although the king was sympathetic to the Central Powers, continued until mid-1917. A revolutionary movement had been gaining strength, however, and the former prime minister, Venizelos, demanded the king's abdication. The French government, which meddled in the situation more than strict interpretation of international law would allow, supported Venizelos. In 1917 a new High Commissioner, M. Celestin Jonnart, arrived from France and forced the king to leave the country, sending him on a French ship to Germany. The king's second son, Alexander, took the throne and called Venizelos as prime minister.

On July 2, 1917, Venizelos declared war on Germany and Bulgaria. Remobilizing the Greek Army, which had been demobilized at French insistence, he provided nine divisions to support the Allies. The year that followed saw little military activity on the Salonika front, although the possibility of developing it was frequently discussed by the Allies. A constant struggle with malaria and other diseases kept the effective strength of the Allied forces at only a fraction of the total strength, and constant bickering between British and French leaders helped to keep action to a minimum. In December, 1917, General Sarrail, who had been less than diplomatic during his period of command at Salonika, was replaced by General Marie Louis Adolphe Guillaumat. He reorganized the forces and raised sagging Allied morale in the area. In May, 1918, he used Greek troops in a small but successful attack west of the Vardar River. Before he could proceed with further offensives, however, he was relieved in July by General Louis Franchet d'Esperey.

Franchet d'Esperey at once inspected the front and elaborated a plan proposed by the Serbian Chief of Staff, General Zivojin Misić, into a major offensive. The main attack was to be a drive across the 4,500-foot-high mountain chain that formed the boundary between Greece and Serbia, and an advance to the Vardar River, to cut the railroads and split the defending Bulgarian forces. Two combined Serbo-French armies (six Serbian, two French divisions) were to execute this operation, while two French groups on the left, and French, Greek, and British units on the right, conducted less ambitious supporting operations. Guillaumat, who had returned to France, helped get French approval for the plan. The British and Italian governments finally agreed also. The attack was to be timed to coincide with the great Allied offensive on the Western Front.

On September 14, while the Americans were moving ahead in the St. Mihiel salient, a powerful artillery bombardment began all along the line in northern Greece. The following day two French divisions and one Serbian division attacked at 5:30 A.M. and fought fiercely to gain the crest of the mountain ridge before them. By 6 P.M. the rest of the Serbs came up through the French lines and, with intense excitement and joy, crossed into their homeland. As they advanced, the French widened the front to sixteen, then to twenty-five miles. Three days after the attack began the Serbian First Army was crossing the Crna River; the following day the Second was across the Vardar, and the Bulgarians, retreating rapidly before them, were split. The Allies on the flanks of the major effort were gaining too, and by September 22 the Bulgarians, and some German units with them, were in full retreat from Lake Doiran to Monastir, on a seventy-five-mile front. British, French, and Greek air units contributed to the victory by bombarding the retreating troops as they struggled through the mountain passes.

One by one Serbian and Bulgarian cities fell to the invaders, until September 29, when French cavalry entered Skoplje. By then some Serb units were eighty miles from where the attack began. The Bulgarians recognized that their position was hopeless and requested an armistice. On September 30 terms were agreed. West of Skoplje the Bulgarian troops became prisoners of war, while east of it the army was to be demobilized and its equipment surrendered. All lines of communication across Bulgaria were to be made available to the Allies for whatever use these might have in fighting the Central Powers.

The Serbs marched triumphantly north through their country, pushing aside scattered German and Austrian units that tried to halt them. Franchet d'Esperey advanced across Bulgaria to the Danube, then crossed into Rumania on November 10 and continued toward Bucharest as the Serbs crossed at Budapest. The following day the war was ended.

The British, meanwhile, never wholehearted in their participation on the Salonika front, had headed east toward the Maritsa River, for British eyes were on Turkey, reeling under British attacks in the Middle East. Bulgaria's surrender had already hastened the Turkish move for peace.

40

The End of the War for Turkey

PALESTINE

After taking Jerusalem in December, 1917, General Allenby
paused during the rainy season, while work on the rail line from
Sinai was completed and the port of Jaffa was opened. Activation
of a port on the Mediterranean would relieve some of the burden
of supplying the British forces all the way from Egypt.

In London the British Cabinet was divided on what Allenby
should do next. Prime Minister Lloyd George strongly favored an
advance to Aleppo and firmly believed that Aleppo's fall would
knock Turkey out of the war. General Robertson, Chief of the Imperial General Staff, and Field Marshal Haig could see in such an
operation a probable diversion of forces from the Western Front,
where they expected the Germans to increase their strength now
that Russia was out of the war. Moreover, the British military
leaders doubted that the capture of Aleppo, so far from Constantinople, would result in the collapse of Turkey.

The Prime Minister's view won out, and General Smuts, the
South African leader, was sent to Egypt in February to consult
with Allenby and representatives from Mesopotamia and develop
a plan to knock out Turkey. From this conference came the decision to halt the advance in Mesopotamia and transfer two divisions to Palestine, to give Allenby ten infantry divisions, three
mounted divisions, a cavalry division from France, and a cavalry
brigade from Mesopotamia. With this force Allenby was to cross
the Jordan River and destroy the Turkish railroad to the Hejaz,
and to advance to Damascus and Aleppo. The Turks had eleven
infantry divisions and one cavalry division to oppose him. In
March, 1918, Von Falkenhayn was replaced as commander of the

Turkish forces by General Liman von Sanders, the defender of Gallipoli.

The first moves of the offensive began on February 19, when the 60th Division entered the Jordan valley and advanced to Jericho. The ANZAC Mounted Division at the same time moved from Bethlehem toward the Dead Sea. Crossing the Jordan proved to be a problem, for the Germans and Turks of the Turks' Fourth Army had blown up the bridge at Ghoraniyeh which the British had planned to cross. At last, on March 23 British units advanced into the mountains east of the Jordan and two days later were in Es Salt. There they stopped, for the Turks had dug in in the hills, and Allenby decided not to undertake the costly job of trying to push on to Amman. Instead he withdrew all but a small detachment to the west bank of the Jordan.

Just as things seemed to be shaping up for a major offensive, Allenby found his strength reduced by almost sixty thousand men, all ordered to France to help halt the German offensives of the spring of 1918. Nevertheless Allenby proceeded with his plan. In early April the XXI Corps tried unsuccessfully to cut the Turkish defense line north of Jaffa, and on April 30 Allenby renewed the offensive in the east. The Australian Mounted Division quickly seized Es Salt, while another force advanced toward the defenses at Shunet Nimrin. But the Arabs who were supposed to cut the railroad line from Shunet Nimrin to Amman did not do so, and the Turks held the units from Es Salt so that they could not move in that direction. When the Turks counterattacked in strength at Es Salt, Allenby once more ordered the British units back across the river and again abandoned the attempt to take Amman.

It was already unbearably hot in Palestine, and Allenby made no attempt to advance for the next few months. He was busy, however, reorganizing and training his troops and planning for a major offensive to take Aleppo. His idea was to break the enemy line near the coast north of Jaffa, then send his cavalry rushing up the coast to enter the Plain of Esdraelon behind the Turkish armies, cutting their main line of retreat. He had about seventy-five thousand men available for this operation, well outnumbering the Turks' forty thousand to fifty thousand. In addition Allenby planned to use the Arabs to cut the railroad line at Déraa, where the railroad from Aleppo branched to the Hejaz and to Palestine.

On September 16 the Arabs struck at Déraa, and the Royal Air Force dropped bombs on the city. Two days later the Arabs cut the railroad in all directions, and the Turks were hastily sending reserves to the Transjordan area from the west. General Chetwode and the XX Corps, in the meantime, had advanced up the road toward Nablus, meeting strong resistance from the Turkish defenders.

These actions in the east had concealed from the Turks the fact that the main bulk of Allenby's forces was being secretly moved to a fifteen-mile front along the coast. There thirty-five thousand infantry, nine thousand cavalry, and almost 400 artillery pieces were confronting about eight thousand Turkish infantry and 120 guns. In a masterpiece of deception Allenby's preparations went undetected.

A brief and effective artillery barrage started the action on the morning of September 19. Almost at once Royal Air Force planes bombed Turkish headquarters at Nazareth with considerable effect, breaking contact between Turkish Eighth Army headquarters at Tulkeram and Liman von Sanders. Communications between the Eighth and Seventh Armies were broken also.

Then the British infantry moved out and in about four hours broke through the Turkish line north of Jaffa. Behind them rode the cavalry. Scarcely hesitating, they headed up the plain. Meanwhile the XX Corps infantry captured Tulkeram, driving the Turks out of the area in confusion, and pushed ahead twelve miles by midday, along the road to Nablus.

Galloping up the coastal plain, the 4th and 5th Cavalry Divisions reached the Carmel Mountains. There they divided. At the Musmus Pass the 4th Division crossed the mountains and poured down into the Plain of Esdraelon at Megiddo, the ancient Armageddon. Farther north the 5th Division took a different pass, and it too emerged onto the plain. Out of the dusk of early morning a Turkish battalion, moving up to guard the Musmus Pass, suddenly encountered a division of British cavalry, with lances in hand, charging at full speed. About fifty Turks fell; the rest were taken prisoner.

At 4:30 in the morning a hard riding detachment of the 5th Division descended on Nazareth, where Liman von Sanders lay asleep, unaware of what had been happening. The British tried in vain to find him, and finally withdrew.

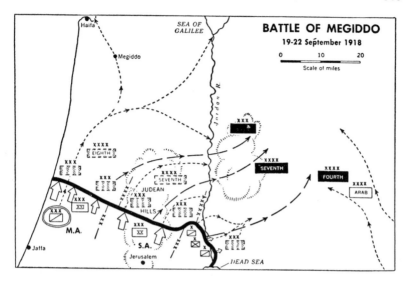

Meanwhile the 4th Division, with one brigade of the 5th, had headed for El Afule, which they took at about 8 A.M. They paused there only long enough to leave a garrison to hold the city, then raced on across the Valley of Jezreel to Beisan on the Jordan River. There at last they halted, having covered almost eighty miles in only thirty-four hours.

The infantry had been busy also. Driving the Turkish Seventh and Eighth Armies north and east, the XXI and XX Corps had converged on Nablus, which they took, along with eighteen thousand prisoners, on October 21. Few escaped from Nablus, but among them was Mustapha Kemal, commander of the Seventh Army.

Continuing their ride, the 5th Cavalry Division seized the seaports of Haifa and Acre on September 23. Two days later Liman von Sanders' vain attempt to defend a line from Semakh to Tiberias and across the Tarmuk valley to Déraa was shattered as British forces took Semakh and Tiberias. Déraa was already isolated, because of the effectiveness of the Arabs' rail-cutting activities, under the direction of Lawrence.

The Arab Northern Army, under Feisal and Lawrence, had also been active east of the Jordan while Allenby's offensive was proceeding. Together with the ANZAC Mounted Division they were pursuing the Turkish Fourth Army. Es Salt and Amman fell to the Anzacs, who also accepted the surrender of the Turkish II Corps, which was hurrying north from the Hejaz. The Arabs went on to Déraa, where they were in command when the 4th Cavalry Division arrived on September 28. Three days later the Arabs and three British divisions entered Damascus.

The pace was beginning to tell on Allenby's gallant men. Many were sick with malaria or had fallen victim to the worldwide epidemic of Spanish influenza. But those who could move started on for Aleppo. The Australians stayed behind in Damascus, and the 4th Division was left at Rayak, after that was taken on October 6. Alone, the 5th Division moved on to Homs by mid-October. Up the coast went the 7th Indian Infantry Division, occupying Beirut and Tripoli. Finally on October 26 the 5th Division, with a column of Arabs, took Aleppo.

Eight miles northwest of Aleppo, Mustapha Kemal had gathered a strong force and was determined to make a stand. In vain two British cavalry regiments tried to dislodge him. When more troops appeared, however, Kemal withdrew. Thus the campaign ended. The 5th Cavalry Division had covered 550 miles in six weeks, while the main army moved 350. In British hands were seventy-five thousand Turkish prisoners and 360 guns, for which the British had paid with about five thousand casualties. The Turks had already sought terms for an armistice.

MESOPOTAMIA

Having gained momentum in 1917, the British advance up the Tigris and Euphrates Rivers continued in 1918. Two tempting targets loomed ahead—Mosul to the north, up the Tigris, and Aleppo to the northwest, up the Euphrates. The road to Mosul was shorter and easier, but an advance on Aleppo, which was also the goal of Allenby in Syria, had attractive strategic possibilities. Although two divisions were transferred away from Mesopotamia to strengthen Allenby's force, the new Chief of the Imperial General Staff, General Sir Henry Wilson, who replaced Robertson in February, ordered Marshall to continue the advance up both rivers.

On March 9, 1918, the Euphrates force captured Hit, an important center for bitumen and lime. A month later the British troops were in Khan Bagdadie, twenty miles farther up the river. On the Tigris, progress was slower. After a series of small operations in the spring, Marshall was again forced by summer heat to wait until October to push ahead toward Mosul.

The Turks were ready to sue for peace by this time, and Spain was already acting in their behalf in discussions with President Wilson. Eager to be in Mosul before the end of hostilities, Marshall accelerated his program. On October 27, after a ride of seventy-seven miles in thirty-nine hours, the 11th Indian Cavalry Brigade drove the Turks under Ismail Hakki north from the Little Zab River. The Turks made another stand on the highlands north of Sharqat, where a fierce battle was fought on October 28. After two days of fighting, the Turkish commander surrendered on October 30.

The way was open to Mosul—open, that is, except for the Turkish commander there, Halil Pasha. Although an armistice between Turkey and Britain had been signed aboard the British battleship *Agamemnon* in the harbor at Mudros on October 30, Halil refused to let the British enter the city without a fight when they appeared on November 1. He was finally persuaded, however, and on November 4 British troops marched into Mosul. For Turkey the war was over.

41

German East Africa

The brilliant commander of the military forces in German East Africa, Colonel Paul von Lettow-Vorbeck, had kept the British on edge during much of 1915 by carrying on a series of raids into neighboring British East Africa. Repeatedly his men damaged the railroad line between Mombasa and Nairobi, and British crews repaired it. The British garrison in East Africa had orders from Lord Kitchener to remain on the defensive. In February, 1916, however, Kitchener decided to send South African General Jan Christiaan Smuts, who had just completed the campaign to take German Southwest Africa, to deal with Von Lettow-Vorbeck.

Smuts arrived at Mombasa on February 19, 1916, and promptly made plans to launch an offensive to take the town of Moshi, head of the railroad from Tanga and center of the best farming country of the colony. Two divisions would move from Voi to Taveta, while a third went west of Mount Kilimanjaro from Nairobi by way of Longido. On March 14 the first troops reached Moshi, to find that Von Lettow-Vorbeck had left the town and taken all the rolling stock with him. Still the British had made progress, and the Germans had lost their best farms.

Smuts next planned to drive Von Lettow-Vorbeck south, in a two-pronged advance. While General Jacob van Deventer took one division west and south, Smuts would take the rest by rail to Tanga and then work south near the coast. Optimistically, Van Deventer started off, and almost at once ran into real trouble. The rains had begun, and what roads there were were turned to thick, sticky mud in which men, animals, and vehicles slipped and slid or stuck fast. Supplies lagged far behind the troops, and hunger added to the misery of men and animals already plagued by ill-

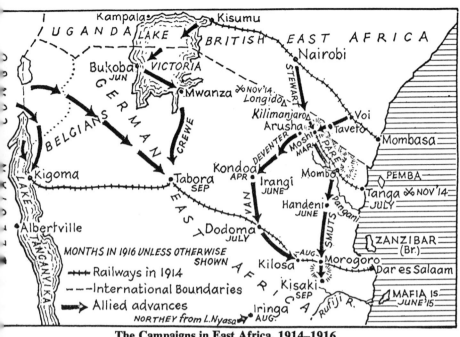

The Campaigns in East Africa, 1914–1916

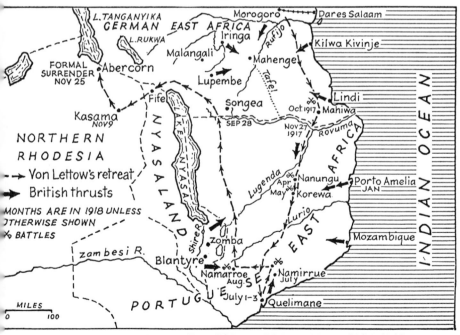

The Campaigns in German East Africa and Mozambique, 1916–1918

ness. On April 19 the sodden, muddy troops at last dragged into Kondoa Irangi, to be met by German troops, carefully entrenched with two guns from the *Königsberg* well placed to provide support. They prevented any further advance, even had the weary British been physically able to continue. For two months the Germans remained in their positions, then disappeared overnight, withdrawing by plan to the south.

Smuts meanwhile had started in May, 1916, his engineers repairing the railroad line ahead of him. Tanga was taken with no resistance, and Smuts continued to Hardeni and then to Morogoro, where he arrived at the end of August. Fifty miles west, Van Deventer was just reaching Kilosa. In the south, General Edward Northey, moving up from Nyasa, arrived at Iringa at about the same time. Belgians, pushing eastward from the Congo, reached Tabora in September. And Dar es Salaam, capital of the colony, surrendered on September 4 to a force that had landed at Bagamoyo and worked its way south.

But Smuts's men were exhausted and their numbers greatly depleted by disease. For three months he stopped, to reorganize and rest his troops. At the end of December the Germans were known to be concentrated at Mahenge, and Smuts planned to attack with two forces, Northey's and another under General A. R. Hoskins, which landed at Kilwa Kivinje. But Von Lettow-Vorbeck escaped across the Rufiji River.

Smuts left the area in January, 1917, and was replaced by Hoskins, who was in turn relieved by Van Deventer in May. A second attempt to take Mahenge was successful, but one group of Germans, led at first by Captain Wintgens, later by Captain Naumann, took off toward Tabora as the Allies moved in. In an almost incredible odyssey this group roamed for the next eight months all over part of German East Africa, attacking or threatening villages and towns that were in Allied hands. Before surrendering, the men covered two thousand miles.

General P. S. Beves, commanding the main body of Allied troops, moved toward Mahiwa, where he attacked nine German companies under command of Major General Wahle. Beves was unaware that Von Lettow-Vorbeck and most of the rest of the Germans were not far away, at Likangara, across the Likangara Mountains. On October 15 Von Lettow-Vorbeck led his men to

Mahiwa and joined the battle. The fight lasted until the evening of October 18, when the British withdrew, having lost fifteen hundred men to the Germans' one hundred, although the Germans had been outnumbered about four to one.

Von Lettow-Vorbeck knew he could not stand up long against such odds, however, and he withdrew to Lukuledi, farther south. There he threw off a British attack before continuing his withdrawal. Reaching the border of Portuguese East Africa, Von Lettow-Vorbeck decided to cross it, leaving behind him about a thousand sick and wounded men for the British to care for. German East Africa was in British hands, but the German commander was not through.

With his small band, Von Lettow-Vorbeck traveled about five hundred miles across Portuguese East Africa. Then he turned and headed back through German East Africa, north of Lake Nyasa, across Nyasaland, and into Northern Rhodesia. On November 13, 1918, he captured Kasama. There he learned that an armistice had been signed in France. At once he offered to negotiate with the British. On November 25 he surrendered, the last German commander to do so in World War I.

Von Lettow-Vorbeck was never defeated. He fought a brilliant campaign in German East Africa, with only the supplies he could get from the land or capture from his enemies, and a single shipload that somehow made it through the British blockade. He held out successfully for four years, inflicting 17,800 casualties and tying down over 70,000 Allied troops, though he never had more than about 3,000 men himself. His achievements in this land far removed from the main theaters of war won well-deserved admiration from his enemies as well as from his own people.

42

The War in the Air— A Comment

World War I started only eleven years after the Wright brothers' successful flight at Kitty Hawk. Much had happened in those years, and the planes available in 1914 were far different from the rudimentary machine the Wrights managed to lift off the ground in 1903. But they were still fragile instruments, many of them made of wood, cloth, and wire, small and awkward and easily damaged.

Some farsighted men had seen the potential for aircraft in warfare, but their attempts to sell their ideas to professional military men had been greeted at first with doubt or scorn and finally with limited acceptance. In 1914 the three powers engaged on the Western Front had planes in considerable variety—Great Britain had 37 of them, France 136, and Germany 180 planes as well as 13 dirigibles and about 200 training planes. But there was no plan to use these aircraft for anything but observation, keeping an eye on what the enemy was up to on the ground and directing the fire of the big guns on the most profitable targets. So it was that on August 12, 1914, when a German Taube passed a French Morane about five thousand feet in the air, the two pilots waved cheerily to each other and went about their business. If they carried revolvers, as some did for the pleasure of it, it would not have occurred to them to fire at one another.

Soldiers on the ground from the first instinctively tried to shoot down these big enemy birds when they flew over. Machine guns and rifles occasionally scored hits and kept the pilots wary when they were low over enemy army units. Then on both sides of the line men started experimenting with weapons for plane-to-plane combat. Small arms, machine guns, even grenades were employed as the notion of aerial combat became generally accepted.

The first months of the war were months of trial and error in the flying services on both sides. Such seemingly routine things as preventive maintenance of planes and their engines had to be learned the hard way as aircraft worn out with overuse and lack of care failed in flight and crashed or, with luck, made emergency landings, often behind enemy lines. Inadequacies of the human eye in reconnaissance from the air were to a considerable extent alleviated by the development of cameras and techniques of photo-mapping. Early attempts at dropping makeshift "bombs" from the air were extended to become planned bombing attacks by large numbers of bombers. And gradually the idea grew that the most effective way of getting rid of the observation planes spying from the sky was to shoot them down in their own element, with other planes.

There were many problems to be solved before the plane was converted into a fighter. The trickiest of these was posed by the whirring blades of the propeller. If the gun was to be handy for the pilot or the copilot in a two-seater to fire, it had to be in or close to the cockpit. But how was he to fire at the target in front of him without cutting off the blades of the propeller or being hit himself by a ricochet? The French stuntman Roland Garros came up with a solution. He installed tough steel deflectors on the edge of each blade, designed to send any bullets which hit the propeller bouncing harmlessly away from the pilot behind it. Garros had great success in scaring off German planes, until at last he was himself forced down in German territory and his plane with its mysterious device fell into German hands. Forty-eight hours later, the Dutch aircraft designer Anthony Fokker had improved on the idea by designing a gun with its rate of fire controlled by the propeller, so that the bullets passed through the spaces between the blades. The Allies stayed away from the new, lethal German aircraft until a German plane forced down in Allied territory gave them the secret. Within a few weeks British and French planes could again shoot it out with the Germans in the air.

The agile little fighter planes soon became the most appealing things in the sordid mess the war had become, and the daring,

often reckless men who flew them were the glamor boys of the
service. Their exploits, only mildly distorted from the remarkable
truth, were widely known on both sides of the line, and their
names and tales of their triumphs brightened the long, dark
months in which nothing but slaughter seemed to be being accomplished on the ground. The Germans and French quickly developed a policy of dubbing pilots who shot down five or more planes
"aces," and awarding them decorations and heroes' acclaim. Os-
wald Boelcke, Max Immelmann, and perhaps the greatest of them
all, Baron Manfred von Richthofen, were three of many whose
names were known throughout Germany, and whose deaths were
mourned by millions when they, like the majority of the first fighter pilots, made their last flights. In France the air heroes had
names like Charles Nungesser, who survived the war, and
Georges Guynemer. Despite British reluctance to distinguish
aviators above the less dramatic man on the ground and refusal
to publicize their names and accomplishments, British pilots too
were soon well known at home. Albert Ball and Edward "Mick"
Mannock led a list of popular names in British hearts.

Pilots on both sides of the front came to know each other and
to admire and respect their most worthy opponents. Everyone
could recognize the great Richthofen, for he alone in the German
air force flew a bright red plane, from which he derived his nick-
name "The Red Knight," or "The Red Baron." When at last
Richthofen was shot down behind Allied lines, a British air
squadron buried him with full military honors.

There are many stories of the deeds of these fighter pilots,
many of whom, even after the advantages of formation flying and
group attacks had been recognized on both sides, continued to
prefer to fly and fight alone. Only slightly atypical of the things
they did is a tale told of Albert Ball.

One afternoon Ball, flying by himself, met two German Alba-
trosses in the air. He attacked, hit them both, and sent them
scurrying home. Although he pursued them, firing until all his
ammunition was gone, they made it safely and landed, much to
Ball's disgust. Annoyed that they had not stood to fight, he
dropped a note on the field, challenging them to meet him above
the base the following afternoon and finish the fight.

The next afternoon, when Ball showed up there were two
planes circling, waiting for him. Immediately he headed in, only

to hear machine-gun bullets all around him. Three more planes had been waiting too, hidden from him by staying between him and the sun. Furious, he chased the closest planes, always having to evade two or three as he tried to close in on others. Then his ammunition ran out. He could not hope to head home, for the Germans stayed carefully between him and Allied territory. Noting a large open field below him, Ball put his plane into a spin, and plummeted toward the earth. The Germans were overjoyed. They had shot down the great Albert Ball. But he pulled out of the spin as he had planned, and landed safely in the field. Two of the Germans quickly followed him down, while the other three flew off to spread the word. As the German pilots leaped from their planes to capture Ball, who was slumped down in his seat, apparently wounded, Ball sprang to life, opened his throttle, took off and headed safely home.

The first bombing done by planes in World War I was haphazard. On August 13, 1914, four four-pound bombs were dropped outside Paris, the first to land on French territory. A British pilot dropped two large bombs on a German cavalry column near Villers-Cotterets on September 1, 1914, causing a stampede of terrified horses. Others dropped hand grenades and various devices, including a collection of small steel arrows which proved useless for that purpose but great for firing at pub dart boards.

The first successful bombing attack on German soil was made by a plane of the British Royal Naval Air Service. From six hundred feet Flight Lieutenant R. L. G. Marix dropped two twenty-pound bombs on the zeppelin sheds at Düsseldorf, destroying a brand-new airship and setting fire to the sheds. Shortly afterward, naval planes successfully attacked airship sheds at Friedrichshafen on Lake Constance. Other bombing attempts, particularly to restrict movements of ground troops, met with less success, and the British and French air leaders soon decided to restrict bombing objectives to enemy headquarters, telephone exchanges, ammunition dumps, railroad crossings, and freight yards.

Almost from the beginning aircraft proved themselves helpful aids to the troops fighting on the ground. At first this was by providing eyes aloft to watch the enemy and report his location and activities to the army command. On August 22, 1914, British pilots reported that great numbers of German troops were approaching the British position at Mons, thereby preventing complete surprise and potential catastrophe. Attempts to disrupt the advance by dropping grenades and gasoline bombs had little effect. Later that month reports of French pilots gave General Joffre information on which to base his plan for counterattack at the Marne. On both sides during 1914 and 1915 planes were used with telling effect to spot targets for artillery.

As the months went by, general staffs of all the armies grew to recognize at least some of the potential values of aircraft, as they proved themselves in action. By the end of 1915 production facilities were working at top speed to build up numbers of aircraft as rapidly as possible. Men were being procured from many sources and quickly trained to fill out newly activated squadrons. Although survival expectancy was very low, there was no dearth of volunteers, many of them eager to avoid the alternative of misery, boredom, fear, and perhaps death in the trenches.

AIRSHIPS

If little was known of the potentiality of the airplane when war began, less was known of the airship. Both England and France had done some experimenting with gas-filled balloons and with nonrigid or semi-rigid airships. In Germany, Count Ferdinand von Zeppelin had achieved great success with a rigid airship that had a bag built around a complicated framework of aluminum alloy. These dirigibles had been enthusiastically promoted by the German public, and when war broke out great things were expected of them. They could fly higher than planes, thanks to the highly flammable hydrogen gas that inflated them, and they promised to provide a secure platform from which to drop bombs with precision on targets below. Both the French and the British feared these sky monsters. The British especially saw in them a real threat to the security that the English Channel and the North Sea had for centuries assured to the island nation. Somehow it was thought that they were practically indestructible, thanks to a nonexistent layer of inert gas thought to be built in around a central bag of hydrogen.

Almost from the beginning German zeppelins were sent out with loads of bombs, which they dropped with remarkable accuracy on military targets in Belgium and France, particularly on the Channel ports. The first attack on England was made in January, 1915, with little effect. Then in May a ship commanded by Hauptmann Linnarz got as far as Southend, where he dropped 120 incendiary bombs, killing one woman, injuring two men, and setting fire to a lumberyard. On May 31 the same pilot reached London around midnight. Flying very high, he dropped his bombs, aiming for the London docks and military targets around the city. Some of them landed on the city, however, killing seven people and injuring thirty-five as well as doing damage to houses and business establishments. This episode caused an increase of the city's gun defenses and the provision of antiaircraft guns to a squadron of light cruisers, with orders to intercept any airships they encountered over the North Sea. When a fleet of four airships tried a few weeks later to bomb London, they were turned back by the intensive antiaircraft fire. But they still dropped 68 bombs on Britain, and caused a move to protect London, under the direction of Sir Percy Scott, a British naval gunnery expert. Scott not only increased the numbers of antiaircraft guns but searched out the best possible weapons, installed searchlights, set up new gun stations, and procured the assignment of forty naval planes to the defense of London. He also urged that pilots be trained in night flying, since the zeppelin attacks came at night.

The first airship to be destroyed by an Allied aviator went down on June 7, 1915. At that time it was believed that the only way to destroy one was to bomb it from above, a difficult feat when airships could fly higher than planes. Flight Sublieutenant R. A. J. Warneford managed to destroy one that way over Belgium, however. From about fifty feet above the ship he dropped six twenty-pound bombs squarely on the big gas bag. It burst into flames, and only skill and luck prevented Warneford from perishing with it. Not long thereafter, Lieutenant Leefe Robinson shot down an airship with his machine guns, and the myth of invulnerability was dispersed.

A very real hazard to zeppelins was nature itself, and more than one pilot had to cope with problems of weather that sometimes proved disastrous. The worst occurred on the night of October 13, 1916. Eleven airships set off to attack London in very light winds, only to find that above ten thousand feet the wind was blowing at forty miles an hour and that at twenty thousand there was a full gale. As was the German practice, when the airships approached the coast of England they ascended, in order to escape detection and to get above the British fighter planes' ceilings. Four of them, after dropping their bombs, found themselves helplessly in the grip of the wind. Blown south across France, one was destroyed by antiaircraft fire; one crashed in southern France; one tried to land but took off again after being fired at, dropped off her car and crew when she passed low over some trees, and finally disappeared from sight over the Mediterranean; the fourth was forced down and captured near Neufchateau.

The accomplishments of the zeppelins were slight in comparison with their cost. Only 557 persons were killed and 1,358 injured, for an expenditure of 196 tons of bombs in fifty-one raids.

AIRPOWER

The Battle of the Somme in June, 1916, saw the perfection of air tactics that had been evolving since the beginning of the war. At Verdun the German Air Force had maintained a constant patrol of the combat zone in a partially successful effort to keep French observation planes off. The French began sending their observation planes with escorts of six or twelve fighters, which kept the Germans at bay. Then the Germans developed the *Jagdstaffeln*, hunting packs of twelve planes in four flights of three. These scored great success. The Allies by this time were bombing behind the German lines, though, and the German air strength had to be used in defense rather than attack. Allied planes attacked German planes in the air and on the ground, and increased production gradually gave the Allies a decisive superiority that they would never lose.

The entry of the United States into the war had no immediate impact in the air, for the U.S. air service was small and weak. Some adventurous Americans had been flying for the Allies almost since the beginning, first individually and then as members of the Lafayette Escadrille. This outfit had made a name for itself, fighting alongside French units, and had its own roster of air heroes, among them Bert Hall and Raoul Lufbery, whose deeds received publicity in papers from one end of the country to the other. When the United States entered the war, most of these pilots joined the U.S. Air Service, although many had to have special waivers because for one reason or another they could not meet U.S. Army physical qualifications.

By the fall of 1918, U.S. aircraft and tactics were really coming into their own. Colonel William Mitchell, Air Planner on the staff of General Pershing, organized and led a combined force of about fifteen hundred American, British, and French planes during the Battle of St. Mihiel. Some of them bombed the German front line and strafed enemy positions, while the rest struck at rear areas in waves. These strikes were so successful that they contributed significantly to the victory on the ground. Similar strikes also assisted the army in the Battle of the Meuse-Argonne.

No battle in World War I was won or lost in the air, nor was the issue ever greatly influenced by airpower, despite its growing contribution to ground action. But World War I had provided an impetus that would not have come otherwise to the development of aircraft and their military uses. Thereafter no country could afford to neglect the potentialities of airpower.

43

The Postwar War in Russia

Although the Allied attempt to capture the Dardanelles and open a warm-water route to Russia failed, in 1916 and 1917 the British delivered large amounts of military equipment and supplies to Russia by the treacherous northern route to Murmansk and Archangel. Much of this material was still there on the docks when the revolutionary government in Russia started negotiating for peace with Germany in 1917. The Allied Supreme War Council, worried that the collapse of the Eastern Front would release more Germans to fight in the west, decided that if they could send an expedition into the Murmansk-Archangel area they might be able to bolster Russian determination to continue fighting, or at least prevent the Germans from using the ports as U-boat bases. Having secured permission from Lenin to send troops to Murmansk with the argument that the supplies should be protected from the Germans or from dissident Russian elements, in March, 1918, some British naval detachments landed at Murmansk. Peace between Germany and Russia had already been signed at Brest Litovsk.

No one was entirely sure what was going on in Russia at that time. To Russia's former allies the most important immediate fact was that fighting had stopped on the Eastern Front. Although some members of the Supreme War Council, including the United States military representative, General Tasker Bliss, thought that nothing practical could be done about it, others believed that if more troops were sent to Murmansk they might give support either to the Bolsheviks, thereby making them able and willing to support the Allies, or conversely to one of the counter-revolutionary movements. If the Bolsheviks were overthrown, some reasoned, the new government might possibly be persuaded to renew the war. In any case the Bolsheviks did not control Murmansk and Archangel, and more British and some French units were sent to that area.

In May, 1918, forty thousand Czech soldiers were being transported across Siberia. Former members of the Austro-Hungarian Army, they had either been captured or had deserted to the Russians, who had formed them into two divisions, known as the Czech Legion. At their request they were being taken to Vladivostok and would be carried by ship to the Western Front, where they were to join the Allies to fight for the liberation of their homeland. Suddenly fighting broke out between the Czechs and the Bolshevik Red Guards. The Czechs overpowered the Guards, grabbed their weapons, and seized control of the Trans-Siberian Railroad from the Urals to Vladivostok. Here was a potential force to open a new Eastern Front, and the Allies decided to try to develop it. By so doing they were also committed to fighting the Bolshevik government, although this was not really understood.

More Allied troops reached Murmansk in the summer of 1918. In August they occupied Archangel, joined by the first of 4,500 American troops to reach the area. After only a brief pause, British Major General F. C. Poole, the Allied commander, in mid-September launched an offensive south from Archangel with the 12,000 men in his command, hoping to rally anti-Bolshevik forces to his support. Although the operation was poorly conceived and inadequately supplied, the advance reached about two hundred miles up the Northern Dvina River on a front about one hundred miles wide before being stopped in October by the new Red Army, led by Leon Trotsky, and the approaching winter.

After months of bitter, snowy cold, the Allies realized that the action was futile. Certainly, with the war against Germany over, there was no longer the incentive of opening a new front. The anti-Bolshevik position had weakened in Russia, and the Bolsheviks were gaining firm control. So the Allies decided to withdraw their troops. The first Americans left Murmansk in June, 1919; the last British troops sailed on October 12.

VLADIVOSTOK AND SIBERIA

At the other end of Russia, small British and Japanese forces had landed at Vladivostok in April, 1918, ostensibly to take charge of military supplies there. This force was increased after the Czech revolt, and more Japanese troops were sent, presumably to help the Czechs from the end of the railroad. The first American troops to reach Vladivostok went there from the Philippines in August, 1918. They were soon joined by more under Major General William S. Graves, whose command numbered ten thousand men. These soldiers, with the twenty thousand Japanese and small British and French contingents, were deployed to guard the Trans-Siberian Railroad from Vladvistok to Lake Baikal in order to assist the Czechs to reach Vladivostok. Although a counterrevolutionary group in central Siberia, headed by Admiral Alexander Kolchak, tried to get American support, Graves carefully avoided giving it as he followed President Wilson's directive to be strictly neutral in the Russian civil war. American troops firmly demonstrated their neutrality by fighting off a number of random attacks by White Russians as well as Bolshevik troops.

American troops remained in Siberia until April, 1920. By that time the Bolsheviks had a secure hand on the Russian government and on most of Siberia. The Czechs had withdrawn or been pushed back along the railroad to the east. By agreement with the Bolsheviks, most of them had been evacuated from Vladivostok and transported back to their own newly independent country. This aftermath of World War I was over.

Postscript

The "war to end all wars" stopped in November, 1918, and the book was closed with the signing of the peace treaties at Versailles on June 28, 1919; St. Germain-en-Laye on September 19, 1919; Neuilly-sur-Seine on November 27, 1919; Trianon on June 4, 1920; and Lausanne on July 24, 1923. The world smiled again, at least in some places, and looked forward optimistically to years of peace stretching indefinitely ahead. The job was done, they said. And twenty years later it all had to be done again.

Selected Bibliography

Albertini, Luigi. *Origins of the War of 1914*. London: Oxford, 1952.

Albion, Robert Greenhalgh. *Introduction to Military History*. New York: The Century Co., 1929.

Allen, George H., Whitehead, Henry C., and Chadwick, F. E. *The Great War*. Philadelphia: George Barrie's Sons, 1916.

Army Times. The Yanks Are Coming: The Story of General John J. Pershing. New York: Putnam, 1960.

Asprey, Robert B. *The First Battle of the Marne*. New York: Lippincott, 1962.

Ayres, Leonard P. *The War with Germany: A Statistical Summary*. Washington: Government Printing Office, 1919.

Bacon, R. H. *The Life of Lord Fisher of Kilverstone*. Garden City: Doubleday, 1929.

Baldwin, Hanson W. *World War I: An Outline History*. New York: Harper & Row, 1962.

Barnett, Correlli. *The Swordbearers; Supreme Command in the First World War*. New York: Morrow, 1964.

Bean, C. E. W. *Official History of Australia in the War of 1914–1918*. Sydney, Australia, 1923.

Bishop, Major W. A. *Winged Warfare*. New York: Doran, 1918.

Blond, Georges. *Verdun*. New York: Macmillan, 1961.

Blücher, Evelyn. *An English Wife in Berlin*. New York: Dutton, 1920.

Bogart, Ernest L. *Direct and Indirect Costs of the Great World War*. New York: Oxford, 1920.

Bordeaux, Henry. *Georges Guynemer, Knight of the Air*. New Haven: Yale University Press, 1918.

Bruce, J. M. *British Aeroplanes 1914–1918*. London: Putnam, 1957.

Buchan, John. *A History of the Great War*. 4 vols. Boston: Houghton Mifflin, 1923.

Buist, H. M. *Aircraft in the German War*. London: Methuen & Co., Ltd., 1914.

Callwell, C. E. *The Dardanelles*. Boston: Houghton, 1919.

Caracciolo, Mario. *Italy in the World War*. Rome: Edizioni Roma, n.d.

Cheesman, E. F. *Fighter Aircraft of the 1914–1918 War.* Letchworth, Herts.: Harleyford Publications, 1960.

Chidsey, Donald Barr. *The Day They Sank the Lusitania.* New York: Award Books, 1967.

Churchill, Winston. *The World Crisis.* 6 vols. New York: Charles Scribner's Sons, 1923–1931.

Corbett, Julian S. *Naval Operations.* London: Longmans, Green and Co., 1920.

Cruttwell, C. R. M. F. *A History of the Great War.* Oxford: Clarendon Press, 1934.

Dupuy, R. Ernest. *The Compact History of the United States Army.* New York: Hawthorn Books, 1961.

Dupuy, R. Ernest, and Dupuy, Trevor N. *Military Heritage of America.* New York: McGraw-Hill, 1956.

Edmonds, James E. *Fighting Fools.* New York: D. Appleton-Century, 1938.

———. *Military Operations, Italy, 1915–1919.* London: HMSO, 1949.

Esposito, Vincent J., ed. *A Concise History of World War I.* New York: Praeger, 1964.

Falls, Cyril. *Armageddon: 1918.* Philadelphia: Lippincott, 1964.

———. *The Great War.* New York: Capricorn Books, 1959.

———. *Military Operations: Macedonia.* 2 vols. London: HMSO, 1933.

Fay, Sidney B. *The Origins of the World War.* New York: Macmillan, 1930.

Fischer, Fritz. *Germany's Aims in the First World War.* New York: Norton, 1967.

Fokker, Anthony G. H., and Gould, Bruce. *Flying Dutchman: The Life of Anthony Fokker.* New York: Henry Holt, 1931.

Gardner, Brian. *The Big Push.* New York: William Morrow, 1963.

———. *On to Kilimanjaro.* Philadelphia: Macrae Smith Co., 1963.

Gibbons, Floyd. *The Red Knight of Germany.* Garden City: Doubleday, 1927.

Gibbs-Smith, Charles H. *The Aeroplane.* London, HMSO, 1960.

Great Britain. Foreign Office. *British Documents on the Origins of the War, 1898–1914.* London: HMSO.

———. Parliament. *Collected Diplomatic Documents Relating to the Outbreak of the European War.* Misc. No. 10 (1915). London: HMSO, 1915.

———. Parliament. *Correspondence Respecting Events Leading to the Rupture of Relations with Turkey.* Misc. No. 13 (1914). London: HMSO, 1914.

―――. War Office. *Statistics of the Military Effort of the British Empire During the Great War, 1914–1920.* London: HMSO, 1922.

Grey, Edward, Viscount of Fallodon. *Twenty-five Years, 1892–1916.* New York: Frederick A. Stokes Company, 1925.

Gullett, H. S. *The Australian Imperial Force in Sinai and Palestine, 1914–1918. Official History of Australia in the War of 1914–1918.* Sydney: Angus & Robertson Ltd., 1923.

Haddow, G. W., and Grosz, Peter M. *The German Giants.* London: Putnam, 1962.

Hamilton, Ian. *Gallipoli Diary.* New York: Doubleday, 1920.

Hankey, Maurice P. *The Supreme Command, 1914–1918.* London: Allen & Unwin, 1961.

Harbord, James G. *America in the World War.* Boston: Houghton, 1933.

―――. *The American Army in France, 1917–1919.* Boston: Little, Brown, 1936.

Hoehling, A. A. *The Fierce Lambs.* Boston: Little, Brown, 1960.

―――. *The Great War at Sea.* New York: Thomas Y. Crowell Company, 1965.

Horne, Alistaire. *The Price of Glory: Verdun, 1916.* New York: St. Martin's, 1963.

Horne, Charles Francis, ed. *Source Records of the Great War.* National Alumni, 1923.

Howland, Charles Roscoe. *A Military History of the World War.* Fort Leavenworth, Kansas: The General Service Schools Press, 1923.

Hoyt, Edwin P. *The Last Cruise of the Emden.* New York: Macmillan, 1966.

Huidekoper, F. L. *The Military Unpreparedness of the United States.* New York: Macmillan, 1916.

Ironside, Sir Edmund. *Tannenberg; the First 30 Days in East Prussia.* London: Blackwood, 1933.

Irving, Commander John. *The Smoke Screen of Jutland.* London: William Kinder, 1966.

Jablonski, E. *The Knighted Skies.* New York: Putnam, 1964.

James, Robert Rhodes. *Gallipoli.* London: B. T. Batsford, 1965.

Johnson, Douglas Wilson. *Battlefields of the World War, Western and Southern Fronts.* New York: Oxford University Press, 1921.

―――. *Topography and Strategy in the War.* New York: H. Holt and Company, 1917.

Johnston, Charles H. L. *Famous Generals of the Great War.* Boston: Page, 1919.

Jones, H. A. *The War in the Air.* Oxford: Oxford University Press, 1937.

Kahn, Herman. *On Thermonuclear War.* Princeton: Princeton University Press, 1960.

Lafore, Laurence. *The Long Fuse: An Interpretation of the Origins of World War I.* New York: Lippincott, 1965.

Lansing, Robert. *The Peace Negotiations.* Boston: Houghton Mifflin, 1921.

Lawrence, T. E. *Seven Pillars of Wisdom.* Garden City: Doubleday, 1926.

Lee, Dwight Erwin. *The Outbreak of the First World War.* Boston: Heath, 1958.

McConnell, James R. *Flying for France.* Garden City: Doubleday, Page, 1917.

McEntee, Girard L. *Italy's Part in Winning the World War.* Princeton: Princeton University Press, 1934.

————. *Military History of the World War.* New York: C. Scribner's Sons, 1937.

McKee, Alexander. *The Friendless Sky.* New York: William Morrow and Company, 1964.

Marder, Arthur J. *From the Dreadnought to Scapa Flow.* 3 vols. London: Oxford University Press, 1961–1966.

Marshall, S. L. A. *American Heritage History of World War I.* New York: American Heritage, 1964.

Mason, Herbert M., Jr. *High Flew the Falcons.* Philadelphia: Lippincott, 1965.

————. *The Lafayette Escadrille.* New York: Random House, 1964.

Middleton, C. E. *The Great War in the Air.* 2 vols. London, 1920.

Mitchell, William. *Memoirs of World War I.* New York: Random House, 1960.

————. *Winged Defense.* New York: Putnam, 1925.

Moorehead, Alan. *Gallipoli.* New York: Harper, 1956.

Nordhoff, Charles, and Hall, James N. *Falcons of France.* Boston: Little, Brown, 1929.

Palmer, Alan. *The Gardeners of Salonika.* New York: Simon and Schuster, 1965.

Parsons, Edwin C. *The Great Adventure.* New York: Doubleday, Doran & Co., 1937.

Pershing, John J. *My Experiences in the World War.* New York: Frederick A. Stokes, 1931.

Pitt, Barrie. *1918, The Last Act.* New York: W. W. Norton, 1963.

————. *Revenge at Sea.* New York: Stein and Day, 1960.

Reynolds, Quentin. *They Fought for the Sky.* New York: Rinehart and Company, 1957.

Richardson, Lewis Fry. *Statistics of Deadly Quarrels.* Pittsburgh: Boxwood Press, 1960.

Ritter, Gerhard. *The Schlieffen Plan; Critique of a Myth.* New York: Praeger, 1958.

Scheer, Admiral. *Germany's High Seas Fleet in the World War.* New York: Peter Smith, 1934.

Society of the First Division, AEF. *History of the First Division During the World War.* Philadelphia: Winston, 1922.

Spears, Edward L. *Liaison, 1914: A Narrative of the Great Retreat.* Garden City: Doubleday, 1931.

————. *Prelude to Victory.* London: Jonathan Cape, 1939.

Stallings, Laurence. *The Doughboys.* New York: Harper & Row, 1963.

Stamps, T. Dodson, and Eposito, Vincent J., eds. *A Short Military History of World War I.* West Point: U.S.M.A., 1950.

Taylor, A. J. P. *Illustrated History of the First World War.* New York: Putnam's, 1964.

Terraine, John. *Ordeal of Victory.* Philadelphia: Lippincott, 1963.

————. *The Western Front, 1914–1918.* New York: Lippincott, 1965.

Thomas, Lowell. *Count Luckner, The Sea Devil.* New York: Garden City, 1927.

Thoumin, Richard. *The First World War.* New York: Putnam's, 1963–1964.

The Times Diary and Index of the War, 1914 to 1918. London: Hodder & Stoughton, 1921.

Tirpitz, Alfred von. *My Memoirs.* New York: Dodd, Mead, 1919.

Tuchman, Barbara. *The Guns of August.* New York: Macmillan, 1962.

————. *The Proud Tower.* New York: Macmillan, 1962.

Tyng, Sewell. *Campaign of the Marne.* New York: Longmans, 1935.

U.S. Department of the Army. Historical Division. *The U.S. Army in the World War.* Washington: Government Printing Office, 1919.

U.S. War Department. *America's Munitions 1917–1918.* Washington: Government Printing Office, 1919.

Villari, Luigi. *The Macedonian Campaign.* London: T. F. Unwin Ltd., 1922.

————. *The War on the Italian Front.* London: Cobden-Sanderson, 1932.

Wavell, Archibald Percival, First Viscount. *Allenby, A Study in Greatness.* London: G. G. Harrap & Co., 1940–1943.

Whitehouse, Arch. *Decisive Air Battles of the First World War.* New York: Duell, Sloan and Pearce, 1963.

————. *Heroes and Legends of World War I.* New York: Doubleday, 1964.

Wolff, Leon. *In Flanders Fields; The 1917 Campaign.* New York: Viking Press, 1958.

Woodward, David. "The Escape of the *Goeben* and *Breslau.*" *History Today,* Vol. X, No. 4 (April, 1960), pp. 232–239.

Index